China
and
the
Three
Worlds

China and the Three Worlds

A FOREIGN POLICY READER

EDITED BY King C. Chen

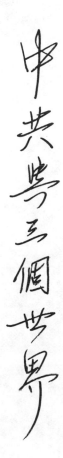

M.E.Sharpe INC.
White Plains, New York

Library of Congress Catalog Card Number: 78-51973
International Standard Book Number: 0-87332-118-9 hardcover
International Standard Book Number: 0-87332-134-0 paperback

Printed in the United States of America

To my sons: David and Donald
May they have a better world!

Contents

Preface

The "reopening" of China in 1971 by President Richard Nixon
has already been regarded as a turning point of China's foreign
policy and international politics. It has facilitated the reestablishment of Peking's diplomatic relations after the Cultural
Revolution, broadened the dimension of China's international
political, economic, and cultural activities, and promoted
China's campaign against hegemonism of the superpowers. Its
impact on China's relationships with the outside world, particularly the United States and Third World countries, is immea-
surable.

In less than a decade after the "reopening" of China, the
main figures who were responsible for the "breakthrough"
were out of the political arena — Richard Nixon resigned in
1974 in the Watergate scandals, Mao Tse-tung and Chou En-lai
both passed away in 1976. But, "the world rolls on," in Mao's
words, "time presses." Sino-American relations continue to
develop. Moreover, China, under a new leadership, is struggling to usher in an era of modernization, ambitiously proposing to build herself into a true world power.

In view of the important events in the past and perceiving
possible significant developments in the future, Michael Ying-
mao Kau and I had planned to co-edit this volume for some
time. After the primary work on my part was finally completed, Ying-mao found himself too tied up with his gigantic
"Mao's writings project" to spare any time for this volume.

xi

He withdrew graciously. I felt a loss. I am indebted to him for his early cooperative effort.

I am grateful to Rutgers University for a research grant which facilitated my research. I am also thankful for the assistance rendered by the Library of Congress, and the libraries of Columbia, Princeton, and Rutgers universities. Several colleagues and students have helped me by offering criticisms and opinions. I thank them.

I would also like to express my appreciation to Douglas Merwin, Chinese Publications Editor, and other staff of M. E. Sharpe, Inc., who have made my preparation of this volume pleasant and smooth.

Finally, I want to thank my wife, Grace, for her constant encouragement and assistance, and my two young sons, David and Donald, for their periodic help in filing clippings and data.

China
and
the
Three
Worlds

Introduction

The "three-world" theory is China's (Mao Tse-tung's) new concept of world politics after the Sino-American rapprochement. This concept, originally developed from the Soviet "two-camp" theory of 1947, has an immediate connection with Peking's "intermediate zone" theory of 1964. On January 21, 1964, Jen-min jih-pao [People's Daily] carried an editorial asserting the existence, between the Western imperialist world and the Communist bloc, of two "intermediate zones" — the first in the "Third World" area, and the second in Western Europe, Oceania, Canada, and other capitalist countries.

In February 1974, when Mao talked with a visiting African leader in Peking, he stated his "three-world" viewpoint:

In my view, the United States and the Soviet Union form the first world. Japan, Europe and Canada, the middle section, belong to the second world. We are in the third world.... With the exception of Japan, Asia belongs to the third world. The whole of Africa belongs to the third world, and Latin America too.[1]

What made Mao shift his world outlook over a period of ten years? A principal reason was the change in the world situation, but a more significant factor was Mao's perception of the world in line with his antihegemonic policy.

As far as the timing is concerned, the Sino-American rapprochement is the watershed that divided China's present foreign relations from the past. From the Chinese standpoint,

3

the rapprochement was a great strategic game played by Chairman Mao Tse-tung and Premier Chou En-lai. It turned the United States from being the "No. 1 enemy" to being a potential friend, played the United States off against the Soviet Union, removed the likelihood of the creation of a "two-China" situation, and switched Japan's formal diplomatic ties from Taipei to Peking. In making full use of the contradictions among the major international actors, it was a masterpiece of the Mao-Chou foreign policy. In this context, a study of China's relations with the three worlds since the rapprochement is a significant challenge.

This volume is an attempt to meet the challenge. It is designed for college students and the general public. An introduction to such an important collection, apart from a short documentary introduction in each section, should not limit itself to dealing with the rapprochement era. It requires a general yet brief treatment of China's foreign relations since 1949 with emphasis on the rapprochement. The purpose of it is to enable the reader to see the continuity and change in Peking's policy. In sum, this introduction includes three parts: Peking's perceptions of the world, China's foreign relations between 1949 and 1970, and foreign relations since 1971, followed by a concomitant conclusion.

I. Peking's Perceptions of the World

1. Objectives of Chinese Foreign Policy

The foreign policy of the People's Republic of China [PRC] can be defined to have short-, medium-, and long-range objectives.[2] Its short-range objectives are to maintain national security, achieve unification, promote international relations and cooperation, increase national power, and enhance national prestige and influence. The most essential among these are unification and security (territorial and national). They have repeatedly been announced by Peking since 1949.

While several medium-range and short-range objectives overlap, such as national power, prestige and influence, one

significant medium-range goal is the establishment of the
PRC's leadership in Asia. When this objective is viewed in
geographical, historical and racial perspectives, it appears
reasonably realistic and attainable. This is not to say, however, that the PRC expects to restore China's traditional leadership in the region in the form of the tributary system, but it
undoubtedly has acted to establish a new leadership in modern
Asia on the basis of its announced five principles of peaceful
coexistence.

The long-range objectives, apart from the continuing promotion of power, prestige and influence, are aimed at a world
leadership. For years, Peking has performed both in words
and deeds, inside and outside the United Nations, as a leader
of the Third World. It has also struggled strenuously against
Soviet "revisionism" to achieve co-leadership of the Communist world. Its recent campaign against the hegemony of the
superpowers indicates the beginning of the PRC's struggle for
a leading position of global dimension.

Whether or not the PRC can achieve its objectives depends
mainly on its capabilities (subjective conditions) and the international environment (objective conditions). A review of the
PRC's capabilities and foreign relations in the past shows successes and failures in achieving the multiple goals.

2. Capabilities

On numerous occasions in the past, the Peking leaders have
repeatedly stated that China is a socialist as well as a developing Third World country. As a socialist nation, its government's control is authoritarian and effective; it maintains a
large army equipped with conventional weaponry. In the past
three decades, it has performed as an influential international
actor; one can rank China among France and Britain. As a
developing Third World country, it has a low stage of economic
development, standing close to Egypt and Pakistan. This unbalanced status, as Robert North puts it, is "anomalous."[3]

To measure the capabilities of this "anomalous" state, a

conventional but useful method is to review briefly its major components of national power. They include geography, natural resources, population, national character and morale, political situation, economic development, and military strength, particularly the last two items.

China's geographical size ranks third (9,761,012 square kilometers) in the world, after the Soviet Union (22,403,000 s.k.) and Canada (9,974,375 s.k.) but ahead of the United States (9,363,387 s.k.). Its impressive size, its dominant position in Asia, and its location in the temperate zone suggest that China can potentially become a great power. In natural resources, China possesses rich coal reserves — about 20 percent of the world's coal deposits. The United States and Canada together possess 49 percent. Its iron ore is not as impressive, although its petroleum production is growing. Some specialists have observed that China does possess relatively rich resources and could become an industrial giant. Such development, nevertheless, must be supported by other favorable conditions, such as a stable political situation, sophisticated management, advanced technology, and even foreign capital.[4] With a population of 850 million people (1978), China is often considered to have a strong human source of military power and economic development, yet its annual 2 percent rate of population growth (approximately 16 million people annually as of 1978) tends to present an everlasting food supply problem. Strict discipline and high morale, after three decades of massive and intensive political socialization, have developed a new value in political culture and national character that has strengthened some aspects of China's capabilities, but the political situation in the past thirty years has recorded both stability and disturbances which have helped increase as well as decrease national strength. For instance, the decade of political upheaval and internal struggle created by the Cultural Revolution (1966-1976) has now been referred to as "ten lost years."[5]

Economically, the PRC remains underdeveloped. Specialists in the field have collected available data on China's GNP and

have ranked China from the fifth to eighth in general economic
growth after the U.S., the USSR, Japan and other industrialized
nations.[6] Yet China's per capita GNP is surprisingly low
(U.S.$410). It stands behind North Korea (U.S.$470), South Korea
(U.S.$670), and Taiwan (U.S.$1,070).[7] These rankings, nevertheless, indicate only one aspect of the PRC's economic situation.

Peking's real concern is still the fundamental problem of
grain production. In the three decades of Communist rule,
China is reported to have eliminated starvation, although it
has annually imported 4.5 to 6 million metric tons of grain
from France, Canada, or Australia since 1961. Grain production has increased from approximately 240 million metric tons
in 1970 to 275 million metric tons in 1977,[8] an amount approximately sufficient for the consumption of a population of 800-
850 million people. Industry and technology remain far behind
those of developed nations. If China continues to compete with
the Soviet Union and the United States in the international arena
without a technological and industrial revolution, it will undoubtedly lag far behind the two superpowers. This is why the slogan of "modernization" is very much in the air in the post-
Mao era.

China's military strength is based mainly on its manpower
and nuclear missile development. It had emphasized manpower
over weaponry during the Mao era; its army of about 2,700,000
is one of the largest in the world with backward military equipment. Its F-9 aircraft (modeled after the MIG-21) cannot
match the Soviet MIG-25. Its navy, the world's third largest,
is twenty years out of date in antisubmarine warfare and other
underwater sensing devices. It was the level of military preparedness which caused James Schlesinger's serious concern
for China's defense capability against Russia after his tour
in China in September 1976.[9]

As of early 1978, the PRC had carried out twenty-one nuclear missile tests. It has developed 1,500-mile medium-
range missiles and may have resumed its ICBM program. The
success of these developments has enormously enhanced China's power status. It makes Peking's participation in the

world disarmament negotiations more desirable, yet, its nuclear capability is still far behind that of the United States and
the Soviet Union.

The above survey suggests one simple conclusion, that is,
the development of China's power components is unbalanced.
While the nation's potential power is impressive, its present
strength is limited. Such a limited capability, regardless of
the factor of the international environment, means that China
can achieve only limited objectives of her foreign policy. Apparently, this was one of the major reasons why Mao and Chou
repeatedly admonished their followers that China should not
seek to become a hegemonous superpower.

II. China's Foreign Relations between 1949 and 1970

The international environment changes in accordance with
the times and events. A review of Peking's foreign relations
from 1949 to the time of rapprochement will not only reflect
the interaction and interrelationship between China and the
world during that period, but will also provide us with information and patterns of successes and failures of Peking's international behavior.

1. Lean-to-One-Side and the Korean War, 1949-1953

Lean-to-One-Side. On June 30, 1949, three months prior to
the establishment of the PRC regime in Peking, Mao Tse-tung
announced that the Chinese Communist foreign policy should
"lean to one side" — to the Soviet side.[10] One day after the
Peking government came into existence on October 1, 1949,
the Soviet Union recognized it. It was followed by the "socialist" countries in Eastern Europe and Northeast Asia. Despite
his past disagreement with and even distrust of the Soviet
leaders, Mao went to Moscow on December 16, 1949, for the
first time, to negotiate with Stalin. He stayed there for nine
weeks (until February 17, 1950). As a result, the Sino-Soviet
Treaty of Friendship, Alliance, and Mutual Assistance was

concluded. The treaty reinforced the "lean-to-one-side" policy.

An agreement that inherited both obligations and rights from the Sino-Soviet Treaty of August 1945, the 1950 treaty included the following items: (1) a thirty-year military alliance directed against Japan and other states allied with it (implying the United States); (2) joint Sino-Soviet administration of the Chinese Changchun Railway in Manchuria; (3) joint use of the naval base Port Arthur until the conclusion of a peace treaty with Japan or at the end of 1952; (4) Chinese administration of the international trading port Dairen; (5) a Sino-Soviet guarantee of the independence of the Mongolian People's Republic (Outer Mongolia); and (6) a Soviet economic credit of U.S.$300 million to cover a five-year period (1950-54). The alliance was extended by other economic agreements on minerals, civil aviation, petroleum, and shipbuilding.[11]

Other diplomatic channels were also opened. From December 1949 to June 1950, the PRC exchanged recognition with five Asian countries: Burma, Pakistan, Ceylon, India, and Afghanistan; and seven European countries: the United Kingdom, the Netherlands, Switzerland, and the Scandinavian states. In addition, Peking, preceding the Soviet Union by thirteen days, granted recognition to the Democratic Republic of Vietnam (North Vietnam) on January 18, 1950.

Intervention in the Korean War. On June 25, 1950, the North Koreans invaded South Korea.[12] They won an initial victory by taking Seoul and pushing the South Korean army to the Pusan area until the Inchon landing by the United Nations forces in mid-September. Little more than one month later, the U.N. forces reached the Sino-Korean border area.

Several factors had contributed to the outbreak of the war: the weak South Korean army versus much stronger North Korean troops, the U.S. exclusion of South Korea from its defense perimeter in the Far East, the greatly reduced U.S. forces in Japan and Korea, and a disarmed Japan. On top of these, there was apparently a well-devised invasion plan developed by Stalin and Kim Il Sung. Although there was no evidence to substantiate Mao's role in decision making on the in-

vasion, he and his associates had undoubtedly been informed of
the war prior to the conflict. One indication was the troop
movement of Lin Piao's and Ch'en I's armies from South and
Southeast China to Manchuria. It began in May 1950, more than
a month before the outbreak of the war.

Peking secretly sent a good number of "volunteers" into
Korea in mid-October. On October 26, the "volunteers" began
to attack the South Korean units and U.N. forces near the Yalu
River. In less than two months, the Chinese pushed the U.N.
forces back below the 38th parallel. Seoul was recaptured. As
the Chinese and U.N. forces seesawed around the 38th parallel
area, the General Assembly of the U.N. passed a resolution on
February 1, 1951, condemning the PRC as an aggressor and
recommending an embargo against it.

Why did Mao, contrary to the traditional practice of consolidation by a new regime, fight against the most powerful nation
on earth only one year after the establishment of his government? There are several explanations: safeguard of national
security, especially Manchuria; Stalin's pressure;[13] prevention
of North Korea from being unified with the South by the U.N.
forces; and promotion of China's influence and leadership in
Asia.

From early 1951 to March 1953, the war and the peace talks
dragged on without any significant progress. The U.S. government threatened Peking through the Indian government with the
possible extension of the war to mainland China and the use of
nuclear weapons. More importantly, Stalin died on March 5,
1953. Four days after his return from Stalin's funeral and
consultations in Moscow, Chou En-lai proposed on March 30
an immediate resumption of armistice negotiations. Both
Kim Il Sung and Molotov endorsed it on April 1, and negotiations resumed at Panmunjom only five days later. On July 27,
the armistice agreement was finally signed. It ended the Korean conflict. Out of a total of 22,500 Chinese and North Korean prisoners of war who refused to return to communism,
14,207 Chinese POWs chose to go to Taiwan in late January 1954.

Peking had achieved several gains from this intervention.
Apart from its internal unity, it had restored China's traditional relationship with Korea, demonstrated its determination
and ability (for the first time in a century) to play a leading
role in opposing Western "imperialism" in Asia, and received
massive military aid from Moscow. Peking's losses, however,
were also heavy. In addition to the loss of tens of thousands
of lives (including Mao's son), economic development was delayed for at least three years, and Taiwan was placed under
the protection of the U.S. Seventh Fleet.

Hostility between Peking and Washington. During this "lean-
to-one-side" period, the United States was depicted as the
"No. 1 enemy" of the Chinese people. Peking and Washington
maintained a hostile attitude toward each other.

On October 24, 1949, the Chinese put Angus Ward, the U.S.
consul-general in Mukden, and four other diplomats under
house arrest on spy charges. The State Department described
the incident as a "direct violation of the basic concept of international relations." On January 10, 1950, the U.N. Security
Council debated the issue of Chinese representation, but a resolution calling for Peking's admission was defeated on January 13. On the following day, the Chinese police in Peking invaded and seized the American consular building there. Secretary of State Dean Acheson declared that the United States
would certainly "not recognize Peking in such circumstances"
and would oppose the seating of the Peking regime in the United
Nations.

After the Korean War broke out, the United States resumed military aid to Taiwan. Although the United Nations invited a Chinese
delegation in August 1950 (headed by Wu Hsiu-ch'üan, arrived in
November) to testify on "the United States invasion of Taiwan," it
resulted in practically nothing. During the Korean War, President
Truman had declined Taiwan's offer to participate in the war under
the U.N. flag, so as not to extend the war beyond the boundary
of Korea. In 1951, when a peace treaty with Japan was signed
in San Francisco by forty-eight countries led by the United
States, both the Taipei and Peking regimes were excluded. In

1952, Taiwan, encouraged by the United States, concluded a separate peace treaty with Japan. Peking, after years of negotiations, finally signed a similar treaty with Japan in August 1978.

2. Peaceful Coexistence, 1953-59

The end of the Korean War meant the conclusion of a period of conflict and the beginning of an era of conciliation. The international environment changed. In this new environment, both the Soviet Union and the PRC practiced almost simultaneously their policies of peaceful coexistence with the outside world. It created a thaw between the East and the West.

Impact of Soviet Aid and De-Stalinization. As soon as the Korean War was over, Peking turned quickly to its First Five-Year Plan. The Korean intervention, however, gave Peking a degree of bargaining power for Soviet aid, and Stalin's death left Mao as one of the most senior Communist leaders in the world. Peking's leverage on the course of events of Sino-Soviet relations increased considerably.

In September 1953, only two months after the Korean armistice, Peking obtained Moscow's aid for the construction or renovation of 141 industrial enterprises. The visit to Peking by Khrushchev and Bulganin in October 1954 was truly important because this was the first post-1949 visit by any top Soviet leader. They reached several agreements with Mao. First, Soviet troops would be completely withdrawn from Port Arthur in May 1955 (the 1952 withdrawal schedule had been delayed because of the Korean War); second, the Soviet Union would help China construct 15 additional industrial projects (U.S.$230 million worth of credit); third, the 4 Sino-Soviet joint-stock companies (minerals, petroleum, civil aviation, and shipbuilding) would be transferred to exclusive Chinese control in 1955; and fourth, the Soviet Union and China would cooperate on projects in the fields of science and technology. The significance lies in the fact that these agreements were carried out in full and on schedule. Soviet aid promoted Sino-Soviet friendship substantially.

However, Khrushchev's de-Stalinization in February 1956 at the Twentieth Congress of the Communist Party of the Soviet Union met with a mixed response from Peking. On April 5, three days after the return of the Chinese delegation to the congress, Peking published its first document on "de-Stalinization" in Jen-min jih-pao. It endorsed the criticism of Stalin's "cult of the individual" and his mistake of expelling Yugoslavia from the Cominform, but praised Stalin's contributions to the world Communist movement.[14] Such a conditional endorsement, apparently solicited by Moscow, was issued two days prior to Mikoyan's visit to China on April 7, 1956. It enabled Peking to request a new Soviet loan for 55 more industrial projects. Twenty days later, Mao made a "fair" evaluation of Stalin: achievement, 70 percent; failure, 30 percent.[15]

The impact of de-Stalinization was broad and profound. The Hungarian Revolution in November 1956 provoked Tito's criticism of Stalinism with which China strongly disagreed. Accordingly, the Sino-Yugoslav relationship deteriorated until the 1970s. The Eighth Congress of the Chinese Communist Party [CCP] in September 1956 elected, for the first time, four vice-chairmen under Mao (Liu Shao-ch'i, Chou En-lai, Chu Teh, and Ch'en Yun) — a move to avoid being criticized for practicing the "cult of the individual." In early 1957 under the impact of the Hungarian Revolution, Mao initiated his "hundred flowers" campaign. It was only short-lived.

When the Middle East Crisis broke out in July 1958 and United States and British troops were requested to land in Lebanon and Jordan respectively to prevent any Iraqi-style coup influenced by Egypt, the Soviet Union, a strong supporter of Egypt, denounced the American and British move as an act of new imperialism and demanded an immediate withdrawal of their troops. To enhance the Soviet position, Khrushchev flew to Peking for support. Mao exercised his leverage and exacted new Soviet aid for another 47 industrial enterprises. In addition, Chou En-lai went to Moscow in February 1959 and obtained another credit for 31 industrial projects. The total number of Soviet-aided projects was 289.

Despite all these efforts and new credits from Moscow, an undercurrent of Sino-Soviet disagreement was growing. It originated in de-Stalinization, as Peking made public in 1963.

The Geneva Conference. Although the Peking government in 1950-54 had given an enormous amount of material and personnel assistance to the Viet Minh (the Vietnam Independence League) led by Ho Chi Minh, China did not fight a second Korean War in Indochina as many observers had feared. Among several important reasons, the most convincing ones were the absence of any "threat" to Chinese security by the war and the fighting ability of the Viet Minh army was such that it required no Chinese help.[16]

The eight years of the Indochina war (1946-1954) ended with a conference at Geneva. The conference (April 26-July 20, 1954) had two issues on the agenda: Korea and Indochina. The Korean issue reached a deadlock and was dropped. Discussions on the Indochina issue began on May 8 with nine participants: France, Britain, the U.S., the USSR, China, the Viet Minh, South Vietnam, Cambodia, and Laos. The Viet Minh victory over the French at Dien Bien Phu on May 7 gave added bargaining power to the Viet Minh delegation. (The U.S. had declined a French request to intervene because of the lack of support from Congress and Great Britain.) At this juncture, the Eisenhower administration had decided to assist South Vietnam to remain non-Communist. Meanwhile, U.S. Secretary of State John Foster Dulles was establishing the Southeast Asia Treaty Organization (SEATO) to defend the region from Communist aggression or subversion.

All the major powers (except the U.S.) exerted some efforts to move the conference toward a successful conclusion. As far as China was concerned, the Chinese delegation led by Chou En-lai also made several contributions. On June 23, Chou met Mendès-France (the new French premier) at Bern. They agreed upon a political settlement in Indochina in addition to an armistice. On July 3-5, Chou met Ho Chi Minh on the Sino-Vietnamese border, presumably to persuade Ho to agree to a political settlement. Moreover, Chou's proposal for the thorny

problem of the components of the International Commission for
Supervision and Control [ICC] was also accepted. The conference concluded on July 20. It registered the end of French
colonialism in Indochina, agreed to a cease-fire throughout
Indochina, and promised a unified Vietnam by national elections
two years after the armistice.

The Chinese press intensively propagandized China's position and prestige at Geneva. It praised China as a "big power"
in the international forum and insisted that Chou En-lai was
not only speaking for China but for Asia as well.[17] As a result
of the performance at Geneva, China's international status was
enhanced considerably.

Peaceful coexistence and the Bandung Spirit. When the
Geneva Conference held a recess between June 21 and July 9,
the chief delegates of the participants returned home for consultation. Chou En-lai visited India on his way to Peking and
concluded with Nehru the well-known Five Principles of Peaceful Coexistence. They were: (1) mutual respect for each other's
territorial integrity and sovereignty, (2) nonaggression, (3) noninterference in each other's internal affairs, (4) equality and
mutual benefit, and (5) peaceful coexistence. These principles
were also endorsed by U Nu (premier of Burma) and Ho Chi
Minh. They became a landmark of the era of peaceful coexistence and had a far-reaching impact on Chinese foreign policy.

The Asian-African Conference (April 18-24, 1955) at Bandung, Indonesia, was another significant development in this
era.[18] It was sponsored by the five Colombo Plan countries
(India, Pakistan, Ceylon, Burma, and Indonesia) and was attended by twenty-nine Asian and African countries. They included two Communist states (China and North Vietnam), twelve
neutral countries, and fifteen anti-Communist states. Its original purposes were to promote goodwill and review the position
of Asia and Africa in the world. As the meeting went on, however, the participants engaged in political quarrels.

Fully realizing the general anti-Communist (and even anti-
Chinese) atmosphere and the conflicting viewpoints among the
participants, Chou En-lai, China's chief delegate, gave an

impressive performance. He first appeared to be a quiet listen-
er, which eased some degree of the anti-Communist attitude.
Later, when the anti-Communist and neutral nations quarreled
over their conflicting views, Chou came out to mediate and
urged them to seek the "common ground" of anticolonialism.
He also announced China's willingness to negotiate with the
United States on Taiwan. His eloquent and moderate attitude
convinced many of the delegates that he was a reasonable man
of goodwill, pursuing a peaceful policy. As the conference concluded, Chou had undoubtedly helped create the so-called "Bandung spirit," which was generally defined to mean peace, goodwill,
conciliation, unity of Asian-African nations, and anticolonialism.

In the four post-Bandung years (1955-59), the international
environment remained quite favorable to China. Peking received diplomatic recognition from nine Asian-African countries. She also began to enter a new world — Africa.

The grand tour of eight Asian nations by Chou En-lai in
1956-57 was an extension of Peking's policy of peaceful coexistence.[19] This was the most extensive visit to Asia ever
made by a Chinese premier. Well received, Chou performed
to strengthen China's relations with these nations on the principles of peaceful coexistence. More significant was the new
flow of Asian leaders to Peking in this era (1954-59). It was a
period of diplomatic growth in which China began to rebuild
her traditional leadership in Asia.

Beginning of the Warsaw Talks. Peking and Washington had
few contacts immediately after the Korean War. But, in December 1954, Washington and Taipei signed the Taiwan-U.S. Mutual
Defense Treaty to protect Taiwan. This formalized the Taiwan
issue as the hard-core problem between the United States and
the PRC.

At the beginning of 1955, Dag Hammarskjold, secretary-
general of the United Nations, visited Peking on behalf of six
U.S. prisoners of war from Korea. As a result, Peking released them later in the year. This development was followed
by the ambassadorial talks on August 1, 1955, at Geneva between China and the U.S.

The crisis over the Chinese Communist shellings at Quemoy and Matsu, islands held by the Chinese Nationalists, in August-October 1958 provided Chou En-lai with an opportunity to offer peace talks with the United States on Taiwan. The U.S. welcomed the offer, but no negotiations took place to settle the shellings. The crisis was eased after Dulles pressured Chiang Kai-shek, the Chinese Nationalist president on Taiwan, to renounce military force as a means to recover mainland China. Washington and Peking returned to the minimum-contact relationship except for the Warsaw talks, which served only as a limited communication line between the two capitals.

3. The Sino-Indian Conflict and
    the Sino-Soviet Dispute, 1959-1965

The outcome of China's First Five-Year Plan (1953-57) was impressive. The combined agricultural-industrial output increased by 60.8 percent, and the GNP in the 1953-57 period rose at an annual rate of 7 to 10 percent (Japan's in the 1950-56 period grew at 8.6 percent). But Mao saw "capitalist forces" appear everywhere as the economy progressed. He was determined to eliminate them. Meanwhile, he decided in 1957, after debates among the leadership, to adopt a radical (as opposed to a moderate) method for economic development. As the pendulum of the nation's policy moved to the left, Peking launched a series of campaigns in 1957-58, such as the Anti-Rightist Movement, the Great Leap Forward, and the commune system.
The radical approach had an important bearing on Peking's foreign relations. Resisting the accelerated steps of communization and unification, Tibet staged a revolt in 1959. The revolt became a sine qua non of the Sino-Indian border conflicts of October 1959. Meanwhile, the radical method of economic and socialist reconstruction "annoyed" (in Khrushchev's words) the Soviet Union. Together with Peking's position on de-Stalinization, Yugoslavia, and the commune system, the anti-capitalist drive developed a link with the antirevisionist cam-

paign against Moscow. It led to the "earth-shaking" Sino-Soviet dispute.

Sino-Indian Border Conflicts.[20] The Tibetan revolt in October 1959 was suppressed by Chinese military force. Fifteen hundred Tibetans, including the Dalai Lama, fled to India. The Indian government granted them political asylum and made the incident known to the world. China disliked it. In securing its border, the Chinese army clashed with the Indian force in the disputed border area in late October. Twelve Indian border policemen were killed.

The conflict alarmed Asia. To demonstrate that the PRC could and would reach agreements by negotiations with neighbors on border issues, Peking concluded in 1960-62 friendship and border treaties with Burma, Nepal, Pakistan, Afghanistan, and Outer Mongolia. No agreement was reached between China and India. While accusing China of illegally building a highway through the disputed Askai Chin area, India actively prepared for self-defense. By September 1962, India had built forty-three outposts and had proudly accepted Soviet military aid (jet fighters) in addition to Britain's and the United States'. One month later, a new war broke out. After a month of fighting (October-November), India suffered a greater defeat than in 1959. The Chinese advanced deep into Indian territory, both in Ladakh and the Northeast Frontier Agency. Peking announced a unilateral cease-fire and withdrew its troops to the original dispute region.

Six Afro-Asian countries (Burma, Cambodia, Ghana, Ceylon, Indonesia, and the UAR) held a conference for mediation at Colombo in December 1962. Their proposal was rejected by Peking in January 1963, and the Sino-Indian border dispute has remained unsettled ever since.

Laos and Vietnam. Events in Laos and Vietnam also reflected the difficulties in maintaining the principles of peaceful coexistence.

In 1958-1960, while the United States offered military and economic assistance to the non-Communist government in Laos, Hanoi and Peking aided the revolutionary Pathet Lao. In

1960-61, Soviet arms for both the Laotian government and the
Pathet Lao were flown in via China and Vietnam. In early 1961,
the Soviet Union became very influential in Laos. The Laotian
crisis then came to a head when the North Vietnam-Pathet Lao
forces overran the Laotian highlands.

As the Sino-Soviet relationship deteriorated, China no longer
provided transit stops for Soviet planes to Laos. The Soviet
Union found it necessary to agree to a conference on peace and
neutrality in Laos in order to check Peking and Washington
there. A lengthy Geneva conference was held from May 1961
to June 1962. In early May 1962, a major Pathet Lao victory
prompted the United States to dispatch 4,000 combat troops to
Thailand to reassure the Thai government. Swiftly, an agreement on Laotian neutrality and foreign troop withdrawal was
reached. Ironically, although the American forces withdrew
on schedule, the Chinese and North Vietnamese military and
economic personnel stayed on.

In South Vietnam, United States military and economic aid
in 1955-59 had significantly strengthened the Ngo Dinh Diem
government. Its military campaign had almost "destroyed"
the South Vietnamese revolutionaries who were restrained
from fighting back by Hanoi's earlier decision on "political
struggle." The years 1958-59 were "the darkest period" of
the South Vietnamese revolution. Its survival was at stake.
In January 1959, Hanoi finally approved the repeatedly requested "military struggle" for the South and sent its first
armed unit to South Vietnam in June 1959 over the Ho Chi Minh
Trail. It was, however, not until December 1963, when the pre-
carious post-Diem military junta in Saigon refused to negotiate
with Hanoi, that the Hanoi leadership decided to adopt an offensive strategy for the South and began to offer massive military
aid to the Viet-Cong. [21]

China, having suffered from its economic failure in 1959-1960,
displayed a cautious attitude toward Vietnam. Publicly supporting the revolt in the South, Peking did not immediately follow
Hanoi's example by intensifying its commitment. In fact,
Peking had repeatedly urged the parties concerned to convene

a new Geneva conference on South Vietnam until the Gulf of Tonkin Incident in August 1964.

The Sino-Soviet Dispute.[22] After 1959, several major issues aggravated the Sino-Soviet dispute. By 1965, more problems were involved, and the polemics had reached a point of no return.

Apart from the problems mentioned earlier (de-Stalinization, Yugoslavia, and the communes), the major issues in dispute in 1959-1965 are succinctly enumerated below:

1) The Secret Atomic Agreement. On October 15, 1957, Peking concluded with Moscow a secret atomic agreement whereby Moscow would help China develop its nuclear capability. Later, Khrushchev asked for a say in China's future nuclear delivery system because he was concerned that a nuclear China might be too powerful to be kept aligned. Mao refused it. Khrushchev then "scrapped" the agreement on June 20, 1959.[23] It almost destroyed Mao's hope of making China a modern military power and seriously hurt his pride.

2) Imperialism, War, and Peace. Peking resented Khrushchev's visit to the United States in September 1959 to promote his peaceful coexistence policy. To patch things up, Khrushchev rushed to Peking on October 1 — one day after his return from the United States — for the tenth anniversary of the founding of the PRC. It was of no avail. On April 16, 1960, Hung-ch'i [Red Flag] published a 15,000-word article entitled "Long Live Leninism" in honor of Lenin's ninetieth birthday. It openly challenged Soviet ideological leadership and stressed Lenin's belief that war was "an inevitable outcome" of the imperialist system. With an eye on Khrushchev's going to a summit conference in Paris, the article warned that "Marxism-Leninism absolutely must not sink into the mire of bourgeois pacifism." Incidentally, the U-2 affair in May 1960 aborted the summit conference. It seemed to "justify" Peking's hard line on imperialism.

3) Withdrawal of Soviet Economic Aid. The Third Congress of the Rumanian Communist Party in late June 1960 unexpectedly witnessed an open confrontation between Khrushchev and P'eng Chen, China's chief delegate to the congress. Peking

later charged that the confrontation was a Soviet "all-out and converging attack" on the CCP. In anger, Khrushchev ordered the withdrawal in August-September 1960 of the entire Soviet economic and technical mission. This came at a time when China was in great economic difficulties.

4) The 1960 Moscow Conference. After long and hard debates, the Moscow conference of eighty-one Communist parties in November 1960 produced a compromise statement. The major propositions contained in the statement included the upholding of Soviet leadership; the acknowledgment of China's influence in Asia, Africa, and Latin America; the condemnation of Yugoslav revisionism; the encouragement of wars of national liberation; the avoidability of world war; and peaceful coexistence among socialist and capitalist (not imperialist) countries. Such a compromise statement registered undisputedly Moscow's loss of its monolithic authority over the world Communist movement, although the Soviet Union had still won a victory over China.[24]

5) The Albanian Issue. The Albanian Communist Party disapproved Khrushchev's de-Stalinization mainly because Enver Hoxha (Party chief) owed his power to Stalin. Albania was also worried that Khrushchev's resumption of his friendship with Tito would bring Albania back under Yugoslav control as in the past. The tiny, poor Albania found help from China. At the 1960 Moscow conference, Hoxha revealed Khrushchev's lobbying for Albania's support against China. At the Twenty-second Congress of the Soviet Party in October 1961, Khrushchev openly criticized Albania and Stalin, whereas China unrestrainedly defended Albania. In strong disagreement, the Chinese delegation walked out of the conference and went home. Khrushchev then attacked the CCP, saying:

...if the Chinese comrades wish to make efforts toward normalizing the relations between the Albania Party of Labor and the fraternal parties, there is hardly anyone who could contribute more to the solution of this problem than the Chinese Communist Party.[25]

Yet, China sided with Albania against Russia.

6) Indian Border Conflicts and the Cuban Missile Crisis.
After the Sino-Indian border conflicts discussed earlier, Peking
repeatedly accused Moscow in November-December 1962 of
helping the Indian "reactionary group" with military weapons
and collaborating with British and U.S. imperialists against
China.

After Khrushchev had ordered the withdrawal of the missiles
from Cuba in late October 1962, Peking railed at him that it
was "purely nonsense" to say that peace had been "saved" by
withdrawing Soviet missiles.[26] Khrushchev replied in kind to
the Chinese attacks. The polemics escalated further.

7) The Sino-Soviet Ideological Meeting and Intensified Dispute. After repeated appeals by several small Communist
parties (the parties of Indonesia, Vietnam, New Zealand, Britain, and Sweden), Peking and Moscow held a two-week meeting
in Moscow in July 1963 on their ideological differences. It
ended in failure and was followed by a year-long (July 1963-
July 1964) intensified exchange of polemics. The Chinese appeared to be much more argumentative than the Soviets.[27]
The dispute reached a new high.

8) The Partial Nuclear Test Ban Treaty. On July 30, 1963,
a partial nuclear test ban treaty was signed by the Soviet Union,
the United States, and Britain. Peking violently condemned the
Soviet signature of the treaty, accusing Moscow of allying with
imperialism against China and deceiving the people of the world.
For propaganda effect, Chou En-lai proposed on July 31, 1963,
to the governments of the world the convening of a world conference on the total and complete prohibition of nuclear weapons. He received only a few favorable responses from small
Communist countries.

9) Border Territories. The Sino-Soviet territorial issue
did not come up until the dispute was brought into the open.
China voiced complaints against Russian and Soviet acquisition
of Chinese borderlands in the past, totaling some 500,000
square miles through the "unequal" Treaties of Aigun (1858),
Peking (1860), St. Petersburg (1881), and others (1861-1894).
The Sino-Soviet treaties of 1945 and 1950, reversing the pro-

visions of the 1924 treaty, severed Outer Mongolia from China.
Bitter in mind, Mao presented a strong argument in July 1964
to a delegation of the Japanese Socialist Party. He not only
wanted to discuss the status of Outer Mongolia with the Soviets,
but also argued for the return of the Kurile Islands to Japan.[28]

Khrushchev fell from power on October 15, 1964. When a
Soviet-proposed, but postponed, international Communist conference was finally held in Moscow on March 5, 1965, nineteen
invited Communist parties attended and seven declined (China,
North Vietnam, North Korea, Japan, Indonesia, Albania, and
Rumania). The conference produced no result. Peking denounced it as a "most serious step to affect an open split in
the international movement."[29]

China Approaches Africa and Latin America.[30] Africa and
Latin America were relatively new to China. The Bandung
Conference of 1955 set the stage for Peking's approach to these
two continents, and the wave of the African independence movement welcomed China with open arms.

To Africa, Chou En-lai announced in 1964 China's "five principles" to promote relations. They were (1) support to the
African peoples in their struggle against imperialism and neocolonialism and in defense of their national independence;
(2) support for their policy of peace, neutrality, and nonalignment; (3) support for their desire to achieve unity and solidarity; (4) support for the settlement of their disputes through
peaceful consultation; and (5) respect for their sovereignty and
opposition to encroachment and interference. In offering economic aid to Africa, China also advocated eight principles,
emphasizing equality and mutual benefit, economic cooperation, respect for recipients' independence, assistance with no
conditions attached, low interest loans, and self-reliance.[31]
The Africans were impressed by this approach. From 1960
to 1965, China gained fifteen nations' recognition and offered
approximately U.S.$296 million in economic aid. In addition,
Chou En-lai's "safari" to eleven nations in 1964 and 1965 promoted China's image and influence there.

The activities of leftist "people's organizations" were also

developing rapidly. The "Afro-Asian People's Solidarity Committee" (1957), an influential offshoot of the Bandung Conference, sponsored three successive meetings in Guinea (April
1960), Tanganyika (February 1963), and Ghana (May 1965).
The delegations of countries and regions grew from thirty-
seven to seventy-two.

The Soviet Union wanted to participate in the scheduled second Asian-African conference in 1965. China opposed Soviet
participation. Several nations, like India and the UAR, intended
to exclude China from this meeting in order to make it a conference of nonaligned nations. In October 1965, one month
prior to the rescheduled conference, China realized her support had declined and proposed an indefinite postponement of
it. Thus, a second Asian-African conference was never held.
In one decade (1955-1965), China's triumph at Bandung had
faded away.

In Latin America, where China had no diplomatic relations
except with Cuba, cultural exchanges were important. Her approach was to use New China News Agency [NCNA] correspondents and friendship societies between China and Latin American countries to engage in "people's diplomacy." Peking sent
numerous delegations, ranging from trade missions to acrobatic teams. A great number of Latin Americans were invited
to China. They included former government officials, legis-
lators, Communist party leaders, workers, intellectuals, newsmen, artists and students. Some of them were received by
Mao Tse-tung and were particularly impressed. As one of
them said, they "had never had the honor of being received
even by the most obscure member of the Central Committee"
in Moscow.[32]

4. Foreign Relations during the Cultural Revolution, 1965-1970

A Policy for the Vietnam War. After the passage of the
Tonkin Gulf Resolution by the U.S. Senate in August 1964,
Peking, in addition to dropping its long-advocated proposal
for a new Geneva conference, shifted to support Hanoi's

offensive strategy. It immediately sent a squadron of MIG-15 and MIG-17 jets to Hanoi, but it took Peking about fifteen months (August 1964-November 1965) to finalize a policy for the Vietnam War. The main reasons were internal debates over the escalating U.S. intervention and the increasing Soviet interest in the war.

For simplicity, Peking's policy is summarized as follows:[33]

1) Increase military and economic aid and encourage self-reliant people's war. The dispatch of the squadron of MIG jets in August-September 1964 was accompanied by the construction of new airfields in Yunnan and Kwangsi as an air sanctuary for Hanoi. After the American bombing of the North began in February 1965, Mao decided not to meet the U.S. air force in kind. Instead, he sent Vietnam some 50,000 "engineer-soldiers" to repair the damage to bridges, roads, and railways caused by U.S. air raids. Meanwhile, Peking increased its military and economic aid to both Hanoi and the Vietcong. More important, it encouraged them to fight their own people's war as Lin Piao's article of September 1965 entitled "Long Live the Victory of the People's War!" had indicated.

2) No Sino-American war over Vietnam. The traditional saying, "We will not attack unless we are attacked" [Jen pu fan-wo, wo pu fan-jen], described Peking's attitude toward the United States on Vietnam. It developed into a "no-war-with-the-U.S." policy throughout the war. Ch'en I (July 1964), Mao Tse-tung (January 1965), Lin Piao (September 1965), and Chou En-lai (April 1966) all made similar statements that China would not "take the initiative to provoke" a war with the United States. The message was clear. Reciprocally, the United States informed China at the Warsaw talks in March 1966 that it had no intention of invading China.

3) Rejection of the Soviet proposal for "united action." As a result of Kosygin's visit to Hanoi in February 1965, Moscow adopted new measures for Vietnam, including the important "united action" proposal to Peking. The proposal contained: (1) transit rights for Soviet military weapons to Hanoi through China by rail; (2) the use of airfields in Yunnan and Kwangsi

and the right to station 500 men there; (3) an air corridor over China; (4) passage rights for 4,000 Soviet military personnel through China to Vietnam; and (5) trilateral talks among Moscow, Peking, and Hanoi on the war. Hanoi eagerly endorsed the proposal, but China, except for the rail transit agreement that was concluded with Russia after some difficulties, formally rejected the rest of the proposal in November 1965.[34] Obviously, Peking was concerned that Moscow might use the "united action" to skillfully achieve not only a stronger Soviet role in Indochina, but also a Sino-Soviet rapprochement and a Soviet military presence in China, both of which would mean the failure of Mao's anti-Soviet policy.

4) No peace talks on Vietnam. After August 1964, Peking actively disapproved any peace negotations on the war. Since China did not have to have any massive military involvement similar to that in Korea, Peking saw advantages in the continuation of the Vietnam War: It served to undermine a possible Soviet-American détente, presented a model for wars of national liberation in the Third World, aroused anti-U.S. sentiment in China and around the world, and promoted the anti-war movement and other domestic problems in the U.S. Mao believed, as he told Edgar Snow in January 1965, that the United States would lose its interest in Vietnam after a short period of time and would withdraw from there. Peking therefore rejected any peace talks proposal on the grounds that "conditions for negotiations" were not yet ripe[35] and advised the Vietnamese to fight until the final victory.

5) Conditions for intervention. It must be made clear that Peking never ruled out the possibility of a Korean-style intervention. Of all the reports and speculations, Anna Louise Strong's letter of May 8, 1965, stated this most clearly to the outside world. She reported that "if the U.S. continues to pour troops and weapons into Vietnam, until the Vietnamese feel the need, the Chinese will be there."[36] It could be understood that in such circumstances North Vietnam would be forced to invite China to intervene.

As of late 1965, China's Vietnam War policy and the pattern

of her involvement in the war had been established. At about
the same time, the tumultuous Cultural Revolution started in
Shanghai.

The Cultural Revolution and Diplomatic Setbacks. In retrospect, we can see a little more clearly than before that the Cultural Revolution, apart from several other known motivations,
was a radical movement directed not only against the old, capitalist, revisionist "poisons" as Mao originally planned, but
also against almost all the Party veterans as the radicals later
revealed. Its final goal was a seizure of power by the radicals,
led by the group now known as the "Gang of Four." Although
partially and temporarily successful due to Mao's support, the
impact of the Cultural Revolution was so devastating that it
wasted a decade for economic development and caused serious
diplomatic setbacks.

On the heels of the postponement (and later cancellation) of
the second Asian-African conference, China suffered a setback
in Indonesia in October 1965. The failure of the September 30
coup, staged by the Indonesian Communist Party [PKI] in cooperation with elements of the air force, resulted in the slaughter of the Communists and the destruction of the Party. It eventually ruined Sukarno's presidency. China was reported to have
been informed of the coup plan and had delivered to the PKI a
large portion of a promised shipment of 100,000 items of small
arms without the knowledge of the Indonesian army authorities.
Many Indonesians blamed China for her involvement.[37]

The great convulsion of the Cultural Revolution aggravated
these setbacks. Less than a year after the Red Guards were
mobilized in mid-1966, all Chinese ambassadors, except
Huang Hua (now foreign minister) in Cairo, were recalled for
reeducation. Charges d'affaires were left in control of other
embassies. The Red Guards made severe verbal attacks on
senior diplomats and the Ministry of Foreign Affairs. Such
criticism reached its height in late spring 1967 when Ch'en I
was forced to "confess" his errors. In August of the same
year, a revolt was staged in the ministry when radicals, led
by Yao Teng-shan who had formally served in Indonesia, were

reported to have "seized power" in the ministry for a few days.[38]

Moreover, the Red Guards turned violently against the Soviet Union (to be discussed later) and several Western missions in Peking. In August 1967, for instance, they set fire to the British mission in the capital. Donald Hopson, the British chargé d'affaires, and several of his staff were beaten when they rushed out of the building. Anti-"imperialist" sentiment ran high. The convulsion and rivalry among the Red Guards even interrupted the arms shipment from Russia to Vietnam via China.

The number of exchanges of delegations between China and all foreign countries dropped from 1,322 in 1965 to 66 in 1969.[39] During the same period, there were five diplomatic suspensions (Indonesia, Dahomey, the Central African Republic, Ghana, and Tunisia) as opposed to two recognitions (Mauritius and South Yemen).

In sum, the Cultural Revolution created a situation in which China experienced a period of contraction in its foreign relations. As China turned inward, most nations adopted a "wait-and-see" policy in dealing with Peking.

Sino-Soviet Border Conflicts.[40] During the same period, the Sino-Soviet dispute escalated and culminated in the border conflicts on the Ussuri River in March 1969.

Early in August 1966, thousands of Red Guards demonstrated in Peking's streets near the Soviet Embassy. Pravda (September 16) denounced them bitterly. In October, Moscow expelled fifty-five Chinese students in reprisal. In late November, Pravda called for Mao's overthrow; this was repeated several times in 1967. In retaliation, Chinese troops joined the Red Guards in late January 1967 in staging a partial siege of the Soviet Embassy for nineteen days. In return, the Soviets invaded the Chinese Embassy in Moscow in early February and beat up several Chinese aides. The Red Guards immediately harassed Soviet dependents and made them bow to Mao's portrait when they evacuated from Peking. Such emotional and vicious interactions continued for some time.

In August 1968 when the Soviet invasion of Czechoslovakia took place, Peking criticized it as being aggression by "social-imperialism." Peking was concerned about the possibility of a similar Soviet move against China. On March 2, 1969, Soviet and Chinese forces clashed on the disputed Chenpao (Damansky) Islands in the Ussuri River. A few hundred men were involved. Whether or not Lin Piao, or even Mao Tse-tung, had provoked such a conflict to promote his authority and leadership, as some specialists have observed,[41] the Chinese gained the upper hand. Unprecedented publicity was made by both the Chinese and Soviets. The sentiment of nationalism on both sides ran high. On March 15, the Soviets struck at the Chinese in the same area. Each side maneuvered thousands of soldiers. This time, the Chinese suffered heavy casualties. Observers wondered whether a large-scale Sino-Soviet war was imminent.

Kosygin visited Peking in September 1969 after attending Ho Chi Minh's funeral in Hanoi. Chou En-lai coolly met him at the airport. He reportedly made conciliatory suggestions for improving relations on three fronts: state-to-state relations, territorial negotiations, and ideological discussions. Although the first two fronts had been quietly but grudgingly improved, the third may last for "9,000 years," as Mao put it.[42]

An Undercurrent of Conciliation with Washington. By the end of 1966, the United States seemed to have developed a consensus in favor of continued containment of China without isolation. As the Cultural Revolution and the Vietnam War ran apace, it became abundantly clear in 1966-67 that neither the turbulent China nor the war-burdened United States had any intention at all of starting a war against the other. In October 1967, Richard Nixon expressed his views in Foreign Affairs that the restoration of domestic tranquillity could be achieved only by defusing the Vietnam War and that China should have its position in the world community. Whereas President Johnson's peace offer to North Vietnam in April 1968 showed Washington's intention to deescalate the war, the Czechoslovakia invasion in August of the same year concerned China. In a surprise shift, Peking proposed on November 26, 1968, to hold a meeting in Warsaw with the Nixon administration's representatives on February 20, 1969, for the purpose of concluding an agreement based on the five principles of peaceful coexistence. The proposed meeting was canceled by Peking on February 19, 1969, on the grounds that the U.S. had granted political asylum to a Chinese diplomat, Liao Ho-shu, who had defected in the Netherlands. Yet Peking's intention was significant.

To move toward conciliation with Peking, Nixon took the initiative. According to the accounts of H. R. Haldeman and other White House aides,[43] Nixon put out a feeler via Secretary of State William Rogers who visited the home of President Yahya Khan of Pakistan in Lahore on May 24, 1969; Rogers expressed Nixon's interest in meeting the top leaders of the People's Republic of China. In June, the U.S. began to withdraw troops from Vietnam. One month later, it acted to relax curbs on travel to and trade with China. On August 1, Nixon repeated his China signal to Yahya Khan in Lahore and flashed it again through President Nicolae Ceausescu of Rumania the next day in Bucharest. In January 1970, the Warsaw talks resumed after almost two years of suspension. A second meeting was held in February. Such moves signaled China's favorable response to Nixon.

The Cambodia incursion by American and South Vietnamese forces in May 1970 interrupted the Warsaw dialogue, but two weeks before the United States completed its withdrawal from Cambodia, Chou En-lai told East European diplomats in Peking that China expected the talks would soon be resumed. Right after the withdrawal, Nixon, in an interview with ABC commentator Howard K. Smith on July 1, reaffirmed his desire to improve relations with China. Meanwhile, Secretary of State William Rogers appealed to China in Tokyo for a settlement in Vietnam. In the same month, China released the Most Reverend James Edward Walsh (an American) after his twelve-year imprisonment, but there was still no definite response to Nixon's meeting proposal from Peking. On October 2, 1970, when Nixon met again with President Yahya Khan in the White House, he knew the Pakistani President was to

visit Peking in three weeks. He asked Yahya Khan to transmit
a message directly to Chou En-lai: Would the Chinese welcome
Nixon's visit to China?

One day in mid-November, Chou En-lai, after his discussions
of Nixon's message with Mao Tse-tung, gave the visiting Yahya
Khan a reply: "We welcome the proposal from Washington for
face-to-face discussions." On December 18, 1970, Mao told
Edgar Snow that he would welcome Nixon's visit to China.
Three weeks after the United States lifted its ban on travel by
Americans to China (March 15, 1971), Mao reversed Chou En-
lai's decision by granting a visa (April 7, 1971) to the U.S.
table-tennis team to visit China from Japan. Now the undercurrent of conciliation was to grow into a main stream of rapprochement.

III. China's Foreign Relations since 1971

From the ping-pong diplomacy of April 1971 to Henry Kissinger's first visit to Peking in early July, the atmosphere of
conciliation enjoyed a gradual and steady growth. Several developments in this period indicated this trend, such as Peking's
endorsement for the first time of the South Vietnamese National Liberation Front peace proposal in early July, the beginning of the flow of American visitors to China, Nixon's order to further ease the trade embargo against China, and the
acceleration of American troop withdrawals from Vietnam.

1. Sino-American Rapprochement

Undoubtedly, the historic move of Nixon's "reopening" of
China which led to the East and West détente was a great surprise to both the Chinese people and the outside world. It is
unnecessary to dwell on the well-known Nixon visit and his
negotiations with Mao and Chou. Yet, what was Peking's real
motivation for the rapprochement? And how did Peking explain such a dramatic move to its own people? These questions are worth exploring.

Motivations and Explanations. The Soviet invasion of Czechoslovakia in August 1968 and the Sino-Soviet border conflicts in
March 1969 must have led Mao to conclude that his dispute with
the Soviet Union might have reached a new stage involving a
possible military confrontation. Meanwhile, the United States
continued withdrawing its troops from Vietnam, and Nixon repeatedly expressed his desire to improve relations with Peking.
These developments seemed to suggest that China's enemy had
shifted from the south to the north. Japan was, and still is, an
American ally and looks to the United States for leadership in
East Asia. Taiwan was, and still is, under the protection umbrella of the United States. Strategically, therefore, Mao must
have calculated that a rapprochement with the United States
would be followed by a thaw with Japan and a clarified U.S.
position on Taiwan. In other words, the advantages would be
as follows:

1) It would change the United States from an adversary to a
potential friend, moving Sino-American relations from confrontation to accommodation.

2) It would make the United States a counterweight against
the Soviet Union so as to strengthen China's position on the
one hand and to drive a wedge in the Soviet-American détente
on the other.

3) It would shift Japan's diplomatic ties from Taipei to Peking and would accordingly eliminate the possibility of Japan's
future "occupation" of Taiwan and reduce the significance of
Japanese-Soviet cooperation in East Asia.

4) It would clarify Taiwan's status as part of China with the
United States and Japan, thus ruling out any possibility of a
"Taiwan independence" or "Two China" situation.

5) It would end China's international isolation which had
been created by the Cultural Revolution and build up new,
broad international relations.

In retrospect, we know from various sources that many
Chinese were puzzled by, and even argued against, the rapprochement. Peking made efforts to explain the motives to
its people. Two weeks after the surprising announcement of

Henry Kissinger's first visit to China in July 1971, a well-
conceived article was published in Hung-ch'i, the Party theoretical journal, on August 2, 1971.[44] It carefully explained the
then forthcoming rapprochement for both domestic and foreign
consumption. It stressed two points of Mao's view on policy —
the importance of formulating and executing policy and the significance of exploiting international contradictions. It quoted
what Mao had said during the Second World War: "Our policy
is to make use of contradictions, win over the many, oppose
the few, and crush our enemies one by one...."[45]

Moreover, Mao explained that a strategy of combining alliance with struggle in a united front is essential: "The (anti-
Japanese national) united front is neither all alliance and no
struggle nor all struggle and no alliance, but combines alliance and struggle."

What was the implication of restating this wartime policy
in 1971? To put it squarely, Mao was preparing in 1971 to
cooperate with the United States, Japan, and possibly other nations against the Soviet Union. It would be a further development of Mao's old strategy of the anti-Japanese united front.
Many people, however, still did not understand how Mao could
cooperate with Richard Nixon, president of "U.S. imperialism."
Lin Piao, among others, even charged that such a Sino-U.S.
rapprochement was a betrayal of revolution and Vietnam. This
prompted Chou En-lai to make a secret explanation to the CCP
officials in December 1971:

Because Nixon has encountered difficulties both domestically and internationally, he has requested eagerly to visit China. When he comes, he has
to bring something along in his pocket; otherwise, he will find it hard to
give explanations when he returns to the U.S. It is to our advantage if the
negotiation succeeds, but it constitutes no detriment to us if the negotiation
fails. We will never give up our principles and sell out our people and revolution.... That U.S.-China relations are a betrayal of principle, of revolution, and of Vietnam-as Lin Piao said, is nonsense and an insult to the
Party....
The USSR and the U.S. are now dealing with us by means of dual tactics.
The U.S. invades Taiwan and Indochina and negotiates with our country at
the same time. The Soviet revisionists deploy millions of soldiers along

the Sino-Soviet border and simultaneously engage in negotiations on the border issue with us. These are dual tactics, and we [should] respond to them with dual revolutionary tactics.[46]

Thirteen months after Nixon's first visit to China, the Chinese authorities at various levels were still giving explanations for the rapprochement. The most revealing were the "secret Kunming Documents" of March 30, 1973, from the Political Department of the Kunming Military Region.[47] Given the background of the Vietnam cease-fire agreement and the Soviet threat, the "documents" offer a convincing interpretation that the thaw was devised to exploit international contradictions. First, it would frustrate the strategic deployment of the Soviet revisionists; second, it would aggravate the contradictions between the United States and the Soviet Union; third, it would step up the contradictions between U.S. imperialism and its lackeys; fourth, it would benefit Peking's liberation of Taiwan; and finally, it would increase Japanese-Soviet and Japanese-U.S. contradictions. As far as the Sino-U.S. relationship was concerned, China considered it necessary "to have problems settled with Nixon, temporarily." The "documents" defended the government's position emphatically:

Our invitation to Nixon to visit China proceeds precisely from Chairman Mao's tactical thinking: "to make use of contradictions, win over the many, oppose the few, and crush our enemies one by one." And this by no means indicates a change in our diplomatic line.

Yet the puzzle was still lingering on, and new skepticism that demanded further explanations was aroused when Mao decided in April 1973 to establish liaison offices in Peking and Washington while tolerating the continuing operation of Taiwan's embassy in the same U.S. capital. It was a compromise substantially different from Mao's practice in the past. At the Tenth Congress of the Party in August 1973, Chou En-lai explained:

...necessary compromises between revolutionary countries and imperialist countries must be distinguished from collusion and compromise between Soviet revisionism and U.S. imperialism. Lenin put it well: "There are compromises and compromises. ..." The Brest-Litovsk Treaty concluded by Lenin with German imperialism comes under the former category, and the doings of Khrushchev and Brezhnev, both betrayers of Lenin, fall under the latter.[48]

In citing Lenin's words and deeds, Chou's explanation was devised not only for Chinese consumption but for the Soviet Union as well. Here we see Mao's intention of promoting a broader Sino-American rapprochement even if it meant compromises. His signal of cooperation with the United States was clear, and yet it must be remembered that this was only the "alliance" aspect of his seemingly contradictory but complementary strategy of "alliance and struggle," as quoted above. The "struggle" aspect, albeit less important than the "alliance" at present, was embodied mainly in Peking's struggle against the hegemony of the two superpowers.

Diplomatic Reestablishment. As discussed earlier, Peking, at the height of the Cultural Revolution, recalled forty-four of its forty-five ambassadors. The forty-fifth, Huang Hua in Cairo, was recalled in July 1969.

China's reestablishment of its diplomatic relations began, however, in mid-May 1969 when Keng Piao was sent to Albania — two months after the Sino-Soviet border conflicts. During the next two and a half months, sixteen other new ambassadors were dispatched to France, Rumania, North Vietnam, Yemen, and other countries.

In 1970, in addition to reestablishing more diplomatic ties, Peking reached an agreement to build a 1,116-mile Tanzania-Zambia (Tanzam) railroad (a five-year project with a Chinese loan of approximately U.S.$413 million). It also received visits of cabinet-level delegations from France (headed by Planning Minister André Bettencourt), Rumania, Tanzania, the Sudan, and others. Meanwhile, it is important to point out that China in that year was the second largest donor (U.S.$620,000) to Peru's earthquake victims — after Japan (U.S.$745,000) but ahead of the United States (U.S.$549,000).

Canada recognized Peking in mid-October 1970 after twenty months of negotiations. The significance of the Canadian recognition lies in the fact that it set a precedent (formula) for handling the Taiwan status which was followed by many other governments. The Canadian government "noted" the Peking government's claim to the Nationalist-ruled Taiwan as an "integral part" of the territory of the People's Republic of China but did not accept it because, as Minister of External Affairs Mitchell Sharp declared, the Canadian government "does not consider it appropriate either to endorse or to challenge the Chinese government's position on the status of Taiwan." [49] This "formula" was adopted in a similar way by Italy, Chile, Austria, Turkey, Belgium, and others when they recognized Peking in 1970-71.

This recognition trend spread to the United Nations. After a week-long, heated debate in late October 1971 on Peking's admission to the U.N., the General Assembly finally voted on the evening of October 25 to adopt the Albanian resolution to seat the Peking government (instead of Taipei) for China. The vote was 76 in favor and 35 opposed. The wave of recognition continued to surge. As of the end of 1977, Peking had established diplomatic ties with 114 nations, whereas Taiwan kept 23. The rapprochement has unprecedentedly broadened the PRC's international relations.

Effects on the Vietnam War. Fully realizing the sensitive implications of the Vietnam situation, Peking informed and explained to Hanoi every development of its rapprochement with the United States, including Nixon's visit to China. Whenever Le Duc Tho, Hanoi's chief negotiator at the Paris peace talks, stopped in Peking en route to or from Paris during the intensive negotiations in 1972, Chou En-lai, though ill, received him.[50] One purpose, of course, was to placate Hanoi's worries and anger over Peking's rapprochement policy.

The stormy spring 1972 offensive by the Communists in South Vietnam scored an early victory. By early May, Anloc, Quangtri, and several other cities had fallen. Saigon was under the Communist threat. To meet the crisis, on May 8 Nixon ordered the mining and blockading of North Vietnamese ports and the bombing of rail lines and other targets. This was a drastic

reescalation and could have resulted in the cancellation of
Nixon's previously scheduled visit to the Soviet Union in late
May. The fact that Moscow continued to welcome the visit
truly upset Hanoi. [51]

Peking kept unusually quiet. The Chinese Ministry of Foreign
Affairs issued only one mild protest statement on June 13 after
Nixon's reescalation. After Henry Kissinger rushed to Peking
on June 20, however, China became silent. There were no personal statements from Mao and no mass demonstrations.
Calmly, Chou En-lai advised Nixon to follow President Eisenhower's example in Korea to end the Vietnam war. [52] Meanwhile, Peking speeded up its military aid, including the construction of two plastic pipelines for fuel supplies to Hanoi.

By late December 1972, several factors had pushed Hanoi
closer than ever to agreeing to a cease-fire accord, but the
decisive forces that compelled Hanoi to sign the Vietnam peace
agreement in January 1973 were the Chinese and Soviet détente
with the United States and the extremely destructive bombing
by the U.S. in December. China made no serious protest against
the massive air raids, but repeatedly urged Vietnam to reach a
peaceful settlement.

After the peace agreement of 1973 was signed, fighting in
South Vietnam went on, but the antiwar mood in the U.S., Nixon's
resignation in the Watergate scandals, and the Congress's limitation of presidential war-making powers prevented the United
States from applying effective measures to curb the continuing
fighting. The sweeping Communist victory in South Vietnam in
the spring of 1975 registered the complete failure of the ten-
year involvement of the United States. Its impact was momen-
tous. The Cambodian Communists (the Khmer Rouge) easily
took Phnom Penh in late April of the same year, and the Pathet
Lao peacefully took over the Laotian neutral government of
Premier Souvanna Phouma in late August.

Riding the tide of the American setback and the total Communist victory in Indochina, China smoothly reaped a major
diplomatic gain. It established full relations with Thailand
and the Philippines. Meanwhile, the trend of conciliation with

China ran through Southeast Asia. This was a logical development of disappointment with the United States and a desire for
accommodation with Peking, even though the nations recogniz-
ing Peking did not approve of the Chinese Communist regime.

Unexpectedly perhaps, two years after Indochina turned Communist, a border war broke out between the Vietnamese and
the Cambodians in Cambodia's province of Svay Rieng (the Par-
rot's Beak region). Minor conflicts began in mid-1977. At the
end of the year, the fighting became serious. Both sides used
division-sized forces with hundreds of pieces of heavy artillery
and armored cars. Each claimed victories over the other. The
conflict was based on nationalism as well as on Communist
politics. In terms of nationalism, the region was a disputed
territory. The Vietnamese Communists used it for sanctuary
during the Vietnam War, and Cambodia under Sihanouk never
filed formal protests against their presence. After the liberation, Cambodia repeatedly had to request Vietnam's troop withdrawal from the area.

In terms of Communist politics, the situation was more complicated. The components of the Cambodian Liberation Army
were extremely complex. Some of them were locally organized,
some were the regular government soldiers, some were trained
by China, and others by Vietnam with the support of the Soviet
Union. After their victory, the Cambodian Communists disbanded the Vietnamese-trained units and sent some of them to
military tribunals for trial.[53] In anger, the Vietnamese
started the battles in the disputed areas.

China's policy in this delicate situation, as stated by its foreign minister, was to support "the stand of Cambodia" and to
serve as a mediator calling for negotiations.[54] Its purpose,
clearly, was to prevent the stronger Vietnam from defeating
the weaker Cambodia in order to curtail the expansion of Soviet
influence in the area.[55] Peking published the statement by
the Vietnamese government of December 31, 1977, which proposed peace talks with Cambodia.[56] Meanwhile, in January
1978 it dispatched Teng Ying-ch'ao (widow of Chou En-lai) to
Phnom Penh, urging negotiations and making a gesture of sup-

port for Cambodia. Sino-Vietnamese relations have not progressed significantly in the post-Vietnam years due to numerous factors, including Soviet influence in Vietnam, China's refusal to negotiate with Hanoi on the sovereignty of the Hsisha
(Paracel) Islands,[57] the reported Sino-Vietnamese border conflicts, and the "ill-treatment" of Chinese residents in Vietnam.
China's support for Cambodia against Vietnam will not improve
her relationship with Hanoi; nor will it promote a settlement
between Cambodia and Vietnam.

2. International United Front against Superpower Hegemonism

After the rapprochement, the PRC's foreign policy began to
have a global dimension: cooperation with the Second and Third
worlds against the two hegemonist superpowers, the United
States and the Soviet Union. Continuing Mao's policy, the new
leadership in Peking now openly calls for the building of the
"broadest international united front"[58] against these two
nations.

Antihegemony Policy. The CCP officially adopted the antihegemony policy at the Tenth Congress of the Party in August
1973 and again at the Eleventh Congress in August 1977. The
1973 Party constitution read:

> The Communist Party of China...firmly unites with the genuine Marxist-
> Leninist Parties and organizations the world over, unites with the prole-
> tariat, the oppressed people and nations of the whole world and fights to-
> gether with them to oppose the hegemonism of the two superpowers — the
> United States and the Soviet Union.[59]

The emergence of the two superpowers is, Peking has asserted, a "new phenomenon" in world politics. Accordingly,
China's antihegemonic policy is a further development of her
long-upheld principle of opposition to great-power chauvinism.
To theorize about this new international struggle, Peking de-
fines "superpower" not merely according to the power's physical size, manpower, economic-industrial strength, and military
might in the general and Western sense, but also according to

its aggressive policy and imperialist behavior. As Teng Hsiao-p'ing said at the United Nations in April 1974, "A superpower is an imperialist country which everywhere subjects other countries to its aggression, interference, control, subversion, or plunder and which strives for world hegemony."[60] More specifically, Peking has described some distinctive features of a superpower as follows:

... its state apparatus is controlled by monopoly capital in its most concentrated form, and it relies on its economic and military power, which is far greater than that of other countries, to carry on economic exploitation and political oppression and to strive for military control on a global scale; each superpower sets exclusive world hegemony as its goal and to this end makes frantic preparations for a new world war.[61]

In this context, we can better understand Mao's strategy of combining "alliance and struggle" in dealing with the United States when we put the rapprochement in the "alliance" column and the antihegemony drive in the "struggle" column. In other words, we are not greatly surprised to learn that Peking has a strong desire for rapprochement on the one hand while campaigning vigorously against American and Soviet hegemony on the other. Naturally, Peking's real target is the Soviet Union. The U.S. superpower, Peking has asserted, has conducted numerous imperialist acts, but its "counterrevolutionary" global strategy has met repeated setbacks; its aggressive power is weakening. On the contrary, the Soviet superpower is more adventurous and deceptive than the United States because it tries hard to "grab areas under U.S. control" just as the postwar United States tried to grab areas under the control of Britain and other old-line imperialists. This is a situation in which, in Mao's words, "the United States wants to protect its interests in the world and the Soviet Union wants to expand."[62] Moreover, the Soviet superpower, due to its social-imperialist nature, also tries hard to expand its control in both socialist and nonsocialist countries — running from Czechoslovakia to Ethiopia. It is the "most dangerous source of war" today.

To enhance their control of the world, the two superpowers

also collude temporarily and opportunistically for a détente.
Peking, however, has said that their "détente is a fraud." This
is proven by the endless Soviet-American competition for hegemony all over the world and by the escalating arms race based
on sophisticated technology and weapons. Their fierce contention is "bound to lead to world war some day." For the interests of independence and revolution, Peking has urged, all nations in the Second and Third worlds should unite into a broad
united front against the two superpowers' hegemonism and
their war policies.[63]

Three-World Theory, Albania and Yugoslavia. Mao Tse-
tung's three-world theory, as discussed at the beginning of
this introduction, is a development of his antihegemonic policy.
This theory has been upheld by the Peking leadership ever
since Mao's death. Its purpose is to place the emphasis on the
Third World and regard it as the principal revolutionary force
against the two superpowers. Unexpectedly, perhaps, China's
old ally, Albania, has disagreed. On July 7, 1977, Zeri I Popullit,
the organ of the Albanian Party of Labor, published an article
attacking China's three-world theory and her policy of cooper-
ating with the Second and Third worlds against the superpowers.
Moreover, the Albanian Embassy in Peking distributed copies
of that article to all other foreign embassies there.[64] At the
United Nations in New York in the fall of 1977, the Albanians,
for the first time, greeted no Chinese diplomats at Kennedy
Airport and accompanied no Chinese comrades to diplomatic
soirees.[65] The Albanian Party accused China of practicing
capitulationism and betraying revolutionary principles, whereas Peking criticized the Albanian Party leadership for falling
into the trap of opportunism and hinted at its colluding with the
"Gang of Four."

Foreign Minister Huang Hua reported that Albania's disagreement with China grew out of the rapprochement. In November 1972, when Beguire Balluku, Albanian defense minister,
led a military delegation to visit China, the difference was felt.
As the rapprochement progressed, Sino-Albanian differences
grew.[66] This is generally true. Specifically, nevertheless, it

was the improvement of Sino-Yugoslav relations after the rapprochement that hurt Albania, although it was not until Peking had decided to invite Tito to visit China in 1977 that Albania brought the dispute into the open. Enver Hoxha owes his leadership to Stalin's expulsion of Yugoslavia from the Cominform in April 1948 and his extension of control over Albania. Stalin's moves saved Albania from being "swallowed" by Yugoslavia — a plan that Stalin was reported to have "agreed" on with Milovan Djilas in January 1948.[67] Khrushchev's de-Stalinization and his thaw with Tito made the Albanians fear that their tiny country might return to stronger Yugoslavia's control. Thus, when China improved her relations with Yugoslavia against the Soviet Union, Albania disapproved. The warm welcome that Peking extended to Tito in China irritated the Tirana leadership. In sum, China's rapprochement policy has caused ideological differences with Albania, and China's cooperation with Tito seems to have weakened Albania's position and strengthened her adversary — Yugoslavia.

While continuing to consider Yugoslavia as "revisionist," Huang Hua attributed China's invitation to Tito to Mao's initiative. He also applauded Yugoslavia's independent line against Russia, commended her role in the cooperation of Third World nations, and praised her support for the PRC's admission to the United Nations. According to the Chinese foreign minister, Tito has behaved more favorably to Peking than have the American "imperialists" and the Soviet revisionists.[68] China consequently "should cooperate" with Yugoslavia against the two superpowers.

Clearly, Peking has become more flexible than ever by adopting a tactic of ch'iu ta-t'ung, ts'un hsiao-i (to reach major agreement while allowing minor differences to exist) in its gigantic struggle against Soviet hegemony. The Chinese leadership hopes to pull Tito closer to Peking, yet, judging by Tito's formal speech in Peking,[69] Yugoslavia seems determined to maintain her own independent policy.

Campaign for the Third World. Early in 1963, the CCP had publicly, and perhaps excessively, emphasized the importance of the role of the Third World in the world communist revolution. In its open letter to the Communist Party of the Soviet Union on June 14, 1963, the CCP asserted:

> The antiimperialist revolutionary struggles of the people in Asia, Africa, and Latin America are pounding and undermining the foundations of the rule of imperialism and colonialism, old and new...therefore, the whole cause of the international proletarian revolution hinges on the outcome of the revolutionary struggles of the people of these areas.[70]

Peking's position on the Third World has been consistent ever since, although its stress on the cooperation of the Second World is a new concept. To encourage the independence and revolutionary movements of the Third World, Peking has often used a slogan that has now become almost a cliché: "Countries want independence, nations want liberation, and the people want revolution." After the adoption of the antihegemony policy and the outbreak of the energy crisis in 1973, however, the PRC broadened the dimension of its policy by advocating a new thesis of "Third World control of Third World resources."

The West has generally accepted the view that the immediate causes of the international energy crisis were the Arab-Israeli war in October 1973 and the ensuing oil embargo. China disagreed. Two days after the outbreak of the war, Foreign Minister Chi P'eng-fei sternly condemned Israel for launching "aggression" against the Arabs. On the same day, October 8, Huang Hua, then chief Chinese delegate to the United Nations, portrayed Israel's policy as "frantic," "aggressive," and "expansionist." Moreover, Peking interpreted the rivalry of the superpowers in the Middle East as the cause of the conflict and harshly denounced the Soviet Union for its "betrayal" of the Arabs.[71] China therefore did not participate in the vote on the United Nations cease-fire resolution or the United Nations Emergency Force.

When the Organization of Arab Petroleum Exporting Countries [OAPEC] used oil embargo as a weapon in the war, Peking praised it as a justified "powerful weapon" against the overexploitation of oil by the capitalists and imperialists.[72]

Moreover, Peking regarded the international economic crisis as a "crisis of the capitalist world." It argued strongly that the crisis was a periodic ill of the capitalist-imperialist system and an inevitable result of the exploitation and hegemony of the superpowers. Such a crisis also aggravated contradictions between imperialist and social-imperialist countries.[73] To oppose such exploitation and hegemony, Peking advocated not only cooperation among the revolutionary peoples, but the protection of the natural resources and rights of the Third World as well. Peking has campaigned for the Third World's economic independence. For this reason, it has endorsed every move relating to Third World control over Third World resources, such as the Declaration on the Establishment of a New International Economic Order adopted by the U.N. (1974), the Dakar (Senegal) Conference on Raw Materials, the Ministerial Meeting of "the Group of 77" in Algeria, the First OPEC Summit Conference in Algeria, the Ayacucho Declaration by eight South American countries, the Declaration of Guyana by six Central American countries, the Lomé (Togo) Convention (all in 1975), the meeting of "the Group of 24" in Jamaica, meetings of the twenty-two-nation Group of Latin American and Caribbean Sugar Exporting Countries [GLACSEC] (all in 1976), the International Economic Cooperation Conference ("North-South Dialogue") in Paris, the Second Association of Southeast Asia Nations [ASEAN] Summit (both in 1977), and so forth. In sum, this drive for the Third World has become the overriding theme of the Chinese position on international economic problems since the energy crisis.

In this campaign, Peking has followed exactly the line of its global strategy of cooperation with the Second and Third World nations for the establishment of a broad international united front as discussed above. Its main target is still the Soviet Union. From the Arab world, to Latin America, to Africa, Peking has accused the Soviets of reaping high profits from the oil and sugar trade and attempting to control resources and strategic positions in the Horn of Africa.

3. Normalization and Taiwan

"Normalization" of the relationship between the United States and China, a euphemism for Washington's establishment of full diplomatic relations with Peking, has experienced ups and downs since the rapprochement. Starting with the issuing of the Shanghai Communiqué in February 1972, the process of normalization surged ahead until 1974; then it declined. The Carter administration, after having pledged to normalize relations with China "in the spirit of the Shanghai Communiqué," offered Peking the reverse-liaison-and-embassy proposal as presented by Secretary of State Cyrus Vance in August 1977. Peking rejected it without hesitation. As Deputy Prime Minister Teng Hsiao-p'ing commented, Vance's offer represented a "retrogression" from the Ford-Kissinger proposals.[74]

As is well known, one of the major "obstacles" to normalization is the Taiwan issue. What are the provisions about Taiwan in the Shanghai Communiqué? What is Peking's attitude toward Taiwan? What is the priority of the Taiwan issue to Peking and will Peking eventually liberate the island by force? An examination of these questions will undoubtedly enhance our understanding of Peking's policy.

The Shanghai Communiqué: Clarity and Ambiguity.[75] On the Taiwan question, the Shanghai Communiqué is a document of both clarity and ambiguity: clarity, because both China and the United States hold the same position that all U.S. forces and military installations will be withdrawn from Taiwan; ambiguity, because both sides have not agreed on how the Taiwan question should be settled.

The clarity is evident in the U.S. troop withdrawals from Taiwan since 1972. The ambiguity is complicated by three nonagreements (not disagreements). First, while the U.S. has reaffirmed its interest in a "peaceful settlement" of the Taiwan issue by the Chinese themselves, the Chinese have insisted that "the liberation of Taiwan is China's internal affair in which no other country has the right to interfere." Second, the U.S. has not "challenged" China's unilaterally declared position of its opposition to "two Chinas," "one China, one Taiwan," "one China, two governments," or other devices,[76] but this position is neither an agreement nor a disagreement. Third, there has been no mention, let alone agreement, on the U.S.-Taiwan Mutual Defense Treaty of 1954. By keeping silent on this issue, the United States may have deliberately left it unsettled for the foreseeable future.

In an attempt to eliminate the ambiguity and to quicken the pace of the normalization process, Peking has set forth three conditions: withdrawal of U.S. troops from Taiwan, severance of U.S.-Taiwan diplomatic relations, and abrogation of the mutual defense treaty. Yet, as of early 1978, apart from the U.S. troop withdrawals, involving a reduction from 9,000 to approximately 1,000, the ambiguity on these three nonagreements remained unchanged.

Peking's Taiwan Unit.[77] It should first be pointed out that after the "reopening" of China in 1971, Peking seems to have organized a special, unpublicized office to handle Taiwan affairs. This office must have arranged numerous meetings and interviews in which the Peking leaders expressed their viewpoints on Taiwan. From the data we have collected, the structure of the unit can be tentatively drawn as follows:

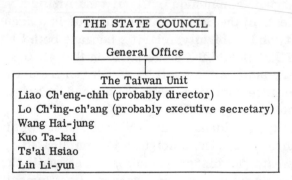

```
┌─────────────────────────────┐
│     THE STATE COUNCIL       │
│                             │
│       General Office        │
└─────────────────────────────┘
┌───────────────────────────────────────────────┐
│              The Taiwan Unit                   │
│ Liao Ch'eng-chih (probably director)           │
│ Lo Ch'ing-ch'ang (probably executive secretary)│
│ Wang Hai-jung                                  │
│ Kuo Ta-kai                                     │
│ Ts'ai Hsiao                                    │
│ Lin Li-yun                                     │
└───────────────────────────────────────────────┘
```

Brief biographical notes may be helpful: Liao Ch'eng-chih is a Party Central Committee member and a veteran of Japanese and Overseas Chinese affairs; Lo Ch'ing-ch'ang is a Party Central Committee member, a leader of the Party's

United Front Department, deputy secretary-general of the
State Council and minister of intelligence of the People's Liberation Army [PLA]; Wang Hai-jung is deputy minister of foreign affairs; Kuo Ta-kai is a member of the New China News
Agency [NCNA] and formerly deputy director of the Information Department in the Ministry of Foreign Affairs; Ts'ai Hsiao
is a Party Central Committee member and is from Taiwan;
Lin Li-yun is a Party Central Committee member, an interpreter, and a Taiwan Chinese from Japan.

In this group, the important figure is Lo Ch'ing-ch'ang, who
is probably in charge of this informal unit. This observation
is made on the basis of his presence at almost all meetings
with persons relating to Taiwan. His triple capacity as one of the
"responsible people" of the Party's United Front Department,
deputy secretary-general of the State Council and minister of
intelligence of the PLA indicates the necessity and significance
of Party-political-military coordination on Taiwan.

Where does the Taiwan unit rank among the government's
agencies? How important is its role in the decision-making
process? These questions cannot be answered in full at present, but preliminary findings suggest that the unit is probably
located in the General Office of the State Council with a cabinet
ranking but without a cabinet status. Unlike the Commission
for Mongolian and Tibetan Affairs in Taipei, it is not a "win-
dow-dressing" agency; nor is it a decision-making unit. Apparently, its functions are to collect information, develop
plans, and submit recommendations for policy deliberation.

Peking's Attitude toward Taiwan. On numerous occasions,
Peking has invited a number of United States officials, legis-
lators, foreign friends, journalists, and Overseas Chinese to
visit China. Through meetings, interviews, and statements,
Peking has made known its attitude toward Taiwan. Apart
from governmental communiqués, Chou En-lai and his associates have elaborated their views on Taiwan in twenty statements to various visitors, especially the Taiwan Chinese.[78]
For the sake of simplicity, I have summarized and reor-
ganized their viewpoints on the following ten major issues

and will discuss them in order of importance.

1) "One China" (the People's Republic of China) and "one legal government" (the Peking government). This principle is unchangeable. With this principle, Peking firmly rules out the creation of "two Chinas," "one China, one Taiwan," "one China, two governments," an "independent Taiwan," or an "undetermined status of Taiwan." The settlement of Taiwan, accordingly, is China's domestic affair. The creation of the "liaison office" in Washington should not be interpreted as a compromise on Taiwan. Rather, it was established to facilitate a future settlement concerning the island.

2) No "self-determination" or "Far Eastern Switzerland" for Taiwan. "Self-determination" is for those nations or areas whose political status is unsettled. Taiwan has already been returned to the motherland. Its status has been settled. There is, therefore, no need for "self-determination," let alone China's "protection" (an imperialist gimmick) of a "self-determined" Taiwan. The "Switzerland formula" is not possible because Taiwan cannot become an independent nation in the Far East. In this context, Peking has thus far not extended an invitation to P'eng Ming-min, a leader of the Taiwan Independence Movement, to visit China.

3) A high degree of autonomy and a long process of social transformation. Whether Taiwan will be a province or an autonomous region after "liberation" is a matter for future decision. Peking is flexible. The island is very likely to have an autonomous status like that of Tibet prior to 1959, and it will require a long process of social transformation to integrate Taiwan into the Chinese political and social system. What is important, Chou En-lai emphasized, is that the Taiwan Chinese must be their own masters, managing their own affairs. All the people in the PRC are equal, it is claimed, and Han chauvinism will never be allowed to exist.

4) Gradual transition of the economic system. Taiwan has large investments of foreign capital from the United States and Japan. Such foreign capital deforms Taiwan's socioeconomic structure. The economic system is a capitalist one under the

exploiting and repressive Kuomintang government and is a humiliation to Taiwan's people. After "liberation," this humiliation must be wiped out. The withdrawal of foreign capital will be made up by government subsidies to prevent an unemployment problem and economic difficulties. There will be no drastic economic measures, and there will be a long and gradual transition from private to public ownership.

5) A high living standard on Taiwan. After "liberation," the Chinese government will not lower Taiwan's living standard, which is now higher than the mainland's. Such a discrepancy is permissible because there are differences in living standards on the mainland, such as in Shanghai and other cities. With the principle of self-reliance, every province, district, city, or commune pursues its own social and economic construction. They all seek to improve the quality of their lives by relying on their own economic and human resources.

6) Peaceful or nonpeaceful liberation of Taiwan. Generally, the question of whether "liberation" will be peaceful or nonpeaceful depends on three conditions: (a) the achievement of socialist reconstruction in People's China; (b) the favorable development of the international situation; and (c) the readiness and collaboration of the people of Taiwan. The first two are now favorable, but the third is yet to develop. Peaceful liberation is Peking's first choice. If peaceful means will not work, however, Peking will employ nonpeaceful means, including armed blockades and attacks. To avoid bloodshed, Peking offers negotiations with delegates from Taiwan, governmental or private.

7) Soviet interest in Taiwan. The Soviet Union is competing for hegemony in Asia with the United States. To this end, Moscow intends to gain access to Taiwan. The Russians tried to explore the possibility of using the naval facilities in the Pescadores, but were rejected by Chiang Kai-shek. This rejection will not end Moscow's interest in the island, but Peking will not allow the Soviet Union to gain what it wants from Taiwan.

8) Recruitment of Taiwan Chinese. Peking is enthusiastic

about recruiting Taiwan Chinese as cadres to serve the people
and government. Professionals in foreign countries are also
welcome to return to China, but this plan requires a few more
years of preparation: China has to prepare the professional
and academic facilities, and the professional people have to
become ideologically and psychologically ready in order to reduce the difficulties of adjustment after they return.

9) Quemoy and Matsu. Peking wants possession of these
islands, but it will not seize them without controlling Taiwan.
This is a complex question, according to Chou En-lai. The bombardment of Quemoy and Matsu in 1958, for instance, was under-
taken under a tacit and complex understanding: Peking understood
that the U.S.-Taiwan Mutual Defense Treaty did not cover the islands, but the PRC had no plan to occupy them; Taiwan understood
that Peking would attack but not seize the islands. Peking wanted
the bombardment to demonstrate the continuity of the civil war,
while Taiwan needed it to support its claim to the mainland. The implication is that as long as the two island groups remain in Taiwan's
hands, Taiwan is in a difficult position to declare independence.

10) Tiao Yu Tai (Senkaku). The Chinese government has repeatedly issued statements to the effect that Tiao Yu Tai is Chinese territory, and it will not change this position. When the
Japanese surveyed that area, China made no protests, but if
Japan should undertake oil or gas drilling, China will stop it.
In terms of nationalism and energy resources, Tiao Yu Tai
is as important as any other offshore island to China. The
April 1978 incident in which thirty-eight Chinese fishing boats
(some armed with machine guns) withdrew from the island
area under Japanese pressure can only be regarded as a tactical move of Peking before a peace treaty with Japan is concluded.

The Priority of the Taiwan Issue. Peking upholds its territorial rights and sovereignty over the island and maintains
that the settlement of Taiwan is a domestic issue in which no
other country has the right to interfere. Yet, how high (or low)
does the Taiwan issue rank among Peking's issue-policy priorities? From the data I have collected, the following ranking seems to apply:

1) Soviet pressure
2) economic development/modernization
3) Taiwan-normalization
4) Japanese cooperation
5) internal stability and unity
6) relations with Second and Third World countries
7) Taiwan-liberation[79]

This tentative list is self-explanatory and does not need any elaboration except, perhaps, a word on the Soviet containment policy against China. Peking is apprehensive that Soviet containment (encirclement) is closing in on the PRC. The Soviet Union has tried hard to gain footholds in Outer Mongolia, Japan, Indochina, and India and is applying growing pressure on China. Although Peking has calculated, as Chou En-lai reported in 1973, that the Soviet Union would not wage a major war with China at present,[80] Peking is very much concerned about the weakness of these nations in dealing with Russia. To protect its own interests, Peking has urged other Asian nations to resist Soviet overtures and has endorsed the continued stationing of U.S. troops in certain areas. Meanwhile, China is trying by every possible means to strengthen its national defense, including holding four unprecedented conferences on national defense in early February 1977. In sum, Peking is making a strenuous effort to cope with the Soviet threat.

It should be pointed out that although Peking fully realizes that it is not possible to "liberate" Taiwan at the present time, the normalization of Sino-American relations as a counter to the Soviet Union is in the best interests of China. Taiwan, however, is one of the major obstacles to normalization, as President Carter has stated. If Peking wants to achieve a speedy normalization, its need to "resolve" this obstacle may prompt Peking to apply more pressure on Washington in the near future.

Liberate Taiwan by Force. Peking has never ruled out a military liberation of Taiwan. Should the situation develop in such a way as to require Peking to take military action, the proposal of "liberating Taiwan by force" will not remain a slogan or an academic issue, but will become a realistic problem. There are two essential questions if Peking is to take Taiwan by force. First, under what circumstances will the PRC employ armed force? Second, what is the Chinese capability for such a military operation?

To answer the first question, it seems that under the following three circumstances the People's Republic would wage a war over Taiwan.

(1) Taiwan's declaration of independence. If this should occur, it is highly likely that Peking would resort to force in an attempt to settle the issue once and for all. (2) The application by the U.S. of the "Japanese formula" (that is, complete withdrawal of U.S. troops, rupture of U.S.-Taiwan diplomatic ties, and abrogation of the U.S.-Taiwan Mutual Defense Treaty, but continuation of trade and cultural relations). If this formula were put into force, Peking would adopt a "talk-talk-fight-fight" strategy. Peking would first offer peace talks; if rejected, it would in due course apply an economic blockade and then military pressure against Taiwan. (3) The application of the "Japanese formula," combined with Soviet access to Taiwan. If the Soviet Union, against all the odds to be sure, should succeed in gaining a naval base in the Pescadores immediately after the execution of the "Japanese formula," a new situation for Taiwan as well as for East Asia would be created which could either escalate the Peking-Moscow conflict or bring about a limited Peking-Moscow rapprochement. The conflict situation might further draw Peking's attention away from Taiwan, but the limited rapprochement, again extremely unlikely, might result in a Moscow-Peking deal to dump Taiwan — an act similar to the U.S. acceptance of the "Japanese formula." The subsequent development is predictable: Taiwan would face military pressure and/or economic blockade by the PRC. Perhaps the only effective deterrent to Peking's military action under such conditions would be the development of a nuclear capability by Taiwan. At present, however, such a deterrent runs contrary to Taiwan's non-nuclear development policy and to U.S. efforts to prevent the proliferation of nuclear weapons.

On the second question — Chinese military capability — there are two major considerations: strategic capability and military strength. The continuance of strong Soviet military pressure in the north will undoubtedly strategically limit Peking's ability to launch a military operation against Taiwan. As long as Sino-Soviet tensions remain unchanged, a war between the Soviet Union and the PRC can never be ruled out. A two-war strategy implemented simultaneously against Russia and Taiwan is very unlikely to be followed by Peking.

China also has only limited military capability with respect to Taiwan. Even if Taiwan lacks nuclear weapons or outside assistance, an invasion would not be a simple operation. While it is clear that the PLA could take Quemoy and Matsu islands without too much difficulty, Taiwan is a different matter. The PRC does not yet have the capability to take the island in a short period of time and, according to one estimate, the PLA could not land more than three divisions of assault troops on Taiwan.[81] In any event, should such an unfortunate war break out, the PLA would face fierce resistance from the well-equipped and well-trained Taiwan army; the casualties on both sides would be extremely high.

From the above discussions, it is clear that the issue of Taiwan and its related problems have serious implications for the process of normalization. If Peking and Washington cannot agree on a "formula" in the very near future, normalization will continue to be a dilemma for both powers. Although Keng Piao said in his August 1976 speech that Peking would, for the time being, "allow the U.S. to guard" Taiwan for China,[82] he also indicated that normalization would come before the "liberation of Taiwan." Judging from Teng Hsiao-p'ing's statement of September 6, 1977, that Peking's patience could not last forever, there would seem to be a sense of gradually increasing urgency on this issue.

As far as the United States is concerned, acceptance of Peking's three conditions (demands) would most likely, in due course, lead Peking to commence an armed blockade of Taiwan and even to armed conflict. As Li Hsien-nien put it,

"There are such a heap of counterrevolutionaries on Taiwan that it cannot be managed without a fight."[83] Such a situation would certainly run contrary to the principle of "peaceful set-tlement" to which Presidents Nixon, Ford, and Carter have re-peatedly committed themselves, let alone the freedom and hu-man rights of the people on Taiwan.

A recent survey of opinion leaders in this country shows a significantly high level of support for Taiwan. Part of the survey reads as follows:

Opinion Leaders' Attitudes toward
U.S.-China Normalization and Taiwan*

Question	Favor %	Oppose %	No Opinion %
1. Accept the PRC's "three demands" as the precondition for normalization	5	93	2
2. Pursue normalization without jeopar-dizing the "independence and freedom" of Taiwan	89	7	4
3. Continue to honor our diplomatic ties and defense treaty with Taiwan if it de-clares independence	75	11	14

Source: Michael Y. M. Kau, Pierre M. Perrolle, Susan H. Marsh, and Jeffrey Berman, "Public Opinion and Our China Policy," Asian Affairs, Vol. 3 (January-February 1978), p. 141.

*Conducted July-August 1977. Data are based on returns from 733 respondents.

This table is self-explanatory. The authors also conclude that in comparison with those of Gallup, Harris, and other polls, this survey clearly indicates that the opinion leaders' support for Taiwan is "uniformly higher than the level of sup-port given by the general public in virtually all the issue areas."[84] If Peking insists on its three conditions (demands) for normalization, one would question why the U.S. govern-ment should accept them without maintaining her own basic principles[85] and contrary to public opinion.

IV. Conclusion

In summing up the PRC's relations with the three worlds,

major emphases should be placed on the model and pattern of its development as well as the implications of its successes and failures. Several significant characteristics can be drawn here from the above examination.

First of all, China has conducted its international relations within the framework of a complex cooperative-competitive-conflicting model.[86] In relations with the First World (by Peking's definition), it has pursued a "competitive-conflicting-cooperative" formula. In relations with the Second World, it has implemented a "competitive-cooperative" model. In relations with Third World countries, Peking's operation has been more "cooperative" than "competitive" or "conflicting." It must be pointed out, however, that Peking has never practiced a "dominant-dependent" type of relationship with any other country. In light of the past and in terms of the revolutionary nature of Peking's policy, it can be predicted that Peking will continue to maintain such "cooperative-competitive-conflicting" relationships with the three worlds.

Second, the development of Peking's foreign relations has formed a pattern of expansion and contraction which corresponds closely to a graph of the nation's growth during the imperial dynasties. When China has been unified and strong, it has expanded its influence, power, and even territory; when China has been disintegrated and weak, it has contracted and retreated. This type of development has been determined more by the internal situation than by external factors. Since 1949, the PRC has scored diplomatic gains and power expansion (during the peaceful coexistence era and the "détente" period) as well as diplomatic setbacks and influence contraction (during the Cultural Revolution). The antihegemony campaign at present has not run contrary to the development of this pattern; rather, it has strengthened it.

Third, the PRC in the past thirty years has achieved an impressive number of its foreign policy objectives. It has been most successful in its short-range objectives of security, unification (except for Taiwan), power, and influence; less successful in its middle-range objective of becoming an Asian leader; and least successful in its long-range goal of attaining world power. For capability and political reasons, it is believable at present that China, as Mao pledged, is not going to become a superpower. If China is to become a "world" leader in the near future, the only attainable goal is to become an influential "Third World" leader through peaceful and cooperative approaches based on the five principles of peaceful coexistence.

Fourth, the fluctuations of China's policy have brought about several changes in China's image. Beginning from the Korean War, China has been seen as an "aggressor" in Korea, a "sponsor" of the peaceful coexistence policy at Bandung, an "aggressor" again on the Indian border, an "ungrateful ally" of Russia, a "weapon supplier" to the revolutionaries in Cambodia and Mozambique, an "advocate" of Third World control of Third World resources, a "critic" of détente, and a "champion" of antisuperpower hegemonism. Such changes have been made in accordance with China's interests as well as ideology. The tactics of zigzags, straightforwardness, and retreats have been flexibly applied, and the implementation of its policy has appeared sometimes peaceful, sometimes violent.

Fifth, after the long, tumultuous struggle of the Cultural Revolution, harmony (peace, unity, and relaxation) seems to be the vital interest of the Chinese people and society. This contradicting but complementing harmony-struggle value is a social norm in China. Originally evolved from the philosophy of yin and yang, this value coincides with the theory of contradiction which Mao employed so often to interpret the Chinese society and revolution. The hardship of struggle is now over, temporarily at least. This is the time for harmony. The Hua Kuo-feng leadership appears to be moving actively in this direction.

In sum, whether or not the PRC will succeed in her antihegemony and antidétente campaign, she will continue to strive for her long-range objective of world power. To this end, Hua Kuo-feng is holding high "the great banner of Chairman Mao" while actually executing the domestic and foreign policies of Chou En-lai (and some aspects of those of purged

Former President Liu Shao-ch'i, such as the material incentive policy). In view of the fact that several fundamental models, patterns, and values as summarized above still remain in force, one should not be greatly surprised if China once again undergoes a cyclical phase of growth and decline, peace and violence.

Notes

1. Editorial Department of Jen-min jih-pao [People's Daily], "Chairman Mao's Theory of the Differentiation of the Three Worlds Is a Major Contribution to Marxism-Leninism," Jen-min jih-pao, November 1, 1977; also in Peking Review, November 4, 1977, p. 11. An excerpt of this article is included in this volume.

2. I have asserted the existence of such a three-level objective of Chinese foreign policy since at least 1965. Many students of international politics and foreign policy have held a similar view on modern nations' foreign policies. See, among others, K. J. Holsti, International Politics: A Framework for Analysis (Englewood Cliffs, N. J.: Prentice-Hall, 1977), Ch. 5. See also King C. Chen, "Foreign Affairs," in Harold C. Hinton, ed., The People's Republic of China: A Handbook (Boulder, Col: Westview, 1978).

3. Robert North, The Foreign Relations of China (Belmont, California: Dickenson, 1969), p. 15.

4. K. P. Wang, "The Mineral Resource Base of Communist China," An Economic Profile of Mainland China, Studies prepared for the Joint Committee, Congress of the United States (New York: Praeger, 1968), p. 169.

5. Foreign Minister Huang Hua's secret report on the world situation (five hours long) on July 30, 1977, in Peking stated that the Gang of Four had caused China "to lose more than ten years." For details, see Huang's text in Fei-ch'ing yüeh-pao [Chinese Communist Affairs Monthly] (Taipei), November 1977, pp. 66-88. A similar report was made by Harrison E. Salisbury from Peking. See New York Times, November 5, 1977, p. 3. Excerpts of Huang's report are in this volume.

6. Bruce M. Russett et al., World Handbook of Political and Social Indicators (New Haven, Conn.: Yale University Press, 1964), p. 152; Alexander Eckstein, Communist China's Economic Growth and Foreign Trade: Implications for U.S. Policy (New York: McGraw-Hill, 1066), pp. 245-59.

7. The figures are from Times, March 13, 1978, p. 27. See also Alexander Eckstein, China's Economic Revolution (New York: Cambridge University Press, 1977), p. 226; Ann Crittenden, "Vital Dialogue Is Beginning Between the Rich and Poor," New York Times, September 28, 1975, p. E3; and New York Times, March 7, 1978, pp. 1, 8.

8. Eckstein, China's Economic Revolution, p. 210.

9. For reports on the Chinese military, see Wall Street Journal, Octo-

ber 12, 1976, p. 26; New York Times, December 18, 1975, p. 1; December 1, 1976, pp. 1, 16; December 2, 1976, pp. 1, 14; March 1, 1978, p. 3. For Schlesinger's concerns, see Ross H. Munro's report, Christian Science Monitor, September 30, 1976, p. 7.

10. Mao Tse-tung, "On the People's Democratic Dictatorship," in Selected Works of Mao Tse-tung, Vol. 4 (Peking, 1961), pp. 415-17.

11. There was apparently no separate military treaty concluded by Mao and Stalin on the same occasion.

12. For China's intervention in the war, see, among others, Allen S. Whiting, China Crosses the Yalu: The Decision to Enter the Korean War (New York: Macmillan, 1960); Harold C. Hinton, Communist China in World Politics (Boston: Houghton Mifflin, 1966), Ch. 8.

13. Consult Mao Tse-tung, "On the Ten Major Relationships," Peking Review, No. 1 (January 1, 1977), p. 24. This version is slightly different from its early version in Mao Tse-tung ssu-hsiang wan-sui [Long Live Mao Tse-tung's Thought], Taipei: Institute of International Relations, reprint, 1974), Vol. 1, pp. 40-59.

14. This Chinese delegation led by Chu Teh stayed in Moscow from mid-February to April 2, 1956. Upon his return to Peking, a Politburo meeting was immediately held. As a result, the "de-Stalinization" document was published. See "On the Historical Experience Concerning the Dictatorship of the Proletariat," Jen-min jih-pao, April 5, 1956.

15. Mao Tse-tung, "On the Ten Major Relationships," p. 24.

16. Melvin Gurtov, The First Indochina Crisis (New York: Columbia University Press, 1970), p. 148.

17. King C. Chen, Vietnam and China, 1938-1954 (Princeton, N. J.: Princeton University Press, 1969), Ch. 6.

18. George McT. Kahin, The Asian-African Conference, Bandung, Indonesia, April 1955 (Ithaca: Cornell University Press, 1958).

19. For details, consult A. Doak Barnett, Communist China and Asia (New York: Harper and Brothers, 1960), pp. 294-97, 529-30.

20. See Neville Maxwell, India's China War (New York: Pantheon Books, 1970); Allen S. Whiting, The Chinese Calculus of Deterrence: India and Indochina (Ann Arbor: University of Michigan Press, 1975), Chs. 4-6.

21. King C. Chen, "Hanoi's Three Major Decisions and the Escalation of the Vietnam War," Political Science Quarterly, Vol. 90, No. 2 (Summer 1975), pp. 239-59.

22. For the origin and development of the dispute, see, among others, Donald S. Zagoria, The Sino-Soviet Conflict, 1956-1961 (Princeton: Princeton University Press, 1962); William E. Griffith, The Sino-Soviet Rift and Sino-Soviet Relations, 1964-65, both (Cambridge: MIT Press, 1964 and 1967).

23. The statement of the Government of the People's Republic of China, Radio Peking, August 15, 1963.

24. For an excellent analysis of this point, see Donald S. Zagoria, The Sino-Soviet Conflict, Ch. 16.

25. For details, see William E. Griffith, Albania and the Sino-Soviet Rift (Cambridge: MIT Press, 1963).

26. Jen-min jih-pao, November 18, 1962.

27. During this year, Peking issued the well-known nine open letters against Moscow; they were published on September 6, September 13, September 26, October 22, November 19, December 12, 1963; February 4, March 31, and July 14, 1964.

28. There are several versions of this particular interview with Mao on July 10, 1964. The most complete one is in Mao Tse-tung ssu-hsiang wan-sui, Vol. 1, pp. 532-45.

29. "A Comment on the March Moscow Meeting," Peking Review, No. 13 (March 26, 1965), pp. 7-13.

30. See a more detailed discussion in King C. Chen, "Relations with Third World and 'Intermediate Zone' Countries," in Yuan-li Wu, ed., China: A Handbook (New York: Praeger, 1973), pp. 367-91.

31. For both the five principles and the eight principles, see Peking Review, No. 7 (February 14, 1964), pp. 7-8.

32. Cited in Ernst Halperin, "Peking and the Latin American Communists," China Quarterly, No. 29 (January-March 1967), p. 119.

33. For both Peking's and Hanoi's policies, see King C. Chen, "Hanoi vs. Peking: Policies and Relations — A Survey," Asian Survey, Vol. 12, No. 9 (September 1972), pp. 808-813.

34. Peking Review, November 12, 1965, pp. 10-21.

35. Quoted in Nguyen Van Vinh's speeches of April 1966, as reported by Beverly Deepe, "How Hanoi Looks at Negotiating," Christian Science Monitor, May 9, 1968, p. 14.

36. Anna Louise Strong, Letters from China, Nos. 21-30 (Peking: New World Press, 1965), p. 165.

37. A good account of the Indonesia coup attempt is given by Arthur J. Dommen, "The Attempted Coup in Indonesia," China Quarterly, No. 25 (January-March 1966), pp. 144-70.

38. Melvin Gurtov, "The Foreign Ministry and Foreign Affairs During the Cultural Revolution," China Quarterly, No. 40 (October-December 1969), pp. 65-102; also Edgar Snow, "A Conversation with Mao Tse-tung," Life, April 30, 1971, p. 46.

39. King C. Chen, "Relations with Third World and 'Intermediate Zone' Countries," p. 380.

40. For this incident, see Thomas W. Robinson, "The Sino-Soviet Border Dispute," The American Political Science Review, December 1972, pp. 1175-1202; Harold C. Hinton, "Conflict on the Ussuri: A Clash of Nationalism," Problems of Communism, January-April 1971, pp. 45-61.

41. For instance, Robinson, "The Sino-Soviet Border Dispute," pp. 1190-94.

42. Edgar Snow, "A Conversation with Mao Tse-tung," Life, p. 48.

43. New York Times, February 16, 1978, p. 23; February 18, 1978, p. 12. Also H. R. Haldeman with Joseph DiMona, The Ends of Power (New York: Times Books, 1978), pp. 88-94.

44. Writing Group of the CCP Hupei Provincial Committee, "T'uan-chieh jen-min chan-sheng ti-jen ti ch'iang-ta wu-ch'i" [A Powerful Weapon to Unite the People and Defeat the Enemy], Hung-ch'i [Red Flag], No. 9 (August 2, 1971). Included in this volume.

45. Ibid.

46. See Chou En-lai's Internal Report to the Party on the International Situation, December 1971. Included in this volume. Lin Piao, former defense minister of the PRC (1959-71), was reportedly killed in a plane crash on September 13, 1971, near Undur Khan, Outer Mongolia. The incident was reported by Chou En-lai to the effect that after Lin Piao's unsuccessful coup plan, which called for the assassination of Mao Tse-tung by bombing his train during the trip from Hangchow to Shanghai on September 12, was discovered by Chou and Mao, Lin nervously escaped by plane (Chinese Air Force Trident jet No. 256), reportedly toward Russia via Outer Mongolia. All nine persons on the jet were burned to death. They included Lin Piao, Yeh Ch'ün (Lin's wife), Lin Li-kuo (Lin's son), Huang Yung-sheng (chief of the general staff), Wu Fa-hsien (Air Force commander), Li Tso-p'eng (first political commissar of the Navy), Ch'iu Hui-tso (director of the Logistics Department), and others. For details, see Michael Y. M. Kau, ed., The Lin Piao Affair (White Plains, N. Y.: International Arts and Sciences Press, 1975).

47. See the "Kunming Documents," included in this volume.

48. Chou En-lai's "Report to the Tenth National Congress of the Communist Party of China," Peking Review, Nos. 35-36 (September 7, 1973). Included in this volume.

49. New York Times, October 14, 1970, pp. 1, 24.

50. Huang Hua's secret speech, July 30, 1977.

51. Note that Premier Pham Van Dong and General Vo Nguyen Giap did not come out to welcome President Nikolai Podgorny in Hanoi in June — an unprecedented snub to the Soviet leader.

52. Harrison E. Salisbury's report from Peking, New York Times, June 17, 1972, p. 4.

53. Huang Hua's secret speech, July 30, 1977.

54. Ibid.

55. Zbigniew Brzezinski, President Carter's advisor on national security affairs, characterized the Vietnamese-Cambodian conflict as a "proxy war" between China and the Soviet Union at a CBS-TV interview on January 8, 1978. His comments drew denunciation and criticism from the Soviet Union and Vietnam. See New York Times, January 10, 1978, p. 8; January 17, 1978, p. 10.

56. Peking Review, No. 1 (January 6, 1978), p. 26. The same issue of Peking Review carried an even longer statement by the Cambodian government.

57. On the Paracel Islands issue, Huang Hua gave some details: "The Vietnamese claim that the islands belong to them. Let them talk that way. They have repeatedly asked us to negotiate with them on the Hsisha issue; we have always declined to do so. Several Vietnamese delegations that came to China recently also brought up this matter. When Pham Van Dong

was here around April 20, he again asked us to discuss the matter, and we declined as before." See his secret speech of July 30, 1977.

58. Jen-min jih-pao, "Chairman Mao's Theory of the Differentiation of the Three Worlds...." Included in this volume.

59. "Constitution of the Communist Party of China," Peking Review, Nos. 35-36 (September 7, 1973), p. 26.

60. Teng Hsiao-p'ing's speech at the Sixth Special Session of the U.N. General Assembly on the problems of raw materials and development on April 1974, Peking Review, No. 16 (April 19, 1974), pp. 6-11. Included in this volume.

61. "Chairman Mao's Theory of the Differentiation of the Three Worlds...."

62. Ibid.

63. Ibid.

64. Huang Hua's secret speech, July 30, 1977. It should be noted that the Albanian Labor Party sent no greetings concerning Hua Kuo-feng's new chairmanship after the downfall of the Gang of Four in October 1976 and that China sent no delegation to attend the Seventh Party Congress of Albania in November of the same year.

65. New York Times, October 8, 1977, p. 2.

66. Huang Hua's secret speech.

67. Stavro Skendi, "Albania and the Sino-Soviet Conflict," Foreign Affairs, April 1962, pp. 471-78; William E. Griffith, Albania and the Sino-Soviet Rift.

68. Huang Hua's secret speech.

69. President Tito's speech, Peking Review, No. 36 (September 2, 1977), pp. 10-13.

70. "A Proposal Concerning the General Line of the International Communist Movement," Peking Review, No. 25 (June 21, 1963), pp. 6-22.

71. Editorial, "Naked Display of Power Politics," Jen-min jih-pao, October 26, 1973.

72. Ch'ang Ch'ien, "Behind the So-Called Energy Crisis," Hung-ch'i, No. 2 (February 1, 1974), pp. 83-86.

73. Chin Nan, "The Present Economic Crisis of the Capitalist World," Hung-ch'i, No. 2 (February 1, 1975), pp. 96-102.

74. Teng Hsiao-p'ing's interview, New York Times, September 7, 1977. Included in this volume.

75. The text of the Shanghai Communiqué is in this collection.

76. The English version differs significantly from the Chinese one. The Chinese text, "pu t'i-ch'u i-i," literally means "not to raise different viewpoints (arguments)." The English version is: "does not challenge that position."

77. This "unit" has been outlined by the author on the basis of the sources in Note 78 and interviews with State Department officials on November 5 and 19, 1976. On December 24, 1977, the director of the Investigation Bureau of the Justice Ministry in Taiwan (Taiwan's FBI) reported that in the past year the Chinese Communist Party and the State Council in Peking had respectively established the "Taiwan Office" and the "Taiwan Unit" and that branch offices

had also been formed in Fukien and Kwangtung provinces as well as in Hong Kong and at the PRC's Embassy in Japan (Central Daily News, December 25, 1977, p. 2). Such a report, albeit significant, remains to be confirmed.

78. Chou's associates include Teng Hsiao-p'ing, Ch'iao Kuan-hua, Lo Ch'ing-ch'ang, Chang Ch'un-ch'iao, Li Hsien-nien, Yü Chan and Keng Piao. In the twenty-two published sources on their talks that we have collected, we found that, due to similar accounts written by different persons from a single group, they have actually held twenty interviews relating to Taiwan. These sources are: (1) Seymour Topping, New York Times, June 3, 1971, pp. 1-2; (2) The Committee of Concerned Asian Scholars, China: Inside the People's Republic (New York: Bantam Books, 1972), pp. 347-52 (an excerpt is in New York Times, July 29, 1971, p. 6); (3) James Reston, New York Times, August 10, 1971, p. 14; (4) William Hinton, "Chou En-lai," New China, January 1976, pp. 39-43; (5) Joseph J. Lee, "Peking's View of Taiwan: An Interview with Chou En-lai," in Yung-Hwan Jo, ed., Taiwan's Future (Tempe, Arizona: Center for Asian Studies, Arizona State University, 1974), pp. 65-70; (6) Sanford Lee, "China Offers to Talk with Taiwan," Toronto Star, October 19, 1972, p. 32; (7) Ts'ai K'an, "Chou En-lai Meets with Taiwan Chinese," Ch'i-shih nien-tai [The Seventies], a monthly, December 1972, pp. 38-39; (8) Parris Chang in Hearings before the Subcommittee on Future Foreign Policy Research and Development, 94th Congress, Parts I and II (Washington, D.C.: Government Printing Office, 1976), p. 278; (9) Yü Yu, "Chou En-lai's Conversations on Taiwan," Ch'i-shih nien-tai, April 1973, pp. 30-31; (10) Ch'u Yen, "Conversations of Ch'iao Kuan-hua and Lo Ch'ing-ch'ang," Ch'i-shih nien-tai, October 1973, pp. 63-65; (11) Fan Lan et al., "Teng Hsiao-p'ing on the Chinese Situation and the Taiwan Question," Ch'i-shih nien-tai, December 1974, pp. 15-17; (12) Mike Mansfield, China: A Quarter Century After the Founding of the People's Republic (Washington, D.C.: Government Printing Office, 1975), pp. 21-24; (13) Murrey Marder, Washington Post, August 3, 1976, p. A3; (14) Daniel Southerland, Christian Science Monitor, November 16, 1976, p. 3; (15) Po-ch'eng ch'ing-miao [Berkeley Newsletter], November 1975, pp. 14-15; (16) Teng Hsiao-p'ing's talks with Cyrus R. Vance, October 11, 1975, in Working Papers (published by the Rockefeller Foundation, New York, October 1976), pp. 76-82; (17) Keng Piao's speech at the Institute of Diplomacy in Peking on August 24, 1976, in Mei-chou fei-ch'ing t'ung-hsin [The Chinese Communist Affairs Weekly], Taipei, No. 503, November 26, 1976, pp. 15-17; (18) Li Hsien-nien's interview, Sunday Times (London), March 27, 1977; (19) Li Hsien-nien's interview, New York Times, August 30, 1977; (20) Teng Hsiao-p'ing's interview, New York Times, September 7, 1977; (21) Yü Chan's interview, Wall Street Journal, October 3, 1977; and (22) Li Hsien-nien's interview, Wall Street Journal, October 4, 1977. All quotations and viewpoints mentioned in this section are based on these twenty-two sources.

79. After this ranking was first drawn up in late November 1976, the author saw on December 17, 1976, the text of Keng Piao's speech of August 24, 1976, which substantiated, surprisingly, the order of priority. Excerpts of Keng Piao's speech are included in this volume. Some other available

information after mid-December 1976 has also supported this ranking. See New York Times, January 27, 1977, p. 3; Hsinhua (Peking), February 6, 1977; Sunday Times (London), March 27, 1977, p. 8; and New York Times, September 7, 1977, pp. 1-2.

80. Chou En-lai's secret speech of March 1973, in this volume.

81. Brian Crozier, "The Art of Survival," National Review, December 6, 1974, p. 1402. Also see New York Times, December 1, 1976, and March 1, 1978, concerning the PLA's strength.

82. Keng Piao's speech, included in this volume.

83. See "China's Vice Premier Reaffirms Rigidity on Taiwan," Wall Street Journal, October 4, 1977, p. 10.

84. For details, see Michael Y. M. Kau et al., "Public Opinion and Our China Policy," Asian Affairs, Vol. 3 (January-February 1978), pp. 133-47.

85. A more detailed discussion on this point is given by Richard H. Solomon, "Thinking Through the China Problem," Foreign Affairs, January 1978, pp. 355-56.

86. Students of international politics suggest different types (models) of international relations. K. J. Holsti summarized four types: collaboration-cooperation, conflict-rivalry, competition, and domination (Holsti, International Politics, Chs. 3, 5). Zbigniew Brzezinski asserts that U.S.-Soviet relations are competitive-cooperative. See his article, "The Competitive Relationship," Research Institute on Communist Affairs Monograph (N. Y.: Columbia University, 1972). Allen S. Whiting used a competitive-conflicting "interaction" model to examine China's relations with India in 1962. See his book The Chinese Calculus of Deterrence (Ann Arbor: University of Michigan Press, 1977), Chs. 2-5. For China's overall international relations, I suggest a complex model of cooperation, competition, and conflict.

I

Theory and perceptions of the Three Worlds

Documentary Introduction

This chapter includes four selections. They are important documents presenting China's perceptions of the present international situation and her theory of the three worlds.

The first selection, "On Policy" by Chairman Mao Tse-tung, was originally released in 1940 during the Sino-Japanese War. It emphasizes the "decisive importance" of the establishment and maintenance of the anti-Japanese united front under which a strategy of combining struggle and alliance with the Kuomintang would be applied. This explanation was necessitated by many people's misunderstanding of the implications of the united front policy at that time.

In 1971, when Mao decided to invite President Richard Nixon to China, a similar but much more complicated international united front against the Soviet Union was being developed in Mao's mind. Yet such a new united front policy, even with the support of a Sino-American rapprochement, was too surprising to be accepted by the Chinese people without an extremely skillful explanation.

The second selection, "A Study of 'On Policy'" carried in Hung-ch'i [Red Flag], was issued by Peking to provide such an explanation. It was published two weeks after the announcement of Henry Kissinger's first visit to Peking in mid-July 1971. In a careful presentation, the article urges the Chinese

to comprehend the significance and implications of Mao's
united front policy in the perspective of the new international
environment. Its central theory is to make use of international
contradictions and combine alliance and struggle in the forthcoming Sino-American rapprochement.

The third selection, "China and the Three Worlds," was Teng
Hsiao-p'ing's speech at the United Nations in 1974, two months
after Mao had expressed his three-world concept. It was the
first official explanation of this new theory with an emphasis
on China's policies concerning the Third World.

An extremely important document is the fourth selection,
abbreviated as "Chairman Mao's Theory of the Differentiation
of the Three Worlds." It fully explains, from political, military, economic, historical, and strategic viewpoints, why the
world should be divided into three at present and how the Second and Third worlds should engage in building the broadest
possible international united front to oppose the two superpowers — especially the Soviet Union. This lengthy article
not only intends to establish China's "three-world theory,"
but also replies indirectly to Albania's open attack on this
theory in July 1977.

Reading through this last document and Foreign Minister
Huang Hua's speech of July 1977 (excerpts in Chapter Four),
one will not fail to comprehend that what Peking has tried to
theorize is actually a strategic world outlook for the present
revolutionary stage. In short, it is a new line of Mao's revolutionary diplomacy in the rapprochement era.

ON POLICY*

(December 25, 1940)

1

Mao Tse-tung

In the present high tide of anti-Communist attacks, the policy
we adopt is of decisive importance. But many of our cadres
fail to realize that the Party's present policy must be very different from its policy during the Agrarian Revolution. It has
to be understood that in no circumstances will the Party change
its united front policy for the entire period of the War of Resistance against Japan and that many of the policies adopted during the ten years of the Agrarian Revolution cannot just be
duplicated today. In particular, many ultra-Left policies of
the latter period of the Agrarian Revolution are not merely
totally inapplicable today in the War of Resistance, but were
wrong even then, arising as they did from the failure to understand two fundamental points — that the Chinese revolution is
a bourgeois-democratic revolution in a semicolonial country,
and that it is a protracted revolution. For example, there was
the thesis that the Kuomintang's fifth "encirclement and suppression" campaign and our countercampaign constituted the
decisive battle between counterrevolution and revolution; there
was the economic elimination of the capitalist class (the ultra-
Left policies on labor and taxation) and of the rich peasants

---

This inner-Party directive was written by Comrade Mao
Tse-tung on behalf of the Central Committee of the Commu-
nist Party of China.
*From Selected Works of Mao Tse-tung, Vol. 2 (Peking, 1965).

(by allotting them poor land); the physical elimination of the landlords (by not allotting them any land); the attack on the intellectuals; the "Left" deviation in the suppression of counterrevolutionaries; the monopolizing by Communists of the organs of political power; the focusing on communism as the objective in popular education; the ultra-Left military policy (of attacking the big cities and denying the role of guerrilla warfare); the putschist policy in the work in the White areas; and the policy within the Party of attacks on comrades through the abuse of disciplinary measures. These ultra-Left policies were manifestations of the error of "Left" opportunism, or exactly the reverse of the Right opportunism of Ch'en Tu-hsiu in the latter period of the First Great Revolution. It was all alliance and no struggle in the latter period of the First Great Revolution, and all struggle and no alliance (except with the basic sections of the peasantry) in the latter period of the Agrarian Revolution — truly striking demonstrations of the two extremist policies. Both extremist policies caused great losses to the Party and the revolution.

Today our Anti-Japanese National United Front policy is neither all alliance and no struggle nor all struggle and no alliance, but combines alliance and struggle. Specifically, it means:

1) All people favoring resistance (that is, all anti-Japanese workers, peasants, soldiers, students and intellectuals, and businessmen) must unite in the Anti-Japanese National United Front.

2) Within the united front, our policy must be one of independence and initiative, i.e., both unity and independence are necessary.

3) As far as military strategy is concerned, our policy is guerrilla warfare waged independently and with the initiative in our own hands within the framework of a unified strategy; guerrilla warfare is basic, but no chance of waging mobile warfare should be lost when the conditions are favorable.

4) In the struggle against the anti-Communist diehards, our policy is to make use of contradictions, win over the many,

oppose the few, and crush our enemies one by one, and to wage struggles on just grounds, to our advantage, and with restraint.

5) In the enemy-occupied and Kuomintang areas our policy is, on the one hand, to develop the united front to the greatest possible extent and, on the other, to have well-selected cadres working underground. With regard to the forms of organization and struggle, our policy is to have well-selected cadres working underground for a long period, to accumulate strength and bide our time.

6) With regard to the alignment of the various classes within the country, our basic policy is to develop the progressive forces, win over the middle forces, and isolate the anti-Communist diehard forces.

7) With respect to the anti-Communist diehards, ours is a revolutionary dual policy of uniting with them, insofar as they are still in favor of resisting Japan, and of isolating them, insofar as they are determined to oppose the Communist Party. Moreover, the diehards have a dual character with regard to resistance to Japan, and our policy is to unite with them, insofar as they are still in favor of resistance, and to struggle against them and isolate them insofar as they vacillate (for instance, when they collude with the Japanese aggressors and show reluctance in opposing Wang Ching-wei and other traitors). As their opposition to the Communist Party has also a dual character, our policy, too, should have a dual character; insofar as they are still unwilling to break up Kuomintang-Communist cooperation altogether, it is one of alliance with them, but insofar as they are high-handed and launch armed attacks on our Party and the people, it is one of struggling against them and isolating them. We make a distinction between such people with a dual character and the traitors and pro-Japanese elements.

8) Even among the traitors and pro-Japanese elements there are people with a dual character, toward whom we should likewise employ a revolutionary dual policy. Insofar as they are pro-Japanese, our policy is to struggle against them and isolate them, but insofar as they vacillate, our policy is to draw

them nearer to us and win them over. We make a distinction between such ambivalent elements and the out-and-out traitors like Wang Ching-wei, Wang I-tang and Shih Yu-san.

9) The pro-Japanese big landlords and big bourgeoisie who are against resistance must be distinguished from the pro-British and pro-American big landlords and big bourgeoisie who are for resistance. Similarly, the ambivalent big landlords and big bourgeoisie who are for resistance but vacillate, and who are for unity but are anti-Communist, must be distinguished from the national bourgeoisie, the middle and small landlords, and the enlightened gentry, the duality of whose character is less pronounced. We build our policy on these distinctions. The diverse policies mentioned above all stem from these distinctions in class relations.

10) We deal with imperialism in the same way. The Communist Party opposes all imperialism, but we make a distinction between Japanese imperialism which is now committing aggression against China and the imperialist powers which are not doing so now, between German and Italian imperialism which are allies of Japan and have recognized "Manchukuo" and British and U.S. imperialism which are opposed to Japan, and between the Britain and the United States of yesterday which followed a Munich policy in the Far East and undermined China's resistance to Japan, and the Britain and the United States of today which have abandoned this policy and are now in favor of China's resistance. Our tactics are guided by one and the same principle: to make use of contradictions, win over the many, oppose the few, and crush our enemies one by one. Our foreign policy differs from that of the Kuomintang. The Kuomintang claims, "There is only one enemy, and all the rest are friends." It appears to treat all countries other than Japan alike, but in fact it is pro-British and pro-American. On our part we must draw certain distinctions, first, between the Soviet Union and the capitalist countries, second, between Britain and the United States on the one hand and Germany and Italy on the other, third, between the people of Britain and the United States and their imperialist governments, and fourth,

between the policy of Britain and the United States during their Far Eastern Munich period and their policy today. We build our policy on these distinctions. In direct contrast to the Kuomintang our basic line is to use all possible foreign help, subject to the principle of independent prosecution of the war and reliance on our own efforts, and not, as the Kuomintang does, to abandon this principle by relying entirely on foreign help or hanging on to one imperialist bloc or another....

A POWERFUL WEAPON TO UNITE THE PEOPLE AND DEFEAT THE ENEMY*

2

A Study of "On Policy"

Writing Group of the CCP Hupei Provincial Committee

At the crucial moment when the War of Resistance against Japan was at its height and when the KMT reactionaries were whipping up an anticommunist high tide in December 1940, our great leader Chairman Mao wrote his glorious work "On Policy." This is an important historical document in which Chairman Mao at that time used dialectical materialism and historical materialism to scientifically analyze the contradictions in society and viewpoints on classes, profoundly criticized and repudiated the Right and "Left" erroneous lines and policies peddled by renegades such as Ch'en Tu-hsiu and Wang Ming, systematically summed up the rich experiences of our Party in waging a protracted struggle against the KMT reactionaries, and clearly elucidated the changes and developments in the Party's policies during the War of Resistance against Japan. He formulated for the Party the tactical principles and various

*"T'uan-chieh jen-min chan-sheng ti-jen ti ch'iang-ta wu-ch'i." Hung-ch'i [Red Flag], No. 9 (August 2, 1971), 10-17. This translation is taken from Selections from China Mainland Magazines (Hong Kong: American Consulate General), Nos. 711-712 (September 7-13, 1971), 1-9. The subtitles are added by the Editor.

concrete policies for forming the anti-Japanese national united
front and helped the Party remain sober-minded in the thick of
an extremely complex struggle so as to ensure the implementation of his correct line and victory in the War of Resistance
against Japan.

The tactical principles and various policies formulated by
Chairman Mao reflect the objective laws in class struggle and
give full play to the spirit of the proletariat and the art of waging struggle in a flexible way. They enrich and develop
Marxist-Leninist tactics and ideas, demonstrating their power
in defeating the enemies and winning victories in various historical stages. They are always the powerful weapon of the
proletariat for uniting the people and defeating the enemies.

In his work "On Policy," Chairman Mao repeatedly stressed
the importance of forming policy and tactics. In light of the
situation at that time, he pointed out in the beginning that "the
policy we adopt is of decisive importance."

The Importance of Forming Policy and Tactics

Chairman Mao has always attached importance to the decisive
role of the policies and tactics of the proletariat, pointing out:
"To win victories, the proletariat must completely rely on the
firm implementation of the correct tactics adopted by its
party — the Communist Party — in waging struggle" ("Oppose
Book Worship"). During various historical stages, Chairman
Mao not only mapped out the general line and policies for the
Party but also formulated the tactical principles and various
concrete policies for the struggle. Policies are determined
by line and reflect line. Chairman Mao's revolutionary tactics
and policies are an embodiment of Chairman Mao's revolutionary line, while the series of erroneous policies pushed by political swindlers such as Ch'en Tu-hsiu, Wang Ming, and Liu
Shao-ch'i are aimed at helping them implement their Right or
"Left" opportunist line. In this sense, the struggle between
the two lines is an embodiment of the struggle between two
policies different in nature. "Policy is the starting point of all

the practical actions of a revolutionary party and manifests
itself in the process and the end result of the Party's action."

Starting from a wrong point, no Right or "Left" policy will
ever find itself on the right track at the end. They will find
themselves manifesting a wrong orientation or a wrong line if
they are allowed to prevail without being corrected in time.
We must view the question of what kind of policy to implement
in light of the struggle between the two lines and must firmly
carry out Chairman Mao's revolutionary line and various proletarian policies. The idea of separating a line from policy,
or setting line against policy, or attaching no importance to
policy is entirely wrong.

To profoundly understand and correctly implement Chairman
Mao's various proletarian policies, it is necessary to have a
thorough understanding of the basis on which tactical principles
and policies are formulated. Our great leader Lenin pointed
out: "Only by objectively examining all the mutual relations
among all classes in a certain society, the objective stages
for the development of this society, and the mutual relations
between this society and other societies will it be possible for
an advanced class to formulate correct tactics on this basis"
(Karl Marx). This tells us that all Marxist tactical principles
and policies are formed on the basis of correct observation
and concrete analysis of the situation in class struggle at home
and abroad and of the mutual relations among classes as well
as the changes in and developments of such relations.

Without drawing distinctions there can be no policy. Marxists
should make a concrete analysis of concrete contradictions.
Chairman Mao has pointed out: "It is necessary to gain a clear
understanding of the mutual relations between classes and to
make a correct class estimate so that we can lay down our
correct tactics in struggle and determine which classes are
the main force of the revolutionary struggle, which classes we
should win over as our allies, and which classes should be
overthrown" ("Oppose Book Worship").

All tactical principles and policies set forth by Chairman
Mao on the basis of class analysis are aimed at correctly

handling the relationships between the enemy and ourselves
and our friends to unite all forces that can be united, to isolate
and strike at the handful of most stubborn enemies, and to lead
the revolution to victory.

During the War of Resistance against Japan, the contradictions between China and Japan became the primary ones, while
class contradictions at home became the secondary or subordinate ones. As a result, changes took place in international
relations and in the various classes within the country, and a
new situation emerged. In his work "On Policy," Chairman
Mao drew extremely profound and concrete distinctions between the complicated class relations at home and abroad under the historical conditions at that time on the basis of a
scientific analysis of the basic features of class struggle. He
said: "We build our policy on these distinctions" in order to
consolidate and develop the anti-Japanese national united front
and to defeat Japanese imperialism.

In analyzing the mutual relations between various classes at
home and their different political attitudes, Chairman Mao
first pointed out emphatically in his work "On Policy": "Within
the united front, our policy must be one of independence and
initiative, i.e., both unity and independence are necessary."
"All people favoring resistance (or all anti-Japanese workers,
peasants, soldiers, students, and intellectuals and businessmen) must unite in the anti-Japanese national united front" to
defeat the then major enemies — Japanese imperialism and
its lackeys, the traitors and pro-Japanese elements.

What attitude did the Party take toward various classes at
home during the anti-Japanese national War of Liberation?
Chairman Mao clearly pointed out: "With regard to the alignment of the various classes within the country, our basic policy is to develop the progressive forces, win over the middle
forces, and isolate the anticommunist diehard forces."

In order to educate the whole Party in implementing this
policy, Chairman Mao concretely pointed out the class content
of the progressive, middle, and diehard forces by saying:
"Developing the progressive forces means building up the

forces of the proletariat, the peasantry, and the urban petty
bourgeoisie, boldly expanding the Eighth Route and New Fourth
armies, establishing anti-Japanese democratic base areas on
an extensive scale, building up communist organizations
throughout the country, and developing national mass movements of the workers, peasants, youth, women, and children."
In criticizing the Right opportunist view of fearing to develop
the anti-Japanese revolutionary forces, Chairman Mao pointed
out: "Steady expansion of the progressive forces is the only
way to prevent the situation from deteriorating, to forestall
capitulation and splitting, and to lay a firm and indestructible
foundation for victory in the war of resistance" (The Tactics
of Fighting Japanese Imperialism: The National United Front).
This policy is based on developing the people's forces, the
starting point from which our Party has defeated the enemies.
Thus have we done in domestic struggles, and so also have we
done in international struggles.

Chairman Mao also pointed out: "The winning over of the middle forces is an extremely important task for us in the period
of the anti-Japanese united front." Thus, he criticized the
"Left" view of attaching no importance to winning over the
middle forces. He further analyzed various conditions for
winning over the middle forces. These are: (1) that we have
ample strength; (2) that we respect their interests; and (3) that
we are resolute in our struggle against the diehards and steadily win victories.

In order to isolate the diehard forces, Chairman Mao made
a concrete analysis of and drew a careful distinction between
the different social forces and political factions of the enemy
camps and the middle-of-the-roaders. He pointed out: "The
pro-Japanese big landlords and big bourgeoisie who are against
resistance must be distinguished from the pro-British and pro-
American big landlords and big bourgeoisie who are for resistance; similarly, the ambivalent big landlords and big bourgeoisie who are for resistance but vacillate and who are for
unity but are anticommunist must be distinguished from the
national bourgeoisie, the middle and small landlords, and the

enlightened gentry, the quality of whose character is less pronounced. We deal with imperialism in the same way. The
Communist Party opposes all imperialism, but we make a
distinction between Japanese imperialism which is now committing aggression against China and the imperialist powers
which are not doing so now and between the imperialist powers
which have adopted different policies in different conditions and
different periods of time."

Applying the revolutionary dialectics of "one divides into
two" in making a scientific distinction between the enemy
camps, Chairman Mao most clearly distinguished between the
primary enemy and the secondary enemy and between the temporary allies and the indirect allies. By making this concrete
and meticulous distinction, he isolated the primary enemy of
the Chinese people at that time, namely, Japanese imperialism
which was committing aggression against China.

In the War of Resistance against Japan, we were able to
overcome interference resulting from various wrong lines, to
organize the masses in their millions, to mobilize a massive
revolutionary army, to develop the people's revolutionary
forces, to win the sympathy and support of the people all over
the world, to smash the attacks of anticommunist diehards,
to completely defeat the primary enemy, Japanese imperialism,
and to win great victory in the war precisely because the whole
Party implemented Chairman Mao's tactical principles and
policies on the basic question of who should be relied on,
united with, or attacked.

The Marxist class differentiation made by Chairman Mao in
his work "On Policy" is a brilliant example for us to follow in
correctly analyzing and handling the complicated alignment of
the various classes at home and abroad, in uniting the people,
in winning allies, and in isolating and defeating the enemies.
Complying with Chairman Mao's consistent teaching on making
a strict distinction between and correctly handling the two different types of contradictions and grasping the struggle between
the two classes, two roads, and two lines as the key link, we
must strengthen the worker-peasant alliance under the leader-

ship of the proletariat, unite with the people constituting more than 90 percent of the population, unite with all the forces that can be united, and isolate and strike at the handful of enemies to the greatest extent so as to consolidate the socialist system and the dictatorship of the proletariat.

A Principle to Exploit International Contradictions

On the basis of thorough analysis of the alignment of the various classes, Chairman Mao, in his work "On Policy," set forth this important tactical principle for the struggle against the enemies: "To make use of contradictions, win over the many, oppose the few, and crush our enemies one by one." This principle arms the whole Party. Not only did it play an important role in the struggle against the enemies in the past, but it remains our sharp weapon in defeating the enemies and winning victories in today's realistic struggles.

There must be close unity and collaboration among the imperialist powers and among all strata, blocs, and groups in the enemy camp whose purpose is to preserve their reactionary forces and exploit and oppress the people. However, because of their class nature, there must also be many contradictions among them resulting in competition with one another. These contradictions are an objective fact, that is, they are independent of the subjective wishes of the reactionaries. The proletariat and its political party must learn to conduct a concrete analysis of the situation in class struggle at home and abroad in different historical stages so that they will be good at grasping the opportunities offered by any struggle, loophole, or contradiction in the enemy camp and use it to combat the principal enemy ("On the Tactics of Fighting Japanese Imperialism").

Facts have shown that Chairman Mao's analysis of the situation in the enemy camp is entirely in keeping with the objective laws governing all developments. Today, there are four major contradictions in the world: the contradiction between the oppressed nations and imperialism and social-imperialism; the contradiction between the proletariat and the bourgeoisie in the capitalist and revisionist countries; the contradiction between imperialist nations and social-imperialist nations and that among the imperialist nations; and the contradiction between the socialist nations and imperialism and social-imperialism.

All of these contradictions are irreconcilable, and their existence and development will inevitably lead to a revolution. For example, United States imperialism and social-imperialism are collaborating and competing with each other. They are intensifying their efforts to expand their aggressive influence in the intermediate zones in the vain hope of redividing the world, and they have become the target of universal condemnation. They are collaborating with each other to suppress the revolutions of the oppressed nations and the oppressed people in the world; they are also vehemently contending with each other for their own imperialistic interests, as shown by their competition in the Middle East, in Europe, in the Mediterranean Sea, and so forth. This competition is becoming more acute with each passing day. Their collaboration and competition will continue to arouse strong opposition from the oppressed peoples of the world. Therefore, Chairman Mao's analysis of the situation in the enemy camp contained in this work still provides good guidance for us to know the present international situation correctly.

The tactical principles formulated by Chairman Mao for struggling against the enemy represent a dialectical unity of firm principles and great flexibility. The purpose of flexible tactics of struggle is to adhere to firm revolutionary principles. Chairman Mao has taught us: "Our principles must be firm. We must also have all permissible and necessary flexibility to serve our principles" (Report to the Second Plenum of the CCP Seventh Central Committee). We deeply realize that the nature of imperialism and all reactionaries can never change. Their subjective wish is always to oppress and exploit the revolutionary peoples of the world and to oppose the revolutionary cause of various peoples.

However, this is but one side of the picture. On the other side, we can see that they still have many objective difficulties in carrying out their counterrevolutionary wishes. Proceeding

from their reactionary nature and their counterrevolutionary
requirements, they always change their counterrevolutionary
tactics and use counterrevolutionary double-dealing. We must
grasp and take advantage of all enemy contradictions and difficulties, wage a tit-for-tat struggle with them, strive for the
basic interests of the people to the maximum extent, and win
victories in the struggle against the enemy.

In order to smash the counterrevolutionary dual tactics of
the enemy, we must also employ revolutionary dual tactics.
While regarding armed struggle as the principal form of struggle, we must wage struggle of various forms against the enemy
in many fields. The art of waging all kinds of struggles in a
flexible way is a requirement for the proletariat in the struggle against the enemy.

A Policy to Combine Alliance and Struggle

To consolidate and develop the revolutionary united front,
the proletariat must have a correct policy. In "On Policy,"
Chairman Mao has concisely generalized the anti-Japanese
national united front policy in the simplest language. He has
pointed out: "This united front is neither all alliance and no
struggle nor all struggle and no alliance, but combines alliance
and struggle."

The relationship between alliance and struggle is that of dialectical unity. The dual policy of alliance and struggle is built
on the dual character of all allies in the united front. In the
War of Resistance against Japanese Aggression, we had to
unite with all social strata that were against Japanese imperialism and form a united front with them. However, if there
was vacillation among them about surrendering to the enemy,
opposing communism, or opposing the people, we had to struggle against them on the merits of each case.

Touching on the relationship between alliance and struggle in
the anti-Japanese united front, Chairman Mao has pointed out:
"Struggle is the means to unity, and unity is the aim of struggle.
If unity is sought through struggle it will live; if unity is sought

through yielding, it will perish" ("On the Tactics of Fighting
Japanese Imperialism: The National United Front").

If we only think of struggle without unity, we will not be able
to unite with the forces that can be united or to consolidate and
develop the united front. We will not be able to force our principal enemy into a narrow and isolated position, and our struggle against the enemy will not be successful.

If we only think of unity without struggle, we will forsake our
revolutionary principles and our Party's leadership in the
united front, the Party will disintegrate ideologically, politically, and organizationally, and the revolution will end in failure.

Chairman Mao sharply pointed out: "All alliance and no
struggle and all struggle and no alliance are two extremist policies which caused great losses to the Party and the revolution."

The lessons learned at the cost of bloodshed from the two
wrong policies in our Party history have an extremely profound
meaning. Political swindlers like Ch'en Tu-hsiu, Wang Ming
and Liu Shao-ch'i have frantically pursued the "Left" and the
Right opportunist line. They have never conducted a scientific
analysis but always obliterated class distinctions and confused
enemies with ourselves. In the period of democratic revolution
as well as the period of socialist revolution, they always opposed class analysis and class distinctions and violated the
proletarian revolutionary line formulated by Chairman Mao
on the basis of a revolutionary and scientific analysis. Liu
Shao-ch'i's counterrevolutionary revisionist line, his Right
opportunist policies which served bourgeois interests, and his
"Left in appearance but Right in essence" policies which dis-
rupted the class ranks were all intended to restore capitalism.
History has shown that the two extremist policies of "all
alliance but no struggle" and "all struggle but no alliance"
were out-and-out opportunist policies. Only those policies of
the united front which underwent the process of alliance and
struggle were Marxist-Leninist policies. China's victories
in the revolution were victories of Chairman Mao's proletarian
revolutionary line and his great tactical principles.

In "On Policy," Chairman Mao summed up our Party's his-

torical experiences and clearly expounded the importance of
raising the Party's tactical principles. He emphatically stated:
"To correct the lopsided views of many Party cadres on the
question of tactics and their consequent vacillation between
'Left' and Right, we must help them acquire an all-round and
integrated understanding of the changes and developments in
the Party's policy, past and present." This great teaching
points out for us the correct way to raise our tactical principles and our level of the understanding of policies. Today, a
restudy of this brilliant work, "On Policy," and a review of
the history of the struggle between the two lines in the Party
tell us that one of the fundamental factors is to arm ourselves
with dialectical materialism and historical materialism and
to attain an all-round and integrated understanding of the
Party's policies and tactics. We must overcome any erroneous
"Left" or Right tendencies.

Chairman Mao's various tactical principles and policies reflect the basic laws of proletarian revolution as well as the
special laws in different historical stages. They are the dialectical unity of the universality and the particularity of contradictions.

We must have an all-round and integrated understanding of
them. If we only use the idealist and metaphysical viewpoint
to explain the various Party tactical principles and policies in
a one-sided and static manner, and absolutely affirm or negate
complicated matters, we will surely go to the extreme "Left"
or the extreme Right in implementing policies.

We must resolutely uphold Chairman Mao's Marxist scientific method of conducting investigation and study of social conditions; conscientiously investigate, analyze, and study the
complex situation of class struggle at home and abroad, the
relationship between different classes, and the changes or
development of this relationship; correctly handle the two different types of contradictions; be good at grasping the various
contradictions in the enemy camp; and deal with each ally in
the appropriate manner. Then, in observing and handling matters, we will be able to avoid subjectiveness, one-sidedness,

and superficiality. We will also overcome absoluteness in
thinking so that our thinking will also be in keeping with the
changing objective conditions. We will also be able to remain
steadfast, overcome vacillation, eliminate blindness, and
strengthen our consciousness in implementing Party policies.

Lenin pointed out: "Revolutionary tactics absolutely cannot
be formulated only according to the revolutionary sentiment"
("The Leftist Infantilism in the Communist Movement"). The
tactical principles and policies of the proletariat are formulated
strictly according to a Marxist-Leninist stand, viewpoint, and
method. Hence, they represent the highest interests of the
whole Party and people throughout the country in a concentrated
way. We can never substitute our feelings for policy. Such bad
practices as adopting pragmatism, deliberately misinterpreting
out of context, and doing whatever is in one's own interest with
regard to Party policies are manifestations of an impure Party
spirit and reflections of a bourgeois world outlook. We must
resolutely struggle against such phenomena.

We must adhere to a Marxist-Leninst stand, the Party spirit,
and Party policies. Taking a serious attitude, we must implement Chairman Mao's tactical principles and policies so as to
ensure the success of our various undertakings.

"The important content for carrying out education in ideology
and political line" is to strengthen education in Party policies
and to further raise the level of the cadres in ideology and policy. Chairman Mao teaches us: "Our policy should be made
known not only to leaders and cadres but to the broad masses."
Only by making the policies and tactics of the Party known to
them can the broad masses raise their consciousness of implementing Chairman Mao's revolutionary line.

In the excellent situation at home and abroad, we must act
on Chairman Mao's teaching "read and study seriously and
have a good grasp of Marxism." In light of our practical work
and thinking, we must conscientiously study works by Marx,
Lenin, and Chairman Mao, strive to remold our world outlook,
adhere to the theory of two points, and oppose the theory of
one point. We must comprehend the policies and tactics of

the Party historically and in an all-round way and "temper ourselves into fighters who have a good grasp of Marxist tactics."

In the protracted, fierce, and complicated class struggle and the struggle between the two lines, we should unite to the greatest extent with all the forces that can be united and isolate and strike at a handful of class enemies at home and abroad to the utmost. Riding on the vigorous East wind and braving high waves, we must closely follow our great leader Chairman Mao to advance triumphantly along the road of continuing the revolution.

CHINA AND THE THREE WORLDS*

3

Teng Hsiao-p'ing

Mr. President,

The special session of the United Nations General Assembly on the problems of raw materials and development is successfully convened on the proposals of President Houari Boumediene of the Council of Revolution of the Democratic People's Republic of Algeria and with the support of the great majority of the countries of the world. This is the first time in the twenty-nine years since the founding of the United Nations that a session is held specially to discuss the important question of opposing imperialist exploitation and plunder and effecting a change in international economic relations. This reflects that profound changes have taken place in the international situation. The Chinese Government extends its warm congratulations on the convocation of this session and hopes that it will make a positive contribution to strengthening the unity of the developing countries, safeguarding their national economic rights and interests, and promoting the struggle of all peoples against imperialism, and particularly against hegemonism.

---

*This is the full text of Chairman of the Chinese Delegation Teng Hsiao-p'ing's speech at the Sixth Special Session of the U.N. General Assembly on the problems of raw materials and development held in April 1974. Peking Review, No. 16 (April 19, 1974), 6-11. The Chinese version can be found in Jen-min jih-pao [People's Daily], April 11, 1974. The title and subtitles are the Editor's.

Great Disorder and the Three Worlds

At present, the international situation is most favorable to the developing countries and the peoples of the world. More and more, the old order based on colonialism, imperialism, and hegemonism is being undermined and shaken to its foundations. International relations are changing drastically. The whole world is in turbulence and unrest. The situation is one of "great disorder under heaven," as we Chinese put it. This "disorder" is a manifestation of the sharpening of all the basic contradictions in the contemporary world. It is accelerating the disintegration and decline of the decadent reactionary forces and stimulating the awakening and growth of the new emerging forces of the people.

In this situation of "great disorder under heaven," all the political forces in the world have undergone drastic division and realignment through prolonged trials of strength and struggle. A large number of Asian, African, and Latin American countries have achieved independence one after another, and they are playing an ever greater role in international affairs. As a result of the emergence of social-imperialism, the socialist camp which existed for a time after World War II is no longer in existence. Owing to the law of the uneven development of capitalism, the Western imperialist bloc, too, is disintegrating. Judging from the changes in international relations, the world today actually consists of three parts, or three worlds, that are both interconnected and in contradiction to one another. The United States and the Soviet Union make up the First World. The developing countries in Asia, Africa, Latin America and other regions make up the Third World. The developed countries between the two make up the Second World.

The two superpowers, the United States and the Soviet Union, are vainly seeking world hegemony. Each in its own way attempts to bring the developing countries of Asia, Africa, and Latin America under its control and, at the same time, to bully the developed countries that are not their match in strength.

The two superpowers are the biggest international exploiters

and oppressors of today. They are the source of a new world
war. They both possess large numbers of nuclear weapons.
They carry on a keenly contested arms race, station massive
forces abroad, and set up military bases everywhere, threatening the independence and security of all nations. They both keep
subjecting other countries to their control, subversion, interference, or aggression. They both exploit other countries economically, plundering their wealth and grabbing their resources.
In bullying others, the superpower which flaunts the label of
socialism is especially vicious. It has dispatched its armed
forces to occupy its "ally" Czechoslovakia and instigated the
war to dismember Pakistan. It does not honor its words and
is perfidious; it is self-seeking and unscrupulous.

The case of the developed countries in between the superpowers and the developing countries is a complicated one.
Some of them still retain colonialist relations of one form or
another with Third World countries, and a country like Portugal
even continues with its barbarous colonial rule. An end must
be put to this state of affairs. At the same time, all these developed countries are in varying degrees controlled, threatened
or bullied by the one superpower or the other. Some of them
have in fact been reduced by a superpower to the position of
dependencies under the signboard of its so-called "family."
In varying degrees, all these countries have the desire of
shaking off superpower enslavement or control and safeguarding their national independence and the integrity of their
sovereignty.

The numerous developing countries have long suffered from
colonialist and imperialist oppression and exploitation. They
have won political independence, yet all of them still face the
historic task of clearing out the remnant forces of colonialism,
developing the national economy and consolidating national independence. These countries cover vast territories, encom-
pass a large population, and abound in natural resources.
Having suffered the heaviest oppression, they have the strongest desire to oppose oppression and seek liberation and development. In the struggle for national liberation and independence,

they have demonstrated immense power and continually won splendid victories. They constitute a revolutionary motive force propelling the wheel of world history and are the main force combating colonialism, imperialism, and particularly the superpowers.

Since the two superpowers are contending for world hegemony, the contradiction between them is irreconcilable; one either overpowers the other or is overpowered. Their compromise and collusion can only be partial, temporary, and relative, while their contention is all-embracing, permanent, and absolute. In the final analysis, the so-called "balanced reduction of forces" and "strategic arms limitation" are nothing but empty talk, for in fact there is no "balance," nor can there possibly be "limitation." They may reach certain agreements, but their agreements are only a facade and a deception. At bottom, they are aiming at greater and fiercer contention. The contention between the superpowers extends over the entire globe. Strategically, Europe is the focus of their contention, where they are in constant tense confrontation. They are intensifying their rivalry in the Middle East, the Mediterranean, the Persian Gulf, the Indian Ocean, and the Pacific. Every day, they talk about disarmament but are actually engaged in arms expansion. Every day, they talk about "détente" but are actually creating tension. Wherever they contend, turbulence occurs. So long as imperialism and social-imperialism exist, there definitely will be no tranquillity in the world; nor will there be "lasting peace." Either they will fight each other, or the people will rise in revolution. It is as Chairman Mao Tse-tung has said: The danger of a new world war still exists, and the people of all countries must get prepared. But revolution is the main trend in the world today.

The two superpowers have created their own antithesis. Acting in the way of the big bullying the small, the strong domineering over the weak, and the rich oppressing the poor, they have aroused strong resistance among the Third World and the people of the whole world. The people of Asia, Africa, and Latin America have been winning new victories in their strug-

gles against colonialism, imperialism, and particularly hegemonism. The Indochinese peoples are continuing to press forward in their struggles against U.S. imperialist aggression
and for national liberation. In the Fourth Middle East war,
the people of the Arab countries and Palestine broke through
the control of the two superpowers and the state of "no war,
no peace" and won a tremendous victory over the Israeli aggressors. The African people's struggles against imperialism,
colonialism, and racial discrimination are developing in depth.
The Republic of Guinea-Bissau was born in glory amidst the
flames of armed struggle. The armed struggles and mass
movements carried out by the peoples of Mozambique, Angola,
Zimbabwe, Namibia and Azania against Portuguese colonial
rule and white racism in South Africa and Southern Rhodesia
are surging ahead vigorously. The struggle to defend sea
rights initiated by Latin American countries has grown into a
worldwide struggle against the maritime hegemony of the two
superpowers. The Tenth Assembly of the Heads of State and
Government of the Organization of African Unity, the Fourth
Summit Conference of the Nonaligned Countries, the Arab Summit Conference, and the Islamic Summit Conference successively voiced strong condemnation against imperialism, colonialism, neocolonialism, hegemonism, Zionism, and racism,
demonstrating the developing countries' firm will and determination to strengthen their unity and support one another in
their common struggle against the hated enemies. The struggles of the Asian, African, and Latin American countries and
people, advancing wave upon wave, have exposed the essential
weakness of imperialism, and particularly the superpowers,
which are outwardly strong but inwardly feeble, and dealt heavy
blows at their wild ambitions to dominate the world.

The hegemonism and power politics of the two superpowers
have also aroused strong dissatisfaction among the developed
countries of the Second World. The struggles of these countries against superpower control, interference, intimidation,
exploitation, and shifting of economic crises are growing day
by day. Their struggles also have a significant impact on the

development of the international situation.

Innumerable facts show that all views that overestimate the strength of the two hegemonic powers and underestimate the strength of the people are groundless. It is not the one or two superpowers that are really powerful; the really powerful are the Third World and the people of all countries uniting together and daring to fight and daring to win. Since numerous Third World countries and people were able to achieve political independence through protracted struggle, certainly they will also be able, on this basis, to bring about through sustained struggle a thorough change in the international economic relations which are based on inequality, control, and exploitation and thus create essential conditions for the independent development of their national economy by strengthening their unity and allying themselves with other countries subjected to superpower bullying as well as with the people of the whole world, including the people of the United States and the Soviet Union.

Mr. President,

The essence of the problems of raw materials and development is the struggle of the developing countries to defend their state sovereignty, develop their national economy, and combat imperialist, and particularly superpower, plunder and control. This is a very important aspect of the current struggle of the Third World countries and people against colonialism, imperialism, and hegemonism.

As we all know, in the last few centuries colonialism and imperialism unscrupulously enslaved and plundered the people of Asia, Africa, and Latin America. Exploiting the cheap labor power of the local people and their rich natural resources and imposing a lopsided and single-product economy, they extorted superprofits by grabbing low-priced farm and mineral products, dumping their industrial goods, strangling national industries, and carrying on an exchange of unequal values. The richness of the developed countries and the poverty of the developing countries are the result of the colonialist and imperialist policy of plunder.

In many Asian, African, and Latin American countries that
have won political independence, the economic lifelines are
still controlled by colonialism and imperialism in varying degrees, and the old economic structure has not changed fundamentally. The imperialists, and particularly the superpowers,
have adopted neocolonialist methods to continue and intensify
their exploitation and plunder of the developing countries.
They export capital to the developing countries and build there
a "state within a state" by means of such international monopoly
organizations as "transnational corporations" to carry out
economic plunder and political interference. Taking advantage
of their monopoly position in international markets, they reap
fabulous profits by raising the export prices of their own products and forcing down those of raw materials from the developing countries. Moreover, with the deepening of the political
and economic crises of capitalism and the sharpening of their
mutual competition, they are further intensifying their plunder
of the developing countries by shifting the economic and monetary crises on to the latter.
    It must be pointed out that the superpower which styles itself
a socialist country is by no means less proficient at neocolonialist economic plunder. Under the name of so-called "economic cooperation" and "international division of labor," it
uses high-handed measures to extort superprofits in its "family." In profiting at others' expense, it has gone to lengths
rarely seen even in the case of other imperialist countries.
The "joint enterprises" it runs in some countries under the
signboard of "aid" and "support" are in essence copies of
"transnational corporations." Its usual practice is to tag a
high price on outmoded equipment and substandard weapons
and exchange them for strategic raw materials and farm produce of the developing countries. Selling arms and ammunition
in a big way, it has become an international merchant of death.
It often takes advantage of others' difficulties to press for the
repayment of debts. In the recent Middle East war, it bought
Arab oil at a low price with the large amount of foreign exchange it had earned by peddling munitions and then sold it at

a high price, making staggering profits in the twinkling of an
eye. Moreover, it preaches the theory of "limited sovereignty,"
alleges that the resources of developing countries are international property, and even asserts that "the sovereignty over
the natural resources is depending to a great extent upon the
capability of utilizing these resources by the industry of the
developing countries." These are out-and-out imperialist
fallacies. They are even more undisguised than the so-called
"interdependence" advertised by the other superpower, which
actually means retaining the exploitative relationship. A socialist country that is true to its name ought to follow the
principle of internationalism, sincerely render support and
assistance to oppressed countries and nations and help them
develop their national economy. But this superpower is doing
exactly the opposite. This is additional proof that it is socialism in words and imperialism in deeds.

Plunder and exploitation by colonialism, imperialism, and
particularly by the superpowers, are making the poor countries poorer and the rich countries richer, further widening
the gap between the two. Imperialism is the greatest obstacle
to the liberation of the developing countries and to their progress. It is entirely right and proper for the developing countries to terminate imperialist economic monopoly and plunder,
sweep away these obstacles, and take all necessary measures
to protect their economic resources and other rights and
interests.

The Importance of the Third World

The doings of imperialism, and particularly the superpowers,
can in no way check the triumphant advance of the developing
countries along the road of economic liberation. In the recent
Middle East war, the Arab countries, united as one, used oil
as a weapon with which they dealt a telling blow at Zionism
and its supporters. They did well, and rightly too. This was
a pioneering action taken by developing countries in their struggle against imperialism. It greatly heightened the fighting

spirit of the people of the Third World and deflated the arrogance of imperialism. It broke through the international economic monopoly long maintained by imperialism and fully demonstrated the might of a united struggle waged by developing countries. If imperialist monopolies can gang up to manipulate the markets at will to the great detriment of the vital interests of the developing countries, why can't developing countries unite to break imperialist monopoly and defend their own economic rights and interests? The oil battle has broadened people's vision. What was done in the oil battle should and can be done in the case of other raw materials.

It must be pointed out further that the significance of the developing countries' struggle to defend their natural resources is by no means confined to the economic field. In order to carry out arms expansion and war preparations and to contend for world hegemony, the superpowers are bound to plunder rapaciously the resources of the Third World. Control and protection of their own resources by the developing countries are essential, not only for the consolidation of their political independence and the development of their national economy, but also for combating superpower arms expansion and war preparations and stopping the superpowers from launching wars of aggression.

Mr. President,

We maintain that the safeguarding of political independence is the first prerequisite for a Third World country to develop its economy. In achieving political independence, the people of a country have only taken the first step, and they must proceed to consolidate this independence, for there still exist remnant forces of colonialism at home and there is still the danger of subversion and aggression by imperialism and hegemonism. The consolidation of political independence is necessarily a process of repeated struggles. In the final analysis, political independence and economic independence are inseparable. Without political independence, it is impossible to achieve economic independence; without economic independence, a country's independence is incomplete and insecure.

The developing countries have great potential for developing their economies independently. As long as a country makes unremitting efforts in the light of its own specific features and conditions and advances along the road of independence and self-reliance, it is fully possible for it to attain gradually a high level of development never reached by previous generations in the modernization of its industry and agriculture. The ideas of pessimism and helplessness spread by imperialism in connection with the question of the development of developing countries are all unfounded and are being disseminated with ulterior motives.

By self-reliance, we mean that a country should mainly rely on the strength and wisdom of its own people, control its own economic lifelines, make full use of its own resources, strive hard to increase food production, and develop its national economy step by step and in a planned way. The policy of independence and self-reliance in no way means that it should be divorced from the actual conditions of a country; instead, it requires that distinction must be made between different circumstances and that each country should work out its own way of practicing self-reliance in the light of its specific conditions. At the present stage, a developing country that wants to develop its national economy must first of all keep its natural resources in its own hands and gradually shake off the control of foreign capital. In many developing countries, the production of raw materials accounts for a considerable proportion of the national economy. If they can take in their own hands the production, use, sale, storage, and transport of raw materials and sell them at reasonable prices on the basis of equitable trade relations, in exchange for a greater amount of goods needed for the growth of their industrial and agricultural production, they will then be able to resolve step by step the difficulties they are facing and pave the way for an early emergence from poverty and backwardness.

Self-reliance in no way means "self-seclusion" and rejection of foreign aid. We have always considered it beneficial and necessary for the development of the national economy that countries should carry on economic and technical exchanges on the basis of respect for state sovereignty, equality, and mutual benefit and the exchange of needed goods to make up for each other's deficiencies.

Here we wish to emphasize the special importance of economic cooperation among the developing countries. The Third World countries shared a common lot in the past and now face the common tasks of opposing colonialism, neocolonialism and great-power hegemonism, developing the national economy and building their respective countries. We have every reason to unite more closely and no reason to become estranged from one another. The imperialists, and particularly the superpowers, are taking advantage of temporary differences among us developing countries to sow dissension and disrupt unity so as to continue their manipulation, control, and plunder. We must maintain full vigilance. Differences among us developing countries can very well be resolved, and should be resolved, through consultations among the parties concerned. We are glad that on the question of oil the developing countries concerned are making active efforts and seeking appropriate ways to find a reasonable solution. We, the developing countries, should not only support one another politically but also help each other economically. Our cooperation is a cooperation based on true equality and has broad prospects.

China's Positions

Mr. President,

The Third World countries strongly demand that the present extremely unequal international economic relations be changed, and they have made many rational proposals of reform. The Chinese government and people warmly endorse and firmly support all just propositions made by Third World countries.

We hold that in both political and economic relations, countries should base themselves on the Five Principles of mutual respect for sovereignty and territorial integrity, mutual nonaggression, noninterference in each other's internal affairs, equality and mutual benefit, and peaceful coexistence. We are opposed to the establishment of hegemony and spheres of influence by any country in any part of the world in violation of these principles.

We hold that the affairs of each country should be managed by its own people. The people of the developing countries have the right to choose and decide on their own social and economic systems. We support the permanent sovereignty of the developing countries over their own natural resources as well as their exercise of it. We support the actions of the developing countries to bring all foreign capital, and particularly transnational corporations, under their control and management, up to and including nationalization. We support the position of the developing countries for the development of their national economy through "individual and collective self-reliance."

We hold that all countries, big or small, rich or poor, should be equal and that international economic affairs should be jointly managed by all the countries of the world instead of being monopolized by the one or two superpowers. We support the full right of the developing countries, which comprise the great majority of the world's population, to take part in all decision-making on international trade, monetary, shipping, and other matters.

We hold that international trade should be based on the principles of equality, mutual benefit, and the exchange of needed goods. We support the urgent demand of the developing countries to improve trading terms for their raw materials, primary products, and semi-manufactured and manufactured goods, to expand their market, and to fix equitable and favorable prices. We support the developing countries in establishing various organizations of raw material exporting countries for a united struggle against colonialism, imperialism, and hegemonism.

We hold that economic aid to the developing countries must strictly respect the sovereignty of the recipient countries and must not be accompanied by any political or military conditions

and the extortion of any special privileges or excessive profits.
Loans to the developing countries should be interest-free or
low-interest and allow for delayed repayment of capital and
interest or even reduction and cancellation of debts in case
of necessity. We are opposed to the exploitation of developing
countries by usury or blackmail in the name of aid.

We hold that technology transferred to the developing countries must be practical, efficient, economical, and convenient
for use. The experts and other personnel dispatched to the
recipient countries have the obligation to pass on conscientiously technical know-how to the people there and to respect
the laws and national customs of the countries concerned. They
must not make special demands or ask for special amenities,
let alone engage in illegal activities.

Mr. President,

China is a socialist country and a developing country as well.
China belongs to the Third World. Consistently following Chairman Mao's teachings, the Chinese government and people firmly
support all oppressed peoples and oppressed nations in their
struggle to win or defend national independence, develop the
national economy and oppose colonialism, imperialism, and
hegemonism. This is our bounden internationalist duty. China
is not a superpower; nor will she ever seek to be one. What is
a superpower? A superpower is an imperialist country which
everywhere subjects other countries to its aggression, interference, control, subversion, or plunder and strives for world
hegemony. If capitalism is restored in a big socialist country,
it will inevitably become a superpower. The Great Proletarian
Cultural Revolution which has been carried out in China in recent years and the campaign of criticizing Lin Piao and
Confucius now under way throughout China are both aimed
at preventing capitalist restoration and ensuring that socialist
China will never change her color and will always stand by the
oppressed peoples and oppressed nations. If one day China
should change her color and turn into a superpower, if she too
should play the tyrant in the world and everywhere subject

others to her bullying aggression, and exploitation, the people of the world should identify her as social-imperialism, expose it, oppose it, and work together with the Chinese people to overthrow it.

Mr. President,

History develops in struggle, and the world advances amidst turbulence. The imperialists, and the superpowers in particular, are beset with troubles and are on the decline. Countries want independence, nations want liberation, and the people want revolution — this is the irresistible trend of history. We are convinced that so long as the Third World countries and people strengthen their unity, ally themselves with all forces that can be allied with, and persist in a protracted struggle, they are sure to win continuous new victories.

CHAIRMAN MAO'S THEORY OF THE DIFFERENTIATION OF THE THREE WORLDS IS A MAJOR CONTRIBUTION TO MARXISM-LENINISM (Excerpts)*

4

Editorial Department of People's Daily

...In his life as a great revolutionary, Chairman Mao inherited, defended and developed Marxism-Leninism both in theory and in practice. His contributions to the Chinese revolution and the world revolution are immortal....

By integrating the universal truth of Marxism-Leninism with the concrete practice of the world revolution, Chairman Mao scientifically analyzed the international situation in different periods and drew illuminating conclusions, thus greatly promoting the revolutionary cause of the proletariat and the liberation of the oppressed nations all over the world....

Chairman Mao put forward the theory of the differentiation of the three worlds at a time when the two superpowers, the Soviet Union and the United States, became locked in a cutthroat struggle for world hegemony and were actively preparing for a new war. This theory provides the international proletariat, the socialist countries and the oppressed nations with a powerful ideological weapon for forging unity and building the broadest united front against the two hegemonist powers and their war policies and for pushing the world revolution forward....

The Differentiation of the Three Worlds Is a Scientific Marxist Assessment of Present-Day World Realities

...In his talk with the leader of a Third World country in

---

*From Peking Review, No. 45 (November 4, 1977).

February 1974, Chairman Mao said, "In my view, the United
States and the Soviet Union form the first world. Japan, Europe
and Canada, the middle section, belong to the second world. We
are the third world." "The third world has a huge population.
With the exception of Japan, Asia belongs to the third world.
The whole of Africa belongs to the third world, and Latin
America too."

This differentiation is a scientific conclusion which is based
on the analysis of the development of the fundamental contradictions of the contemporary world and the changes in them in
accordance with Lenin's theses that our era is the era of imperialism and proletarian revolution, that the development of
imperialist countries is uneven and the imperialist powers inevitably try to redivide the world by means of war, and that,
as imperialism has brought about the division of the whole
world into oppressor and oppressed nations, the international
proletariat must fight together with the oppressed nations. . . .

In appearance, this theory of Chairman Mao's seems to involve only relations between countries and between nations in
the present-day world, but, in essence, it bears directly on
the vital question of present-day class struggle on a world
scale. In the final analysis, national struggle is a matter of
class struggle. The same holds true of relations between
countries. Relations between countries or nations are based
on relations between classes, and they are interconnected and
extremely complicated. . . .

Marxist-Leninists invariably adhere to the stand of the international proletariat, uphold the general interests of the revolutionary people of all countries in international class struggle and persist in the replacement of the capitalist system with
the communist system as their maximum program. But the
situation with regard to this struggle is intricate and volatile.
The international bourgeoisie has never been a monolithic
whole; nor can it ever be. The international working-class
movement has also experienced one split after another, subject as it is to the influence of alien classes. In waging the
struggle in the international arena, the proletariat must unite

with all those who can be united in the light of what is impera-
tive and feasible in different historical periods, so as to develop the progressive forces, win over the middle forces and
isolate the diehards. Therefore, we can never lay down any
hard and fast formula for differentiating the world's political
forces (i.e., differentiating ourselves, our friends and our enemies in the international class struggle).

Following the emergence of the first socialist country,
Lenin, referring to the two kinds of diplomacy, the bourgeois
and the proletarian, said in 1921 that "there are now two
worlds: the old world of capitalism ... and the rising new
world. ..." Stalin said in 1919, "The world has definitely and
irrevocably split into two camps: the camp of imperialism
and the camp of socialism." ...

After the October Revolution and World War I Lenin made
a report in 1920 on "The International Situation and the Fundamental Tasks of the Communist International" at the Second
Congress of the Communist International in which he explicitly
divided the countries of the world ... into three categories —
the oppressed colonial and semicolonial countries and van-
quished countries, countries which retained their old positions,
and countries which had won the war and benefited by the par-
tition of the world; he placed socialist Russia and the oppressed
nations and countries in the same category. ...

Stalin more than once spoke of the capitalist and the socialist worlds opposing each other, but in concretely differentiating the world political forces in different periods, he proceeded
from the overall situation in the changing international class
struggle. As early as 1927, at the Fifteenth Congress of the
CPSU (B) [Communist Party of the Soviet Union-Bolshevik],
he made the following division of the existing world political
forces, saying: "Judge for yourselves. Of the 1,905 million
inhabitants of the entire globe, 1,134 million live in the colonies and dependent countries, 143,000,000 live in the USSR,
264,000,000 live in the intermediate countries, and only
363,000,000 live in the big imperialist countries, which oppress the colonies and dependent countries." In March 1939,

at the Eighteenth Congress of the CPSU (B), he defined Germany, Italy and Japan as aggressor countries and Britain, France and the United States as nonaggressor countries. Immediately after Hitlerite Germany attacked the Soviet Union in 1941, Stalin saw to it that the Soviet Union became allied to the United States, Britain and other countries to form an antifascist camp. In 1942 he said that "it may now be regarded as beyond dispute that in the course of the war imposed upon the nations by Hitlerite Germany, a radical demarcation of forces and the formation of two opposite camps have taken place: the camp of the Italo-German coalition and the camp of the Anglo-Soviet-American coalition" and that "it follows that the logic of facts is stronger than any other logic." ... Can we blame Stalin for not strictly following the formula of the capitalist world versus the socialist world in this instance? Can we doubt the great significance of the division of the world's political forces at the time into the fascist camp and the antifascist camp? Can the division of the world's political forces be based not on the logic of facts but on a logic that transcends facts?

...It is thus plain that all the revolutionary teachers of the proletariat differentiated the world's political forces by relying on an objective and penetrating analysis of the overall situation in the international class struggle in different periods, instead of following any hard and fast formula. The differentiation of the present-day political forces into three worlds by Chairman Mao, the greatest Marxist of our time, is a historical product of his creative application of Marxism over the years to the observation and analysis of the development of the world's fundamental contradictions and the changes in them. ...

In the days following World War II, U.S. imperialism raised an incessant anti-Soviet clamor. With exceptional perspicacity Chairman Mao exposed the real purpose of this hue and cry. He pointed out that "the United States and the Soviet Union are separated by a vast zone which includes many capitalist, colonial and semicolonial countries in Europe, Asia and Africa" and that "at present, the actual significance of the U.S. slogan of waging an anti-Soviet war is the oppression of the American people and the expansion of the U.S. forces of aggression in the rest of the capitalist world." ...

The Suez Canal incident of 1956 brought to light the sharpening contradictions between the imperialist powers. Chairman Mao pointed out at the time: "From this incident, we can pinpoint the focus of struggle in the world today. The contradiction between the imperialist countries and the socialist countries is certainly most acute. But the imperialist countries are now contending with each other for the control of different areas in the name of opposing communism.... In the Middle East, two kinds of contradictions and three kinds of forces are in conflict. The two kinds of contradictions are: first, those between different imperialist powers, that is, between the United States and Britain and between the United States and France and, second, those between the imperialist powers and the oppressed nations. The three kinds of forces are: one, the United States, the biggest imperialist power, two, Britain and France, second-rate imperialist powers, and three, the oppressed nations." Did this analysis of Chairman Mao's correspond to the objective realities of international class struggle at that time? Again, it obviously did. No one can doubt this, because events then and since have likewise borne out the validity of his analysis.

It is not difficult to see that Chairman Mao's analysis of the three kinds of forces was the forerunner of his theory of the three worlds....

This theory makes it clear: The two imperialist superpowers, the Soviet Union and the United States, constitute the First World. They have become the biggest international exploiters, oppressors and aggressors and the common enemies of the people of the world, and the rivalry between them is bound to lead to a new world war. The contention for world supremacy between the two hegemonist powers, the menace they pose to the people of all lands and the latter's resistance to them — this has become the central problem in present-day world

politics. The socialist countries, the mainstay of the international proletariat, and the oppressed nations, who are the worst
exploited and oppressed and who account for the great majority
of the population of the world, together form the Third World.
They stand in the forefront of the struggle against the two hegemonists and are the main force in the worldwide struggle
against imperialism and hegemonism. The developed countries
in between the two worlds constitute the Second World. They
oppress and exploit the oppressed nations and are at the same
time controlled and bullied by the superpowers. They have
a dual character, and stand in contradiction with both the First
and the Third Worlds. But they are still a force the Third
World can win over or unite with in the struggle against hegemonism. This theory summarizes the strategic situation concerning the most important class struggle in the contemporary
world in which the people of the whole world are one party and
the two hegemonist powers the other. The internal class struggles of various countries are actually inseparable from the
global class struggle. Therefore, this theory of the differentiation of the three worlds is the most comprehensive summing-
up of the various fundamental contradictions in the contemporary world. . . .

The Two Hegemonist Powers, the Soviet Union and the United States, Are the Common Enemies of the People of the World; the Soviet Union Is the Most Dangerous Source of World War

The emergence of the two superpowers is a new phenomenon
in the history of the development of imperialism. . . . Lenin
said, "Imperialism means the progressively mounting oppression of the nations of the world by a handful of Great Powers;
it means a period of wars between the latter to extend and
consolidate the oppression of nations." Today, this handful
of imperialist powers has been reduced to only two superpowers, the Soviet Union and the United States, which are
capable of contending for world hegemony, and all the other

imperialist powers have been relegated to the status of second-
or even third-rate powers. The distinctive features of a superpower are as follows: its state apparatus is controlled by
monopoly capital in its most concentrated form, and it relies
on its economic and military power, which is far greater than
that of other countries, to carry on economic exploitation and
political oppression and to strive for military control on a
global scale; each superpower sets exclusive world hegemony
as its goal and to this end makes frantic preparations for a
new world war....

In the postwar period, the concentration of U.S. monopoly
capital and its expansion abroad assumed startling propor-
tions.... While direct private investments abroad stood at
11.8 billion dollars in 1950, they jumped to 137.2 billion dollars in 1976.... For many years it acted as the world's gen-
darme and perpetrated numerous bloody crimes against the
revolutionary people (the people of the United States included)
and the oppressed nations of the world. But however much
this enemy of the world's people blustered, it had to take
crushing blows from the people of Asia in wars of aggression
which it thought it could win hands down. The heroic Korean
people were the first to explode the myth of U.S. invincibility.
In their war against U.S. aggression and for national salvation,
the people of Vietnam, Cambodia and Laos plunged U.S. imperialism into military, political and economic crises and
hastened its decline. In the meantime, Western Europe and
Japan steadily recovered, grew in economic strength and hard-
ened their positions in competing with the United States. Thus
U.S. imperialism was obliged to concede that it could no longer
have its own way in the world. However, it remains the most
powerful country in the capitalist world and is trying its utmost to retain its supremacy.

As the United States got bogged down in wars and its strength
began to decline, Soviet social-imperialism came up from behind. The Khrushchev-Brezhnev renegade clique, which had
snatched the fruits of the socialist construction carried out
by the Soviet people for over thirty years, gradually trans-

formed what had been a socialist power into an imperialist power.... As we all know, the Soviet revisionist renegade clique has converted a highly centralized socialist economy into a state monopoly capitalist economy which is centralized to a degree unattainable even by the United States.... It has caught up with the United States in nuclear armament and surpassed it in conventional weaponry. As its military and economic power increases, Soviet social-imperialism becomes more and more flagrant in its attempts to expand and penetrate all parts of the world. It makes great play with its ground, naval and air forces everywhere and engages the United States in a fierce struggle for supremacy on a global scale, thus betraying its aggressive ambitions which are unparalleled in world history.

The United States exploits other countries mainly through exporting capital in the form of overseas investment. According to U.S. official statistics, in 1976 it recouped profits, earnings from patents included, amounting to 22.4 billion U.S. dollars from its direct private investments overseas, the rate of profit exceeding 16 percent. Such is the sordid record of how U.S. monopoly capital sucks the blood of the people of the world. Although the Soviet Union falls short of the United States in the total volume of profits grabbed from other countries, it is not in the least inferior to the latter in its methods of plunder. It is chiefly through "economic aid" and "military aid" to Third World countries that the Soviet Union buys cheap and sells dear and squeezes enormous profits in the process. For example, the Soviet Union has been selling commodities to India in the name of "aid" at prices sometimes 20 to 30 percent, and even 200 percent, higher than on the world market. On the other hand, it purchases commodities from India at prices sometimes 20 to 30 percent lower.... It was reported in the Western press that in the Arab-Israeli War in October 1973, "Russia not only demanded payment in cash for the arms it sold but jacked up their prices when the war reached its height." After the principal oil-exporting Arab countries paid this sum in U.S. dollars, the Soviet Union used it to extend a

Euro-dollar loan at an interest rate of 10 percent or more.

. . .

The United States has gone in for selling arms on a world scale in order to extract huge profits from other countries and dominate them. Between 1966 and 1976 it exported arms to the value of 34.9 billion dollars. In the same period and for the same purpose, the Soviet Union sold arms amounting to 20.2 billion dollars. According to data issued by the U.S. Arms Control and Disarmament Agency, already in 1974 arms sales by the Soviet Union amounted to 5.5 billion dollars, accounting for 37.5 percent of the world total in that year and making it the second biggest merchant of death after the United States. . . .

The United States has some 400,000 of its armed forces stationed in foreign lands. The Soviet Union has about 700,000 troops in other countries and has put Czechoslovakia, which is a universally recognized sovereign country, completely under prolonged (actually indefinite) military occupation.

The United States has turned the territories of many countries into U.S. military bases through military treaties. The Soviet Union has got military bases or installations in Eastern Europe, the People's Republic of Mongolia, Cuba and Africa, and in the Mediterranean and the Indian Ocean; it has also insolently tried to perpetuate its occupation of Japan's northern territories and territorial seas. . . .

The conduct of the Soviet Union in international affairs is quintessential imperialism and hegemonism, without a trace of a socialist proletarian spirit; nor is that all. Of the two imperialist superpowers, the Soviet Union is the more ferocious, the more reckless, the more treacherous, and the most dangerous source of world war.

Why must we say so ? . . .

First, Soviet social-imperialism is an imperialist power following on the heels of the United States and is therefore more aggressive and adventurous. Lenin said long ago that late-comers among the imperialist countries always wanted the world to be divided anew and since they "came to the

capitalist banquet table when all the seats were occupied,"
they were "even more rapacious, even more predatory." "Without a forcible redivision of colonies the new imperialist countries cannot obtain the privileges enjoyed by the older (and
weaker) imperialist powers." To attain world supremacy,
Soviet social-imperialism has to try and grab areas under
U.S. control, just as Germany under Kaiser Wilhelm II and
under Hitler and the postwar United States had to try and grab
areas under the control of Britain and other old-line imperialists. This is a historical law independent of man's will. Therefore, Chairman Mao pointed out in a talk in February 1976:
"The United States wants to protect its interests in the world,
and the Soviet Union wants to expand; this can in no way be
changed." ...

Second, because, comparatively speaking, Soviet social-
imperialism is inferior in economic strength, it must rely
chiefly on its military power and recourse to threats of war
in order to expand. ... At present, the Soviet Union's armed
forces are double those of the United States, and it has over
400 strategic nuclear weapon carriers more than the United
States. It has vastly more tanks, armored cars, field guns
and other items of conventional weaponry. ... Soviet military
spending for fiscal year 1976 has been estimated at 127 billion
dollars, which is about 24 percent more than the projected U.S.
outlay of 102.7 billion. All this shows that the Soviet Union
will inevitably adopt an offensive strategy and resort chiefly
to force and threats of force in its contention with the United
States for world hegemony.

Third, the Soviet bureaucrat-monopoly capitalist group has
transformed a highly centralized socialist state-owned economy into a state-monopoly capitalist economy without its equal
in any other imperialist country and has transformed a state
under the dictatorship of the proletariat into a state under
fascist dictatorship. It is therefore easier for Soviet social-
imperialism to put the entire economy on a military footing
and militarize the whole state apparatus. The Brezhnev clique
has appropriated 20 percent of the national income for military

expenditures and is clamoring for getting "ready at any time to switch the economy to the military program." The clique is continuing to strengthen the state apparatus and is striving to fasten the Soviet people to its war chariot....

Fourth, Soviet social-imperialism has come into being as a result of the degeneration of the first socialist country in the world. Therefore, it can exploit Lenin's prestige and flaunt the banner of "socialism" to bluff and deceive people everywhere. United States imperialism has been pursuing policies of aggression and hegemonism for a long period and has time and again met with resistance and been subjected to exposure and denunciation on the part of the proletariat and oppressed people and nations throughout the world and of all fair-minded people including those in the United States.... Although more and more people have come to see the Soviet Union's policies of aggression and hegemonism in their true colors and the paint on its signboard of "socialism" is peeling day by day, it must not be supposed that the Soviet Union has completely lost its capacity to deceive. In carrying out aggression, intervention, subversion and expansion, it always dons the cloak of "fulfilling internationalist obligations," "supporting the national-liberation movements," "combating old and new imperialism," "safeguarding the interests of peace and democracy," and the like. It takes some time to recognize its essence, and China has had its own experience in this respect. It must be admitted that this duplicity peculiar to the Soviet Union increases the special danger it poses as an imperialist superpower.

These objective historical features of the Soviet Union undoubtedly make it more dangerous than the United States as a source of world war.

. . .

The Countries and People of the Third World Constitute the Main Force Combating Imperialism, Colonialism and Hegemonism

... In a message dated October 25, 1966, Chairman Mao said,

"The revolutionary storm in Asia, Africa and Latin America will certainly deal the whole of the old world a decisive and crushing blow." This is Chairman Mao's scientific prediction and high evaluation of the role of the Asian, African and Latin American people as the main force in the worldwide anti-imperialist revolutionary struggle.

What are the grounds for our saying this? Since the end of World War II, the revolutionary people of Asia, Africa, Latin America and other regions, standing in the forefront of the anti-imperialist and anticolonialist struggle, have waged one revolutionary armed struggle after another and scored a series of magnificent victories that have changed the face of the world.... The victorious Chinese revolution in 1949, the victory in the Korean war of resistance against U.S. aggression and for the defense of the fatherland in 1953, the Bandung Conference of Afro-Asian Countries in 1955, the Egyptian people's victory in the war over the Suez Canal in 1956, the victories in a series of national democratic movements in Latin America from the Cuban revolutionary war of 1959 to Chile's struggle for democracy in the early 1970s, the victory in the Algerian national-liberation war in 1962, the world-shaking heroic struggles waged by the people of many Asian and African countries to win and safeguard their independence in the 1960s, the restoration of China's legitimate seat in the United Nations in 1971, the victories won by the people of Vietnam, Cambodia and Laos in their war against U.S. aggression and for national salvation in 1975, the victorious wars of independence in Guinea-Bissau and Mozambique and the progress of the wars of independence in other countries in the 1970s, the powerful blows dealt by Egypt, the Sudan and other countries to Soviet schemes for control and subversion, the Zairian people's success in repelling invasion by Soviet mercenaries in 1977, the persistence of the Arab countries and the Palestinian people in waging wars and other forms of struggle against aggression over the past two decades, the African people's mounting resistance to white racism, the deepening of the national democratic movements of the people of Southeast Asia despite all obstacles, and the independence won by more than eighty countries in Asia, Africa, Latin America and other parts of the world over the past three decades — all these magnificent victories constitute a powerful force promoting revolutionary change in the postwar world. . . .

The Third World has become the main force in the worldwide struggle against imperialism, colonialism and hegemonism, and this has ushered in a new and unprecedented situation. How are we to evaluate it?

First, the roughly 3,000 million enslaved people who make up the overwhelming majority of the world's population have shaken off or are freeing themselves from the fetters of colonialism. This means that a radical and historic change has taken place in the balance of world class forces.

Second, subjected as they were to the most ruthless oppression, the countries and people of the Third World have been the most resolute in their resistance. Lenin said, "Colonies are conquered with fire and sword." Similarly, it is only with fire and sword that the colonial people can win complete emancipation. World imperialism cannot develop or survive without plundering colonies, semicolonies and oppressed nations and countries. The liberation struggles of the colonial people have shaken and will finally destroy the foundation on which imperialism depends for its survival. It is natural that imperialism will put up a desperate struggle.

. . . In order to be independent, to survive and to develop, the countries and people of the Third World have no choice but to wage a sustained and fierce life-and-death struggle against the aggressive and expansionist activities of imperialism and above all of the superpowers. New national-liberation wars are bound to break out. These inevitable contradictions and struggles between the Third World on the one hand and imperialism and superpowers on the other determine the long-term role of the Third World as the main force in the struggle against imperialism and hegemonism.

Third, the countries and people of the Third World have immensely enhanced their political awareness and strengthened

their unity in the course of struggle.... In his well-known
statement of May 20, 1970, Chairman Mao said: "Innumerable
facts prove that a just cause enjoys abundant support while an
unjust cause finds little support. A weak nation can defeat a
strong, a small nation can defeat a big. The people of a small
country can certainly defeat aggression by a big country if
only they dare to rise in struggle, dare to take up arms and
grasp in their own hands the destiny of their country. This is
a law of history." This statement of Chairman Mao's...is a
tremendous inspiration to all the people of the Third World....

The nonaligned movement has become an important world
force in coordinating the interests of its numerous member
countries and in jointly combating hegemonism, a force that
has to be reckoned with. Growing unity in struggle has made
it possible for the Third World countries to broaden their anti-
hegemonist struggle, wage it on a higher level and achieve
more striking results. For example, the struggle initiated
by the Latin American countries against superpower maritime
hegemony, the struggle waged by the Arab and other oil-
exporting countries in the Third World to defend their oil
rights and the struggle of other raw material producers have
inflicted unexpected and severe defeats on imperialism and
hegemonism....

Fourth, from an overall viewpoint, not only are there limits
to the imperialist countries' capacity for suppression in the
vast areas of Asia, Africa, Latin America and Oceania where
the 120 or more countries of the Third World are located, but
their interests in these areas clash in one way or another.
This provides the anti-imperialist revolutionary forces of the
Third World with a favorable condition in which to grow in
strength over the long period....

Does recognition of the Third World as the main force in
combating imperialism and hegemonism mean any reduction
of the responsibility or role of the international proletariat
in this struggle? The struggle against the two hegemonist
powers, which is an essential component of the world proletarian socialist movement, is extremely arduous and complex.

The proletariat of all countries must make an effort to study and disseminate Marxism-Leninism, play the exemplary role of vanguard in this struggle, fulfill their internationalist obligations and give all-out support and assistance to the people of all countries in their fight against imperialism and hegemonism so that this struggle can advance along the correct path and win final victory. Thus, the fact that the Third World has become the main force in combating imperialism and hegemonism in no way reduces the responsibility and role of the international proletariat in this struggle....

In affirming that the Third World countries are the main force in the struggle against imperialism and hegemonism, do we mean to deny the differences among these countries with respect to their social and political conditions and their conduct in the international struggle? Their social and political systems differ, the level of their economic development is not uniform, and there are constant changes in the political situation in each country. Hence it is often the case that the authorities of these countries adopt different attitudes toward imperialism and the superpowers and toward their own people. Owing to certain historical causes, and especially owing to the fact that the imperialists and social-imperialists keep sowing dissension among the Third World countries, certain disputes have arisen and even armed conflicts have occurred between some of them. But taken as a whole, the majority of these countries are for struggle against imperialism and hegemonism. There are of course struggles between different political forces within the Third World countries themselves. Some people are revolutionaries who firmly stand for carrying through the national democratic revolution. Others are progressives and middle-of-the-roaders of various descriptions. A few are reactionaries. And there are even some agents of imperialism or social-imperialism. Such phenomena are inevitable so long as there are classes, so long as there is a proletariat, a peasantry and a petty bourgeoisie and a variegated bourgeoisie and landlord and other exploiting classes. However, this complex situation does not affect the

basic fact that the Third World countries are the main force
in the struggle against imperialism and hegemonism....

China has proclaimed that she belongs to the Third World.
This is precisely an indication that China adheres to the socialist road and upholds Leninist principles. When Lenin put
Russia and the oppressed nations in the colonies in the same
category, could he possibly have forgotten that Russia was already a socialist country? Can it be said that Lenin had thus
altered the socialist orientation of Russia's development?
Nothing of the kind. His stand completely accorded with the
interests of the cause of the international proletariat and he
truly upheld the socialist orientation of Russia's development.
Today, China and other socialist countries stand together with
the rest of the Third World countries, and they support and
help each other and are advancing shoulder to shoulder in the
struggle against imperialism and hegemonism. In so doing
they have faithfully inherited this great concept of Lenin's
and are carrying it forward.

...On April 10, 1974, at the Special Session of the U.N. General Assembly, Comrade Teng Hsiao-p'ing solemnly declared
on behalf of the Chinese Government and the Chinese people,
"If one day China should change her political color and turn
into a superpower, if she too should play the tyrant in the
world, and everywhere subject others to her bullying, aggression and exploitation, the people of the world should put the
label of social-imperialism on her, expose it, oppose it and
work together with the Chinese people to overthrow it." We
would like to ask: Is there any other power today that dares
to make such a candid and honest statement?

However, the Soviet revisionist renegade clique had the
cheek to revile China as a country "seeking hegemony" in the
Third World. Such shameless slander is ludicrous. In China's
relations with other Third World countries over the years and
in the provision of aid to them within her capacity, is there a
single instance to indicate that she is seeking hegemony? Has
China ever sent a single soldier to invade and occupy any country? Has she ever demanded a single military base from any

country? Has she ever extorted a single penny from any country or held any country to ransom? Has she ever, in giving
aid, ordered any recipient country about, requiring it to conduct itself towards China this way and that? Chairman Mao
always held that the people of the world support each other in
their just struggles. There is never a one-way street from
donor to recipient. In her relations with other Third World
countries, China has initiated and faithfully observed the well-
known Five Principles of Peaceful Coexistence and the eight
principles of economic aid to other countries. This is plain
to all. The vain attempt by the Soviet revisionist renegade
clique to confound the friendly tics between the Chinese people and the people of the Third World only serves to expose
once again its reactionary features....

The Second World Is a Force That Can Be United with in the Struggle against Hegemonism

... How is it that the Second World countries constitute a
force which can be united with in the struggle against hegemonism? The reason is that an important change has taken
place in their role in international political and economic relations during the last thirty years.

Through twenty to thirty years of struggle against U.S. control and simultaneously through taking advantage of the severe
worldwide setbacks suffered by the United States in its policy
of aggression, the West European countries have succeeded in
altering the situation prevailing in the early postwar years
when they had to submit to U.S. domination. Japan is in a
similar position. The establishment of the Common Market
in Western Europe, the independent policies pursued by France
under DeGaulle, the passive and critical attitude taken by the
West European countries toward the U.S. war of aggression in
Vietnam, Cambodia and Laos, the collapse of the dollar-
centered monetary system in the capitalist world and the
sharpening trade and currency wars between Western Europe
and Japan on the one hand and the United States on the other —

all these facts mark the disintegration of the former imperialist camp headed by the United States. True, the monopoly capitalists of the West European countries, Japan, etc., have a
thousand and one ties with the United States and, in face of the
menace posed by Soviet social-imperialism, these countries
still have to rely on the U.S. "protective umbrella." But so
long as the United States continues its policy of control, they
will not cease in their struggle against such control and for
equal partnership.

But today Soviet social-imperialism obviously represents
the gravest danger to the West European countries, for Europe
is the focal point in the Soviet strategy for seeking world hegemony. The Soviet Union has massed its military and naval
forces in Eastern Europe and on the northern and southern
European waters, which are deployed to encircle Western
Europe. At the same time it has stepped up its seizure of
strategic areas along the line running from the Red Sea through
the Indian Ocean via the Cape of Good Hope to the eastern
shores of the South Atlantic, endeavoring to outflank and encircle Europe and seriously menacing the main lines of communication vital to Western Europe. This poses a grave
threat to the security of the West European countries and com-
pels them to strengthen their defenses, coordinate their relations with each other and maintain and enhance their unity economically, politically and in defense. In the Far East, Japan
is also faced with a serious threat. The massive Soviet military buildup in the Far East, aimed at China as it is, is directed primarily against the United States and Japan. The
Soviet Union has forcibly occupied Japan's northern territories and territorial seas, and it is posing a growing threat
to Japan and intensifying its infiltration of the latter. This has
aroused strong indignation and resistance on the part of all
Japanese patriotic forces. Australia, New Zealand and Canada
too have heightened their vigilance against Soviet expansion and
infiltration.

. . .

The East European countries have never ceased waging

struggles against Soviet control. Since the Soviet occupation of Czechoslovakia the people's resistance has continued to grow. In 1976 the Polish people repeatedly launched widespread movements to protest the inclusion of a provision on the Polish-Soviet alliance in the new constitution, and there were workers' strikes and demonstrations in which slogans like "We want freedom," "We want no Russians" were raised.... As the Soviet Union steps up its contention for world hegemony, Eastern Europe becomes a forward position in Soviet preparations for war against Western Europe and the United States. Soviet control and interference in the East European countries through the Warsaw Treaty Organization has become increasingly intolerable. Thus, uneasiness is growing among the East European people and the struggle to defend their independence, security and equal rights is gathering momentum.

Of course, it must be realized that some Second World countries will not easily relinquish their deep-rooted exploitation of and control over many Third World countries. For the Third World to establish relations of equality and mutual benefit with the Second will involve a long and arduous struggle. However, as already indicated, the Second World is being subjected to interference, control and bullying by the two hegemonist powers and to their war threats, particularly on the part of the Soviet Union. This has become a grim reality and will become more so....

Since the Soviet Union regards Europe as the strategic focal point, countries in both Eastern and Western Europe will have to bear the brunt of its attack. They face a grave problem of safeguarding their national independence....

Today, the European countries are faced with the grave threat of invasion and annexation from the Soviet social-imperialists. Chairman Mao told the political leaders of West European countries more than once that "the Soviet Union has wild ambitions. It wants to lay hands on the whole of Europe, Asia and Africa." If West European countries were to fall under the iron heel of the new tsars, they would be reduced to dependencies and their people to the status of second-class citizens, who would be doubly oppressed by the foreign conquerors and domestic capitulationists....

Since the Second World countries are faced with the super-powers' growing threat of war, it is necessary for them to strengthen unity among themselves and their unity with the Third World and other possible allies, so as to advance in the struggle against the common enemy. United struggle is the only correct path for them to take in defense of their national independence and survival, even though this path is strewn not with roses but with thorns.

Build the Broadest International United Front and Smash Superpower Hegemonism and War Policies

The current fight of the people of the world against the hegemonism of the two superpowers and the fight against their war policies are two aspects of one and the same struggle. Hegemonism is their aim in war as well as their means of preparing for it. The danger of war resulting from Soviet-U.S. contention for hegemony is a growing menace to the people of the whole world. What attitude should we take toward this problem?

The people of China and the people of the rest of the world firmly demand peace and oppose a new world war.... As Chairman Mao consistently stated, our attitude toward a world war is: first, we are against it; second, we are not afraid of it....

What are our tasks then?

First of all, we must warn the people of the danger of war. The two superpowers are making frenzied efforts to muster all their strength for war....

Since the rivalry between the two hegemonist powers is intensifying and especially since Soviet social-imperialism is on the offensive, the conflict between them cannot possibly be settled by peaceful means, when the chips are down. In the course of their fierce rivalry, these two superpowers may sometimes come to some agreement or other for a specific purpose.

Chairman Mao said: "They may reach some agreement, but I wouldn't take it as something solid. It's transitory, and deceptive too. In essence, rivalry is primary." Such rivalry inevitably leads to war. At present, the factors for war are visibly growing. The two hegemonist powers are stepping up their war preparations while harping on the shopworn theme of "détente" and "disarmament." Why don't they simply stop it and destroy their huge arsenals lock, stock and barrel? Instead, they are spending huge sums of money on further research into new nuclear weapons and missiles and their manufacture and on the development of still more efficient and still more lethal chemical, biological and other weapons. Their armed forces are so deployed that they can swiftly go into action, and they are constantly holding various kinds of military exercises. Each has massed hundreds of thousands of troops in Central Europe. Their fleets keep each other under surveillance as they prowl the oceans. Spies are sent out on new assignments, submarines embark on new missions, and new military satellites orbit in outer space. They are gathering military intelligence and readying themselves to wipe out each other's war potential. All this makes it abundantly clear that the two superpowers are actively preparing for a total war....

Second, we should make every effort to step up the struggle against hegemonism, that is, we should fight to put off the outbreak of war and in the process strengthen the defense capabilities of the people of all countries.

· · ·

Chairman Mao said: "The United States is a paper tiger. Don't believe in it. One thrust and it's punctured. Revisionist Soviet Union is a paper tiger too."... Going all out as it does for arms expansion and war preparations, the Soviet Union finds that "it's strength falls short of its wild ambitions," and it is "unable to cope with Europe, the Middle East, South Asia, China and the Pacific Region."

· · ·

History has repeatedly shown that unity in struggle forged

by the people of all countries is the main force in defeating the
war instigators. The people of every country must work hard
and step up their preparations materially and organizationally
against wars of aggression, closely watch the aggressive and
expansionist activities of the two hegemonist powers and resolutely defeat them. The people must see to it that these two
superpowers do not violate their country's or any other country's sovereign rights, do not encroach on their country's or
any other country's territory and territorial seas or violate
their strategic areas and strategic lines of communication, do
not use force or the threat of force or other maneuvers to
interfere in their country's or any other country's internal affairs; moreover, both powers must be closely watched lest
they resort to schemes of subversion and use "aid" as a pretext to push through their military, political and economic
plots. The people must also see to it that they do not establish,
enlarge, carve up and wrest spheres of influence in any part of
the world. So long as all this is done, it will be possible to hold
up the timetable of the two hegemonists for launching a world
war, and the people of the world will be better prepared and
find themselves in a more favorable position should war break
out. . . .

Third, we must redouble our efforts to oppose the policy of
appeasement because it can only bring war nearer. There are
people in the West today who in fact adopt a policy of appeasement toward the Soviet Union. In striving to work out an "ideal"
formula for compromise and concessions in the face of Soviet
expansion and threats, some people have dished up such proposals as the "Sonnenfeldt doctrine" in the fond hope of as-
suaging the aggressor's appetite or at least gaining some
respite for themselves. Others intend to build a so-called
"material basis" for peaceful cooperation and the prevention
of war by means of big loans, extensive trade, joint exploitation of resources and exchanges of technology. Still others
hope they can divert the Soviet Union to the East so as to free
themselves from this Soviet peril at the expense of the security of other countries. But aren't all these nostrums just a

revamping of what was previously tried and found totally bankrupt in the history of war? Did the Munich agreement to sacrifice Czechoslovakia, cooked up by Chamberlain, Daladier and company, stop or slow down the march of the voracious Hitler? True, Hitler did go east and overrun Poland, but didn't he follow this up by turning west to occupy France? The United States, Britain and France gave Germany and Japan a shot in the arm by extending aid and loans to them and selling them war materials. And did they succeed in saving themselves? Today's activities are indeed far more hectic than those before World War II, what with the SALT [Strategic Arms Limitation Talks] talks between the United States and the Soviet Union, the talks on the reduction of forces in Central Europe and the conference on European security and cooperation. But hasn't the war crisis in Europe worsened rather than abated despite the intensified efforts to keep these conferences going and make deals? Haven't the weapons of all kinds installed on both sides of the European front grown in number rather than diminished? The more highfalutin the talk of détente and the more intense the efforts at appeasement, the greater the danger of war. This is not alarmist talk. It is a truth repeatedly borne out by history. It is high time that these appeasers woke up.

. . .

In 1968 Chairman Mao stated that the Soviet revisionists and the U.S. imperialists "have done so many foul and evil things that the revolutionary people the world over will not let them go unpunished. The people of all countries are rising. A new historical period of struggle against U.S. imperialism and Soviet revisionism has begun." Today, the world forces fighting the hegemonism of the two superpowers are growing in strength, building as they are the broadest international united front. . . . As time passes, this main trend increasingly testifies to the correctness of Chairman Mao's theory of the differentiation of the three worlds and to its power as the guiding concept for the international proletariat and the people of the world in building the broadest possible international united front against hegemonism.

Much importance is attached to Chairman Mao's theory of
the differentiation of the three worlds by the forces ranged
against the superpowers throughout the world. Why? Because,
first, this theory gives immense confidence to the international
proletariat and the people of the socialist countries and enables
them to see clearly the essential relationships between the
three forces — ourselves, our friends and our enemies — in
the present-day world and visualize their eventual victory in
the struggle against imperialism and hegemonism and the
triumph of communism. Second, this theory gives immense
confidence to the masses and countries of the Third World
and enables them to realize their own gigantic strength; it enables them to see that in their struggle they not only enjoy
the sure support of the socialist countries and the international proletariat and the solidarity of the people of the First
and Second worlds, but they can to a certain extent also obtain
cooperation from the countries of the Second World and take
advantage of the contradictions between the two superpowers.
Third, this theory not only holds out high hopes to the people
of the First and Second worlds, but shows the way ahead for
all the political forces of the Second World striving to safeguard state sovereignty and national survival under the menace of aggression by the two superpowers. In a word, this
theory is powerful because it accords with the objective realities of world politics and illuminates the bright future of
mankind.

Chairman Mao always pinned high hopes on the people of
all countries. He said that "the masses of the Soviet people
and of Party members and cadres are good, that they desire
revolution and that revisionist rule will not last long." On another occasion he said, "I place great hopes in the American
people." With regard to the Japanese people Chairman Mao
said, "Tortuous as is the road of struggle, the prospects for
the Japanese people are bright." In a talk with personages
from Africa and Latin America he pointed out: "We all stand
on the same front and need to unite with and support each
other." "The people of the world, including the people of the

United States, are our friends." Obviously, by the people of the world Chairman Mao meant, first and foremost, the international proletariat.

. . .

Proletarians and the oppressed nations of the world, unite! All countries subjected to aggression, interference, control, subversion and bullying by the two hegemonist powers, unite! Victory belongs to the people of all countries fighting the two hegemonist powers, the Soviet Union and the United States!

II

Sino-American rapprochement

Documentary Introduction

In this chapter, we have included four selections on the documentation, motives, and explanations for the Sino-American rapprochement.

The first selection, the well-known Nixon-Chou joint communiqué of 1972, has become the basic document relating to the United States' relations with the People's Republic of China and Taiwan.

The second, "Why Did Our Country Accede to Nixon's Request for a Visit?" was originally delivered by Chou En-lai in December 1971, three months after Lin Piao's death and two months before Nixon's visit. It explained why China should flexibly employ the "dual revolutionary tactics" of negotiating and simultaneously struggling with the United States.

The third selection, "the Kunming Documents," is a really important piece of material on why the Sino-American rapprochement should be promoted and accepted. Originally secret military educational material of 1973, the documents reveal China's deep concern over the "Soviet threat," state Peking's plans to settle problems with Nixon temporarily, and make clear Mao's strategies to exploit international contradictions among the United States, the Soviet Union, and Japan.

The last selection, "Necessary Compromise," was part of

Chou En-lai's speech in 1973, four months after the establishment of the respective American and Chinese liaison offices
in Peking and Washington. Although Chou's speech did not
state outright that the coexistence of the PRC's liaison office
and Taiwan's embassy in the U.S. capital was a compromise
with the United States, the allusion of the message was clear.
It was devised to modify the disagreement among the Chinese
concerning such an intriguing compromise.

THE NIXON-CHOU SHANGHAI COMMUNIQUÉ*

(February 27, 1972)

President Richard Nixon of the United States of America visited the People's Republic of China at the invitation of Premier Chou En-lai of the People's Republic of China from February 21 to February 28, 1972. Accompanying the President were Mrs. Nixon, U.S. Secretary of State William Rogers, Assistant to the President Dr. Henry Kissinger, and other American officials.

President Nixon met with Chairman Mao Tse-tung of the Communist Party of China on February 21. The two leaders had a serious and frank exchange of views on Sino-U.S. relations and world affairs.

During the visit, extensive, earnest, and frank discussions were held between President Nixon and Premier Chou En-lai on the normalization of relations between the United States of America and the People's Republic of China, as well as on other matters of interest to both sides. In addition, Secretary of State William Rogers and Foreign Minister Chi P'eng-fei held talks in the same spirit.

President Nixon and his party visited Peking and viewed cultural, industrial, and agricultural sites, and they also toured Hangchow and Shanghai where, continuing discussions with Chinese leaders, they viewed similar places of interest.

The leaders of the People's Republic of China and the United States of America found it beneficial to have this opportunity,

---

*"Joint Communiqué." Peking Review, No. 9 (March 3, 1972), 4-5.

after so many years without contact, to present candidly to one
another their views on a variety of issues. They reviewed the
international situation in which important changes and great
upheavals are taking place and expounded their respective positions and attitudes.

The Chinese side stated: Wherever there is oppression,
there is resistance. Countries want independence, nations
want liberation, and the people want revolution — this has become the irresistible trend of history. All nations, big or
small, should be equal; big nations should not bully the small,
and strong nations should not bully the weak. China will never
be a superpower, and it opposes hegemony and power politics
of any kind. The Chinese side stated that it firmly supports
the struggles of all the oppressed people and nations for freedom and liberation and that the people of all countries have
the right to choose their social systems according to their own
wishes and the right to safeguard the independence, sovereignty,
and territorial integrity of their own countries and oppose foreign aggression, interference, control, and subversion. All
foreign troops should be withdrawn to their own countries.
The Chinese side expressed its firm support to the peoples of
Vietnam, Laos, and Cambodia in their efforts for the attainment of their goal and its firm support to the seven-point proposal of the Provisional Revolutionary Government of the
Republic of South Vietnam and the elaboration of February
this year on the two key problems in the proposal, and to the
Joint Declaration of the Summit Conference of the Indochinese
Peoples. It firmly supports the eight-point program for the
peaceful unification of Korea put forward by the Government
of the Democratic People's Republic of Korea on April 12, 1971,
and the stand for the abolition of the "U.N. Commission for
the Unification and Rehabilitation of Korea." It firmly opposes
the revival and outward expansion of Japanese militarism and
firmly supports the Japanese people's desire to build an independent, democratic, peaceful, and neutral Japan. It firmly
maintains that India and Pakistan should, in accordance with
the United Nations resolutions on the India-Pakistan question,

immediately withdraw all their forces to their respective
territories and to their own sides of the ceasefire line in
Jammu and Kashmir and firmly supports the Pakistan Government and people in their struggle to preserve their independence and sovereignty and the people of Jammu and Kashmir
in their struggle for the right of self-determination.

The U.S. side stated: Peace in Asia and peace in the world
requires efforts both to reduce immediate tensions and to eliminate the basic causes of conflict. The United States will
work for a just and secure peace: just, because it fulfills the
aspirations of peoples and nations for freedom and progress;
secure, because it removes the danger of foreign aggression.
The United States supports individual freedom and social progress for all the peoples of the world, free of outside pressure
or intervention. The United States believes that the effort to
reduce tensions is served by improving communication between
countries that have different ideologies so as to lessen the
risks of confrontation through accident, miscalculation, or
misunderstanding. Countries should treat each other with
mutual respect and be willing to compete peacefully, letting
performance be the ultimate judge. No country should claim
infallibility, and each country should be prepared to reexamine
its own attitudes for the common good. The United States
stressed that the peoples of Indochina should be allowed to
determine their destiny without outside intervention; its constant primary objective has been a negotiated solution; the
eight-point proposal put forward by the Republic of Vietnam
and the United States on January 27, 1972, represents a basis
for the attainment of that objective; in the absence of a
negotiated settlement the United States envisages the ultimate
withdrawal of all U.S. forces from the region consistent with
the aim of self-determination for each country of Indochina.
The United States will maintain its close ties with and support
for the Republic of Korea; the United States will support efforts
of the Republic of Korea to seek a relaxation of tension and
increased communication in the Korean peninsula. The United
States places the highest value on its friendly relations with

Japan; it will continue to develop the existing close bonds.
Consistent with the United Nations Security Council Resolution
of December 21, 1971, the United States favors the continuation
of the ceasefire between India and Pakistan and the withdrawal
of all military forces to within their own territories and to
their own sides of the ceasefire line in Jammu and Kashmir;
the United States supports the right of the peoples of South Asia
to shape their own future in peace, free of military threat, and
without having the area become the subject of great power
rivalry.

There are essential differences between China and the United
States in their social systems and foreign policies. However,
the two sides agreed that countries, regardless of their social
systems, should conduct their relations on the principles of
respect for the sovereignty and territorial integrity of all
states, nonaggression against other states, noninterference
in the internal affairs of other states, equality and mutual
benefit, and peaceful coexistance. International disputes should
be settled on this basis, without resorting to the use or threat
of force. The United States and the People's Republic of China
are prepared to apply these principles to their mutual relations.

With these principles of international relations in mind the
two sides stated that:

— progress toward the normalization of relations between
China and the United States is in the interests of all countries;

— both wish to reduce the danger of international military
conflict;

— neither should seek hegemony in the Asia-Pacific region
and each is opposed to efforts by any other country or group
of countries to establish such hegemony; and

— neither is prepared to negotiate on behalf of any third
party or to enter into agreements or understandings with the
other directed at other states.

Both sides are of the view that it would be against the interests of the peoples of the world for any major country to
collude with another against other countries or for major
countries to divide up the world into spheres of interest.

The two sides reviewed the long-standing serious disputes
between China and the United States. The Chinese side reaffirmed its position: The Taiwan question is the crucial question obstructing the normalization of relations between China
and the United States; the Government of the People's Republic
of China is the sole legal government of China; Taiwan is a
province of China which has long been returned to the motherland; the liberation of Taiwan is China's internal affair in
which no other country has the right to interfere; and all U.S.
forces and military installations must be withdrawn from Taiwan. The Chinese Government firmly opposes any activities
which aim at the creation of "one China, one Taiwan," "one
China, two governments," "two Chinas," an "independent Taiwan" or advocate that "the status of Taiwan remains to be
determined."

The U.S. side declared: The United States acknowledges that
all Chinese on either side of the Taiwan Strait maintain there
is but one China and that Taiwan is a part of China. The United
States Government does not challenge that position. It reaffirms its interest in a peaceful settlement of the Taiwan question by the Chinese themselves. With this prospect in mind,
it affirms the ultimate objective of the withdrawal of all U.S.
forces and military installations from Taiwan. In the meantime, it will progressively reduce its forces and military installations on Taiwan as the tension in the area diminishes.

The two sides agreed that it is desirable to broaden the understanding between the two peoples. To this end, they discussed specific areas in such fields as science, technology,
culture, sports, and journalism in which people-to-people contacts and exchanges would be mutually beneficial. Each side
undertakes to facilitate the further development of such contacts
and exchanges.

Both sides view bilateral trade as another area from which
mutual benefit can be derived and agreed that economic relations based on equality and mutual benefit are in the interest of the
peoples of the two countries. They agree to facilitate the progressive development of trade between their two countries.

The two sides agreed that they will stay in contact through various channels, including the sending of a senior U.S. representative to Peking from time to time for concrete consultations to further the normalization of relations between the two countries, and continue to exchange views on issues of common interest.

The two sides expressed the hope that the gains achieved during this visit would open up new prospects for the relations between the two countries. They believe that the normalization of relations between the two countries is not only in the interest of the Chinese and American peoples but also contributes to the relaxation of tension in Asia and the world.

President Nixon, Mrs. Nixon, and the American party expressed their appreciation for the gracious hospitality shown them by the Government and people of the People's Republic of China.

WHY DID OUR COUNTRY ACCEDE TO NIXON'S REQUEST FOR A VISIT?

2

Chou En-Lai's Internal Report to the Party on the International Situation, December 1971 (Excerpts)*

A. Characteristics of the Current International Situation

1. The characteristics of the current international situation can be summarized into four phrases: "one trend," "two possibilities," "three parts," and "four contradictions."

"One trend" reflects what Chairman Mao said in his statement of May 20: "The main trend in the world today is revolution."

The "two possibilities" are the possibility of circumventing war by revolution and the possibility of revolution triggered by a war. The possibility of a war still exists; we must maintain vigilance.

The "three parts" refer to the two superpowers, the United States and the Soviet Union, and to the third world. We are resolutely on the side of the third world.

"Four contradictions" are the basic contradictions of the contemporary world manifested by the contradiction between the two superpowers, the U.S. and USSR, and the people throughout the world; the contradiction between the U.S. and USSR for

---

*"Chou En-lai tsai i-chiu-ch'i-i nien shih-erh yüeh tui tang-nei so-tso ti kuo-chi hsing-shih pao kao." Fei-ch'ing yüeh-pao [Chinese Communist Affairs Monthly], XIX: 6 (December 1976), 90-93. This translation is adapted with permission from Issues & Studies, XIII: 1 (January 1977), 113-120. The title is changed by the Editor.

gaining world hegemony; the contradiction among the imperialist countries shifting [the causes] for the economic crisis on each other; and the contradiction of the medium-sized and small countries struggling together against the U.S. and USSR.

2. The present global strategy of the U.S. is contained in five phrases mentioned by Kissinger: "the Americas as the base," "western Europe as the pivotal point," "Asia as the flank," "the Middle East as the throat," and "the oceans being the center of the world struggle in the future." The strategy of the USSR is to step up the contention for hegemony with the U.S., with their arms stretching out ever further and their ambition ever increasing. The U.S. and USSR are both contending and compromising. They compromise when their contention is without result and contend again when compromise is fruitless. The Soviet revisionists compromised with Western countries on the Berlin issue with an eye to consolidating their foothold in Western Europe in preparation for contention. The key points for which the USSR is contending with the U.S. are: (a) Europe, (b) Middle East.

3. The general strategy of our nation for the present is: to push forward [preparations against] war and promote revolution.

a) In Asia: Korea is our No. 1 comrade-in-arms. We are closely united with her and we support each other, seeking common ground while maintaining our differences and resisting enemies jointly. With respect to "differences," there were two of them recently: The first is that while we say there is no longer a socialist camp presently, Korea still adheres firmly to a proposition that there is; the second is that while we say that "anti-imperialism" is not to be mentioned in the Afro-Asian ping-pong games, Korea is determined to mention it, saying that it is revisionist not to.

The relations between Vietnam, Laos, Cambodia and us are like those between the front line and the rear. But, for the present, it is not appropriate to praise Vietnam excessively; we should treat her as we do the other two nations. The contradictions among them should be solved by themselves. Vietnam shows anxiety over Nixon's visit to China. We have pro-

vided explanations. If she cannot figure it out for the moment,
just let her watch the development of the truth.

Burma has restored normal relations with our country. Ne
Win has visited our country this year and made three major
points: (1) He was sorry for the events of 1967 in which the
Chinese Embassy in Burma was assaulted; (2) He was appre-
ciative of [our] permitting him to visit China; (3) He wondered
what he should do about the losses of the overseas Chinese
[in Burma] incurred by the 1967 events. To the third point,
we answered that he should compensate for the losses. After
he returned to Burma, a special committee was immediately
organized by a vice foreign minister to handle the matter of
reparations for losses suffered by overseas Chinese [in
Burma].

India and Pakistan. While the Soviet revisionists back India,
we support Pakistan. In supporting Pakistan, we support her
resistance to Indian aggression. But there are mistakes in the
domestic policy of Pakistan, [such as] the massacre in East
Pakistan and the lack of a policy toward nationalities. India is
the head of the reactionaries among the imperialists, revisionists and reactionaries. In spite of this, we still want to restore
normal diplomatic relations with her at an opportune moment,
for the purpose of furthering the people's revolution in India.

Singapore and Malaysia. Lee Kuan Yew said that, with respect to the problem of improving relations with China, Singapore will move one step when Malaysia moves two. In short,
he follows others and is not eager to improve relations with
China. He is very much interested in the investments of the
U.S., Japan, and the USSR. The potential influence of Britain
in Singapore is still strong. Although overseas Chinese comprise seventy percent of the population of Singapore, we cannot
count Singapore as Chinese territory. This demarcation must
be clear.

If Singapore [proposes to] establish diplomatic relations
with us, we can take it into consideration. But, presently, it
would be better [just to maintain] commercial relations.
Malaysia upholds neutralism and wants to improve relations

with us. We have complied with her demands, and relations will also develop step by step from now on. There is also the possibility of establishing diplomatic relations [with us] in the future. The Soviet revisionists take great interest in this area, but Britain, the U.S., and Japan will not relinquish the area.

The Philippines already has commercial relations with our country and relations will continue to develop. Yet it remains to be seen how things will develop in the future.

Japan. Sato is increasingly unstable. But, for the time being, it is the Japanese Communist revisionists and the Komeito that are best able to appeal to the masses. There are only one thousand-odd people who are real leftists. Wang Kuo-ch'üan did a good job when he was sent to Japan for a couple of days. He helped to revive the cooperation between the two factions of Hisao Kuroda and Seimin Miyazaki and a celebration was held on that occasion. It will take time for the Japanese revolution to create unity out of division.

b) It is necessary to do a good job of dealing with the people of the U.S. Chairman Mao said: "Place great hope in the people of the United States." As the people's revolution in the U.S. gradually gains momentum, we have to do more work.

c) In the areas of Africa and Latin America, generally speaking, we support national revolution, chiefly with moral support. Lately the Soviet revisionist have been engaged in sabotage. Recently the situation in Zambia became unstable mainly because the Soviet revisionists are playing tricks.

d) In the Middle East, we [aim] mainly to uncover the intrigues of deception and division of the U.S. and USSR. The Soviet revisionists are not faring well in the Middle East. Egypt toppled Ali Sabri and Sudan crushed the coup d'état machinated by the Soviet revisionists. But the Soviet revisionists have increased their influence in Syria, Iraq, Yemen, and South Yemen. The current situation in Palestine is not very good, with a decrease to 20,000 people from 50,000. Struggle is complicated.

e) Europe: The ten countries of the European Economic Community will deal a heavy blow to the USSR and U.S. Heath

said that "The era of the control of the two superpowers over
the world has already come to an end." This is indeed the
truth. However, Britain, France, and West Germany all have
their own plans; contradictions do exist. That the rise of European power has broken down the power division between the
U.S. and USSR is one of the signs of global upheaval. The linch-
pin of the diplomatic relationship between China and Britain
lies in the Taiwan issue. The British said that "The uncertain
status of Taiwan, as Churchill called it, has become law. It is
now inappropriate to change our position." We must persist
in this matter. As long as this problem remains unsolved, the
Chiang gang in Taiwan will reapply for admission to the United
Nations at any time. We cannot give way.

f) The Balkan Peninsula: Brezhnev asked Tito: "Who is the
hypothetical enemy when you practice military maneuvers?"
Tito answered: "Whoever attacks us is the enemy." The petty
revisionists of Eastern Europe are now also beginning to fall
away from the USSR. Moreover, with regard to the matter of
invectives unleashed against us by the newspapers and radios
of the petty revisionists of Eastern Europe, Chairman Mao
said: "They are ordered to call [us] names and cannot do
otherwise."

B. Why Will Nixon Come to Our Country
for Negotiations?

1. The visit of the head of U.S. imperialism to China is a
victory for the people of the entire world and renders bankrupt the China policy of the U.S.

2. It is the outcome of the development of the four basic
contradictions in the world.

3. [It is due to] the immense internal pressure of the people
in the U.S. demanding improvement in U.S.-China relations.

4. When the U.S. got stuck in Vietnam, the Soviet revisionists used the opportunity to extend vigorously their sphere of
influence in Europe and the Middle East. The U.S. imperialists have no choice but to improve their relations with China

in order to counter the Soviet revisionists.

5. Improving relations with China is great capital in the coming presidential election. Therefore, Nixon is "dressing up elaborately and presenting himself at our door."

C. Why Did Our Country Accede to Nixon's Request for a Visit?

1. Chairman Mao made it clear in his talk with Snow. It will not do to discuss the problems of the world only with leftist or middle-of-the-road or ordinary rightist opponents. Problems cannot be solved. Until the people hold power, only by negotiating directly with the head of the rightists will what has been said count.

2. At this stage, it is necessary to take full advantage of the contradiction between the U.S. and USSR and to magnify it.

3. After improving U.S.-China relations, it will be easier to do a good job in dealing with the people of the U.S. The strength of the U.S. people's revolution is growing little by little; this problem must be handled seriously. As long as relations between countries [the U.S. and us] remain unimproved, our work will be difficult to carry out.

4. Because Nixon has encountered difficulties both domestically and internationally, he has requested eagerly to visit China. When he comes, he has to bring along something in his pocket; otherwise, he will find it hard to give explanations when he returns to the U.S. It is to our advantage if the negotiation succeeds but it constitutes no detriment to us if the negotiation fails. We will never give up our principles and sell out our people and revolution. If Vietnam does not comprehend this, we can persuade her gradually. That U.S.-China relations are a betrayal of principle, of revolution, and of Vietnam, as Lin Piao said, is nonsense and an insult to the Party. Furthermore, some say that we are helping Nixon to run for president. How should this be viewed? The Republicans and Democrats are of the same ilk. How can it be said that it is right to help the Democrats? Any question should be studied from the viewpoint of class analysis.

D. The Current Situation of Soviet Revisionism

1. The development of new internal power struggles and
Brezhnev's reckless power grabbing are exemplified by the
postponement of the Soviet revisionist Communist Party's
twenty-fourth congress. Their domestic economy is in a mess,
their five-year plan is unfulfillable. Their agricultural production targets have fallen through, the supply of commodities
in cities is under stress, their social morality is decadent,
and their society is tending to polarize into the two extremes
of rich and poor.

2. The petty revisionists of Eastern Europe are unstable
and discontented with the USSR. The USSR sold out East Germany to win over West Germany. But both the stick and carrot used on Yugoslavia and Rumania have been ineffective. A
new phase will appear in Eastern Europe, namely, one of turning against [the Soviet Union] by all and desertion by their kin.

3. In the Middle East, the Soviet revisionists have expanded
their military bases in Iraq, Syria, Yemen, and South Yemen.
Although they have intensified their control over Egypt, they
have also increased the contradictions. Sudan's Nimieri im-
placably hates the Soviet revisionist tyrant. In Asia, Afghanistan is leaning toward the Soviet revisionists. Nepal has received much aid [from the Soviet revisionists], but her basic
policy is to balance the power among the USSR, China, the U.S.,
and India. For the present, Burma is not buying [the Soviet]
line. Kosygin passed through Burma twice and Ne Win met
with him only the second time. The collusion between the Soviet revisionists and Japan is developing somewhat, but, when
the Soviet revisionists want the Japanese to exploit Siberia,
the Japanese answer: What we really want to exploit is Sakhalin.
The contradiction between the two countries is irreconcilable.
In Asia only India is comparatively receptive to the Soviet revisionists and the Soviet revisionists have supported Indian
moves against Pakistan. Yet, India is a heavy burden; to have
the Soviet revisionists bear it is a good thing.

The struggle between the U.S. and USSR for hegemony over

the Mediterranean Sea is a heated one. Previously the Mediterranean Sea was part of the world of the U.S. Now the Soviet fleet has increased from six or seven ships to fifty or sixty (and more than seventy, at times). Their ambition is ever increasing.

E. The Problem of the Expansion of the International United Front

1. Our strategy is: The U.S. and USSR are our main enemies. The first intermediate zone comprises Asia, Africa, and Latin America; the second includes Western Europe, Japan, Canada, and Oceania.

2. The Japanese people belong to the sphere of the Asian, African, and Latin American revolutionary forces while Japan's rulers belong to the category of the second intermediate zone.

3. When de Gaulle assumed the reins of French government, Chairman Mao said: "It is a good thing and, at the same time, a bad thing for de Gaulle to come to power. It is a bad thing because he is anti-Communist and a good thing because he is a man with backbone."

Toward Britain, France, and West Germany, we must use abusive language less frequently and must apply strategy.

4. The work of dealing with high-level people in the capitalist countries must be furthered vigorously. They are transitional figures; the power will in the end fall into the hands of the people. Nevertheless, doing a good job of dealing with these people will spare us an enemy and give us one more indirect ally.

F. Correctly Understanding the Five Principles of Peaceful Coexistence

1. The five principles are applicable to the two intermediate zones and the two superpowers, the U.S. and USSR. But [the superpowers], in reality, do not want these principles.

2. Correctly utilize these principles to win over the two intermediate zones.

3. The normalization of a country's relations [with us] makes it easier [for us] to bolster the people's revolution of that country. That Lenin established relations with China's northern warlords while simultaneously helping China's revolution in a big way is an example of this.

4. The "peaceful coexistence" of the Soviet revisionists is capitulationism; our "peaceful coexistence" is for the purpose of revolution.

G. The Problem of Fully Taking Advantage of the Contradictions and Weaknesses of the Enemy

1. Lenin taught us that we must discreetly and extremely cautiously exploit all the contradictions and weaknesses of the enemy camp. This is both a strategy and a matter of revolutionary principle.

2. It is necessary to adhere to principle while strategy can be changed considerably and manipulated flexibly. The contradictions between the U.S. and USSR, the contradictions between the U.S. and Japan, and the contradictions between the U.S. and Europe must all be exploited.

H. Appropriate Use of Dual Revolutionary Tactics to Oppose Dual Counterrevolutionary Tactics

1. Chairman Mao's "Chungking negotiations" were a typical precedent.

2. The USSR and U.S. are now dealing with us by means of dual tactics. The U.S. invades Taiwan and Indochina and negotiates with our country at the same time. The Soviet revisionists deploy millions of soldiers along the Sino-Soviet border and simultaneously engage in negotiations on the border issue with us. These are dual tactics and we [should] respond to them with dual revolutionary tactics.

3. Properly employ dual revolutionary tactics to win the sympathy and support of the people.

I. Push Forward [Preparations against] War and Promote
   Revolution. But It Is Still Necessary to Be Ready for a
   Surprise Attack by the Enemy at Any Time and We Must
   Continue to Do a Good Job of Preparing for War.

J. Oppose Great Power Chauvinism

1. Great power chauvinism is the mortal wound of the U.S.
and USSR. This is the point that creates the most antipathy in
the Third World. The Third World admires China primarily because China opposes great power chauvinism.

2. The better the situation is and the more help we give to
other countries, the more we should pay attention to opposing
great power chauvinism.

3. We must oppose the "favor-granting viewpoint." The
help given to other countries is not a favor but mutual aid.

THE "KUNMING DOCUMENTS"*

3

(Secret)

Instructions

The great leader Chairman Mao teaches us: we "should
teach Party members how to use Marxist-Leninist methods to analyze the political situation and assess the class
influence." In order to implement the spirit of the Sym-
posium on Criticizing Lin Piao and Rectifying the Style
of Work held by the General Political Department and the
Enlarged Meeting of this Region's Party Committee, we
recently conducted an education on situation test at the
8th Company, 118th Regiment, 40th Division in accordance
with the above-mentioned instruction of Chairman Mao.
The entire education is composed of five lessons. These
five lessons are now disseminated to various companies
for reference in conducting their education on situation.
(These materials may be disseminated to platoons in the
border defense companies.)

---

*The original title of these secret documents is "Hsing-shih
chiao-yü ts'an-k'ao ts'ai-liao" [Reference materials concerning
education on situation], Nos. 41-43. They are composed of
five lessons and are designed for distribution to companies and
above. Edited and printed by the Propaganda Division of the
Political Department of the Kunming Military Region on March 30,
1973, they were reprinted on April 20, 1973, by the Political Department, Eleventh Regiment, Yunnan Production Construction
Corps of the Chinese People's Liberation Army. Three lessons
out of the five are selected here. The English translation is taken
from Issues & Studies (Taipei), Vol. 10 (June 1974), 94-108.
The subtitles are added by the Editor.

Outline of Education on Situation for Companies

(Lesson One)

The Historical Current of the People's Revolution in the World Is Irresistible

Chairman Mao teaches us: "We should constantly publicize to the people the progressive situation and bright future of the world." What is the current international situation like? Is it excellent or pitch-dark? This is an important question facing us and requiring our answer.

The International Situation

The current international situation, on the whole, is excellent. The whole world is changing its appearance in the process of great commotion, great demarcation, and great reorganization. Countries want independence, nations want liberation, and people want revolution. This has become an irresistible historical current. The situation is developing in a direction favorable to the people's revolution in the world and unfavorable to the enemy. This is the mainstream and substance. It is the basic indication of the excellent current international situation.

At present, the revolutionary struggles of all people of the world are rolling forward like a torrent.

In Asia, the people of Vietnam, persisting in their protracted people's war, have defeated the aggression of U.S. imperialism, a superpower, and have won a great victory. The people of Laos, long persisting in their war of national salvation against the United States, have now triumphantly realized a ceasefire. The people of Cambodia have been fighting well for three years. Now they have their own people's arms and have liberated 90 percent of the territory and 80 percent of the population. The situation is developing very well.

In Africa, which used to be a stagnant pond and was considered backward, things are becoming noisy and ebullient.

Africa is now an advanced continent. It had only three independent states before World War II. The number of independent states has grown now to twenty-one [sic], making Africa the continent with the greatest number of independent states. In the past, imperialism had an idealistic outlook, hoping that these countries would stop advancing after gaining independence and would be satisfied with the change of flags. But the people of Africa have not stopped. They want to gain economic independence, to develop their own national culture, to build their national armed forces, and to obtain real independence. Furthermore, African unity is developing very fast and is better than Asian unity. Forty-one countries in Africa have joined the Organization of African Unity, which is becoming a separate force. These medium and small countries support one another and struggle against the superpowers. In the United Nations, they do not listen to the superpowers. Among the seventy-five countries which voted in the U. N. General Assembly for restoration of our legitimate seat in the United Nations, many were African countries. When the U. N. General Assembly adopted the resolution requiring India to discontinue its aggression against Pakistan, many African countries voted for the resolution. The United States and the Soviet Union found it hard to manipulate these issues.

In Latin America, which used to be called the backyard of U.S. imperialism, the fire has been lit. Not long ago Latin American countries jointly acted to oppose the two superpowers' unreasonable limitation of the width of territorial waters. They insisted that American countries had the right to define the bounds of their territorial waters and firmly defended the 200-nautical mile territorial right over the waters.

In the Middle East, the people of the Arab countries are becoming increasingly awake. They are strengthening their unity and waging just struggle against U.S. aggressors. The Middle East has become an important battlefield where the Arab people and the people of the world strike at U.S. imperialism.

Furthermore, the people in the United States are not satisfied with the present state of things and have risen up to oppose their government's aggressive policy and war policy. Workers strike, students suspend classes, and antiwar demonstrations spread all over the nation. The American people are actively seeking revolutionary truth and agitating for revolution.

The Soviet people are becoming increasingly discontented with the fascist rule of Soviet revisionism. Minority people's struggles against oppression and pan-Russianism are waged here and there. In their opposition to the fascist rule of Soviet revisionism, the Soviet people walk out of factories, suspend class, stage demonstrations, disseminate leaflets, and wage resistance struggle. They are agitating for the second October Revolution. They are sure to rebuild proletarian dictatorship.

Some comrades ask: Since the situation of revolutionary struggles of the people of the world is excellent, how then should we look at the adverse current of the revisionist clique headed by the Soviet Union and how should we look at the superficial phenomenon of the temporary decrease of truly socialist countries?

To revolutionaries, how to analyze and look at the situation is a very important question. One can correctly analyze the situation only by insisting on the Marxist stand, viewpoint, and method. Chairman Mao teaches us: "What determines everything is whether or not the ideological and political line is correct." In order to make a correct assessment of the situation, one must analyze it in terms of the line. First, we should be able to see that countries want independence, nations want liberation, and people want revolution. This is the general trend of development in the current world situation. The emergence of a small counterrevolutionary adverse current in the process of development of world history is not surprising. It is an inevitable phenomenon in the development of the class struggle. The counterrevolutionary adverse current is but a tributary in the excellent situation. It is a temporary phenomenon. In the end, it will not be able to alter the historical fate of capitalism, which will perish eventually; nor will it be able to undermine the revolutionary struggles of the people of the world to stop the onward rolling wheel of history. After the

Soviet revisionist social-imperialism betrayed the people of
the world, the revolutionary struggle of the people of the world
has developed faster than before. In the past, revisionism and
Marxism-Leninism were intermingled in the international
Communist movement, and they were not clearly distinguished
from each other. Now that revisionism has been separated
out, the demarcation between genuine and sham Marxism-
Leninism is clear. Even though countries ruled by genuine
Marxist-Leninist parties have apparently decreased in number,
their ranks are purer, their quality is better, and their combat
strength is greater. After revisionism has been separated out,
Marxist-Leninist parties and organizations in the world have
distinguished between the genuine and the sham and have one by
one come over to the side opposing Soviet revisionism. In the
world today, there are sixty-eight genuine Communist parties
and organizations. The strength is not less but greater. It is
recalled that Chairman Mao once said the following: When the
Red Army of more than 300,000 men arrived at northern Shensi
after the 25,000-li Long March in 1935, it only had some 30,000
men left. Chairman Mao then asked: Did our strength become
less or greater? He said that it became greater, for the re-
maining 30,000 men were the cream of the revolution; they had
been trained in the bitter revolutionary struggle, and their revolutionary determination had become stronger. Later historical developments completely verified Chairman Mao's wise
judgment.

In the following, we shall concentrate on the great victory of
the Vietnamese people in their struggle against the United
States for national salvation. Through this victory, we shall
see further that countries want independence, nations want liberation, and people want revolution. This is an irresistible
historical current that shall triumph.

The Meaning of the Vietnam Ceasefire

Vietnam is a glorious example of the revolutionary struggle
of the people of Asia, Africa, and Latin America. The Vietnam

War lasted for twelve years. The twelve years of arduous
struggle forced U.S. imperialism to sign the armistice agreement. The signing of this agreement has far-reaching significance. What is this significance?

1. The signing of the armistice agreement in Vietnam established for the world a glorious model of a weak country tri-
umphing over a strong country and a small country defeating
a large country.

The Vietnam War began in 1955 when U.S. imperialism violated the Geneva Agreement. The war passed through three
stages: U.S. imperialism supporting a South Vietnamese puppet government to slaughter and persecute patriotic people,
U.S. imperialism's "special warfare," and U.S. imperialism's
direct aggression by sending troops. In the twelve years counting from 1961, U.S. imperialism despatched more than 540,000
men in their ground forces or a total of more than 1,000,000
men including Navy, Air Force, and logistic troops. It committed the 7th Fleet and up to 10,000 aircraft dropping nearly
8,000,000 tons of bombs (over two and one half times the total
of bombs dropped during World War II and the war of aggression against Korea combined). They sprayed up to 10,000 tons
of toxic chemical agents, spent nearly US $200 billion in direct
military expenditures, and used all new weapons except atomic
bombs. Even at such a great cost, the United States could not
save itself from the fate of certain defeat. Under the blows of
the Vietnamese people, it was forced to sign the armistice
agreement on January 27 this year, ending the longest war of
the twentieth century. This is a huge victory for the Vietnamese
people in their protracted struggle on the military, political,
and diplomatic fronts. It is also a huge victory for the people
of the world. The victory of the Vietnamese people has formid-
ably demonstrated that no matter how strong a superpower is,
it is bound to fail if it intends to conquer the people of other
countries by force. Those who are on the side of justice will
receive much help, and those who are not on the side of justice
will receive little help. A small country can defeat a large
country, and a weak country can triumph over a strong country.

It is a steadfast truth that just causes shall win and that agression shall fail. The victorious Vietnamese people have set the most glorious example for people all over the world who wage struggles against imperialism and colonialism and for national liberation.

2. The signing of the Vietnam armistice agreement is in the interests of gradual reunification of the North and the South free from external intervention.

The greatest victory of the Vietnam armistice agreement is the expulsion of U.S. troops from Vietnam. In the past, the Vietnam war was resumed after an armistice because the United States intervened directly and breached the Geneva Agreement thoroughly. Before now, because of the U.S. involvement, the whole thing was hard to accomplish. Now that the "god of plague" has been sent away, it is easier to do. In the past, the Vietnamese people had to deal with U.S. imperialism and Nguyen Van Thieu simultaneously. Now that U.S. imperialism has been expelled, Nguyen Van Thieu is easier to cope with. After more than ten years of fighting, the National Liberation Front in South Vietnam has liberated large expanses of territory, established revolutionary base areas, trained people's armed forces, and set up the South Vietnam Republican Provisional Revolutionary Government, thus creating favorable conditions for the final solution of the Vietnam problem.

3. The Vietnam Armistice is also in our interests and in the interests of the revolution of the Southeast Asian people.

The ceasefire in Vietnam first had an impact on Indochina and then a direct impact on the whole of Southeast Asia. After the Korean Armistice, the game on the Southeast Asian chessboard became unplayable. The game has now been revived by the Vietnam Armistice. Once the United States departed, its running dogs in Asia became very uneasy. The rulers of countries like Thailand, Singapore, and the Philippines, realizing that the United States could not hang on, all wanted to enter into relationships with us. The heads of these countries were originally set on following the United States; now they are beginning

to waver. This wavering is good for the development of our
work. In the past, Soviet revisionism intervened in Southeast
Asia under the pretext of supporting Vietnam. Now that the
Vietnam War has stopped, we can, by working harder, more
effectively expose and strike at Soviet revisionism. Britain
has great influence in Southeast Asia. It both welcomes and is
displeased with U.S. imperialism's withdrawal and Soviet revisionism's intervention in Southeast Asia. Some other capitalist countries have their own ideas about Southeast Asia. All
this is very favorable to our use of contradictions to develop
our work.

4. The signing of the Vietnam armistice agreement dealt a
blow to Soviet revisionism and aggravated the contradictions
between the United States and the Soviet Union.

Holding the socialist banner, Soviet revisionism gave some
assistance to Vietnam. But it wanted to make use of the Vietnam War for achieving unmentionable objectives. One of its
objectives was to place several hundred thousand U.S. imperialist troops at the gate of our country to threaten our security
and contain our forces. Its second objective was to have the
United States pinned down in Vietnam to contain the U.S. forces
so that it could contend with U.S. imperialism for world hegemony. Now that the Vietnam War has stopped, this ideal plan
of Soviet revisionism has come to nought, which is indeed a
blow to it. Furthermore, U.S. imperialism will shift its forces
from Vietnam to Europe, the Middle East, and other regions
to contend with Soviet revisionism for hegemony. In this way,
the contradictions between them will become acute. This is an
excellent development favorable to us and the people of the
world.

The signing of the Vietnam armistice agreement is a great
victory for the people of Vietnam and the people of the world
and has great significance. This is positive. We should see,
however, that after the armistice two possibilities lie ahead:
one is the settlement of the Vietnam question by peaceful means
or peaceful reunification of Vietnam; the other is that the peaceful means do not work, that Nguyen Van Thieu uses force first,

and that the question is finally settled through war. From the viewpoint of class struggle and from historical experience, the probability of peaceful settlement of the question is not great. It will still be necessary to settle the question by war. No matter how the question is settled, the struggle from now on will still be complex and ardous. Our troops are stationed in the southwestern border region of the motherland. We must pay close attention to developments in the Vietnamese situation and be ready to fight at all times.

At present, the international situation is excellent. Under this excellent situation, we must never forget why the situation is so excellent, and we must never let peace benumb us. We must seriously implement Chairman Mao's instruction, "Dig tunnels deep, store grain everywhere, and never seek hegemony," deeply develop the campaign to criticize revisionism and rectify the style of work, do our work well at home, and support with concrete actions the revolutionary struggles of the people of the world.

Topics for discussion

1. Having correlated the ideology, reality, and the revolutionary struggles of the people of various countries, what is the historical trend of the contemporary world?
2. What is the significance of the victory of Vietnam's war of resistance against the United States for national salvation?

Outline of Education on Situation for Companies

(Lesson Two)

Soviet Revisionism Is Our Country's Most Dangerous and Most Important Enemy

The great leader Chairman Mao teaches us: "Soviet revisionism and U.S. imperialism, working hand-in-glove, have done so many bad things and ugly things that the revolutionary people of

the whole world will not spare them." From these remarks,
we can see clearly that both Soviet revisionism and U.S. imperialism are our arch enemies. At present, Soviet revisionism is our most important enemy. After World War II, at first
it was U.S. imperialism which lorded it over the world; so we
said that U.S. imperialism was the No. 1 enemy. Later, Soviet
revisionist social-imperialism emerged. A situation presented
itself in which the United States and the Soviet Union contended
for hegemony in the world and demarcated spheres of influence.
These two big villains carried out aggression, subversion, control, and intervention everywhere and bullied the people of all
countries, turning the world into a very unpeaceful place. Since
then, U.S. imperialism and Soviet imperialism, the two superpowers, have been the common enemies of the people of the
world. The present situation is: U.S. imperialism's counterrevolutionary global strategy has met with repeated setbacks;
its aggressive power has been weakened; and hence, it has had
to make some retraction and adjustment of its strategy. Soviet
revisionism, on the other hand, is stretching its arms in all
directions and is expanding desperately. It is more crazy,
adventurist, and deceptive. That is why Soviet revisionism
has become our country's most dangerous and most important
enemy.

Soviet Expansion

1. Soviet revisionism's aggression and expansion have fully
exposed its imperialist reactionary nature.

When the great mentor Lenin severely rebuked the revisionism of the Second International for supporting the imperialist
policy and neocolonialist policy of the bourgeoisie, he pointed
out that these renegades were a group of social-imperialists
who were "socialists on their lips but imperialists in essence,
or in other words, opportunists turned imperialists." The
Soviet revisionist renegade clique today is a group of genuine
social-imperialists through and through. After this clique,
usurped the party and state leadership in the Soviet Union, they,

on the one hand, fully restored capitalism at home. On the
other hand, they frantically carried out an imperialist policy
abroad, treating some countries as colonies which they brutally
plunder and enslave. Through the so-called economic "assistance" and military "assistance," they infiltrate and control
these countries. They display the signboard of "socialism,"
but their real business is imperialism. In 1968 their armed
invasion of Czechoslovakia was a full exposure of the ugly features of their social-imperialism. Today, the aggressive ambition of the Soviet revisionist social-imperialism has grown
even larger, and their claws have been stretched even farther.
     In Asia, Soviet revisionism is expanding actively. In 1971,
it instigated India to start a war of aggression against Pakistan,
resulting in the dismemberment of Pakistan. On the Indochina
question, Soviet revisionism has carried out sabotage in all
imaginable ways and tried to make deals with U.S. imperialism.
At the same time, it has made great efforts to sow discord in
a wild attempt to undermine our relations with Vietnam and
other countries. As of now, it is still maintaining diplomatic
relations with the Lon Nol rightist clique and has not recognized
Sihanouk, whose government it disparagingly calls a government "in exile." In substance, it is also opposed to the peaceful reunification of Korea. It thinks that possible peaceful reunification of Korea resulted from Nixon's visit to China, and
it is afraid that this will cause the reunification of East and
West Germany to its disadvantage. At heart, it disapproves of
the reunification, but in public it cannot say so. So it has kept
quiet. Regarding the Japan question, Soviet revisionism always
wants to drag Japan to its side, and yet it does not want to return the four northern islands to Japan, fearing that the return
of the islands to Japan may start a chain reaction affecting its
occupation of many territories in Romania and other countries.
It is trying to sabotage the normalization of Sino-Japanese relations. In addition, it is intensifying infiltration into Afghanistan, Burma, Malaysia, Indonesia, and Singapore, and has designs
on Taiwan. We can see very clearly that all actions of Soviet
revisionism in Asia are intended to encircle China. Its spear-

head is pointed at us in an attempt to achieve a great strategic encirclement of us.

In Europe, Soviet revisionism is strengthening control over East Europe, trying to win over West Europe, and contending with U.S. imperialism for the control of the whole of Europe. Brezhnev has declared publicly: "We pay special attention to Europe." Soviet revisionism controls East European countries in all imaginable ways and has become these countries' super-czar and paternal party. Politically and economically, it is practicing homogeneity. Diplomatically, East European countries must listen to it. Even the leaders of these countries must be appointed by Soviet revisionism. Militarily it assigns Soviets to be the commander in chief and chief of staff of its "Warsaw Pact" organization. Soviet revisionism maintains massive amounts of troops in East Germany, Poland, Czechoslovakia, and Hungary. It has turned East Europe into a base for external expansion. From there, it can attack West Europe westward and stretch to the Mediterranean Sea southward. Under the banner of "relaxing" European tension and through the Warsaw Pact Organization, Soviet revisionism proposed the so-called "Conference on European Security and Cooperation." This serves the purpose of consolidating its sphere of influence in Europe as far as possible, dividing NATO, and expelling U.S. influence from Europe. At the same time, it serves to maintain temporary stability in the West so that it may increase its strength to confront us.

In the Middle East the main interest of Soviet revisionism is to contend with U.S. imperialism for oil and strategic positions. The United States produces over 800 million tons of petroleum a year, more than any other country in the world. But its reserves are very limited. In ten years there will practically be no domestic petroleum. Consequently, some [American] people propose to ship Middle East oil to the United States and store it in exhausted oil wells as reserves for World War III. Soviet revisionism is the second largest oil producer, second only to the United States. Like the United States, it is expanding its armed forces and preparing for war, and it needs large

quantities of oil. At the same time, it resells the oil obtained
from the Middle East to East Germany, Czechoslovakia, and
some West European countries to earn foreign exchange. In
addition, the Middle East is situated at the junction between
Europe, Asia, and Africa, and the Suez Canal connects the
Mediterranean Sea, the Red Sea, and the Indian Ocean. The
Middle East is thus a pivotal area. Via the Mediterranean Sea
and the Suez Canal, a ship leaving Soviet revisionism's Odessa
only has to sail 7,000 nautical miles to arrive at Haiphong. If
the Suez Canal is not open, the ship will have to go around the
Cape of Good Hope in Africa and sail 15,000 nautical miles.
This is why Soviet revisionism wants to control this area. The
Middle East and the Mediterranean Sea used to be the sphere
of influence of Britain, France, and the United States. The
United States regards the Mediterranean Sea as its "throat,"
and of course it cannot let Soviet revisionism put its hand
around its throat. That was how the Soviet-U.S. contention began there. After the June 5, 1967, war between Egypt and Israel,
Soviet revisionism sent a fleet to the Mediterranean Sea. Displaying the banner of "assistance" to the Arab countries in
opposing Israeli aggression, it controlled Egypt and some other
Arab countries. It wanted at all times to expel the influence
of the United States and the West from Arabia. It made a lot
of weapons sales; its military assistance to Egypt alone
amounted to US $6 billion, which may be added to economic
assistance of US $2 billion, making a total of US $8 billion.
Egypt incurred much debt and got the weapons but is not permitted to fight. The better weapons are controlled in the hands
of Soviet revisionist soldiers. U.S. imperialism supports
Israel. Soviet revisionism feared that a war between Egypt
and Israel might embroil itself in a confrontation with the
United States. Therefore, in their own respective interests,
both Soviet revisionism and U.S. imperialism want to maintain
in the Middle East a situation of "neither war nor peace." Nor
is this all. Soviet revisionism has asked for special privileges
and military bases. What is even more enraging is that Soviet
revisionism has now agreed to let 30,000 Jews emigrate to

Israel each year. In substance, this means making available
to Israel a source of military manpower. Hence, Soviet revisionism is nominally a friend of the Arab countries, while,
in reality, what it does are criminal acts supporting and incit-
ing Israel to encroach on the Arab countries.

The actions of Soviet revisionism have fully exposed its aggressive nature. Where there is the presence of Soviet revisionists,
the terms "revolution," "friendship," and "cooperation" will mean
"aggression," "control," and "subversion." Soviet revisionism
has become the common enemy of the people of the whole world.

Soviet War Preparation

2. Soviet revisionism is expanding its armed forces and preparing for war under the cover of the high tone of "disarmament."

Some comrades are not clear as to what is meant by Soviet
revisionism's extravagant talk about "disarmament." This
problem must be properly solved. In appearance it would seem
that Soviet revisionism is very concerned about the question of
"disarmament." In fact, everything that it says is a lie that
must be effectively exposed and refuted. What are the facts?

a) In May last year, the Soviet Union and the United States
signed the so-called "Agreement on Strategic Nuclear Arms
Limitation," which was nothing but a fraud to fool the people
of the world. The facts have now shown that the Soviet-U.S.
Agreement on Strategic Nuclear Arms Limitation only limits
the number of ICBMs but not the equivalent worth of warheads.
This was because they had enough numbers of warheads. Their
main problem is that of quality improvement. Since the signing
of the agreement, Soviet revisionism has started a qualitative
race with the United States in ballistic missiles with emphasis
on the development of multiple warheads. Soviet revisionism
has also built twenty-five silos capable of launching missiles,
each of which carries twenty warheads of the half-megaton
class. It is also developing a multiple-warhead missile similar
to, but smaller than, the U.S. "Minuteman," and for this it has
built sixty-six silos. In the estimate of U.S. Defense Secretary

Laird, by this year or next, Soviet revisionism will have multiple-warhead ICBMs that can be used in real war. On the one
hand, Soviet revisionism clamors for a nuclear weapons ban in the
United Nations. On the other hand, it is desperately doing experi-
ments on nuclear weapons and new ICBMs. This fully exposes the
agressive nature of Soviet revisionist social-imperialism.

b) The alleged nonuse of force in international relations is
an even bigger lie. In the first place, Soviet revisionism, itself, cannot do this. Its invasion of Czechoslovakia and its
support for India in aggression against Pakistan are instances
of the use of weapons. "War is the continuation of politics." In order to oppose the use of force in international relations, one must
oppose the policy of aggression and wars of imperialism and social-imperialism. One must oppose unjust wars and support just
ones. If no distinction is made and if the use of force is opposed
indiscriminately, this will only benefit imperialism.

c) The so-called permanent ban of nuclear weapons may,
at first hearing, sound similar to our country's proposition.
Actually, it is completely different. Our government consistently favors a total ban and complete destruction of nuclear
weapons. As a first step, a formal agreement should be reached
in which everybody declares that he will not use nuclear weapons first. However, Soviet revisionism is troubled by a guilty
conscience, and it dares not make such a declaration. How,
then, can this be called a "permanent ban of nuclear weapons"?
As for the so-called "ban of all nuclear tests," it is proposed
because Soviet revisionism has had enough testing and because
now it wants to limit the development of nuclear weapons by
countries without nuclear weapons, especially by our country.
We develop nuclear weapons for defensive purposes, while
Soviet revisionism wants to maintain its monopoly of nuclear
weapons in order to effect nuclear blackmail and nuclear
threats against us and the people of the world. We shall never
play into its hands.

We must fully realize that Soviet revisionism's so-called
"disarmament" is false, while its frantic expansion of armed
forces is true.

The Soviet Threat

3. Soviet revisionism is our country's most threatening enemy.

Numerous facts show that Soviet revisionism is our country's most threatening enemy as we claim. There are historical facts and contemporary facts.

Historically, since its coming to power, Soviet revisionism has regarded socialist China, which persists in Marxism-Leninism and holds high the anti-imperialist and antirevisionist banner, as a thorn in its side. It has been trying to control us and subvert us and destroy us. At home and abroad it has unleashed one anti-China wave after another. It has made unreasonable demands for building longwave radio stations in our country and forming a joint fleet with our country in a vain attempt to control our country militarily. It has tried vainly to limit our nuclear weapons. It has joined with India in opposing China. It supported Indian reactionaries in launching large-scale attacks against us on the Sino-Indian border. It has also tried to join with Japan in opposing China. In an attempt to subvert our proletarian dictatorship, it has given maximum support to renegades, secret agents, and counter-revolutionary revisionist elements unmasked by us. It has gone back on its words and unilaterally decided to withdraw experts and scrap contracts, undermining our country's socialist construction and causing us to sustain heavy losses. It has carried out large-scale subversive activities in Sinkiang in a vain attempt to separate Sinkiang from our country. It has invaded and occupied our territory, disturbed the status quo at the border, and incessantly provoked armed clashes. But none of its schemes has subdued us or made us collapse. As a result, it is waiting for an opportunity to wage large-scale aggressive war against our country.

It terms of contemporary facts, Soviet revisionism is politically creating anti-China public opinion on a large scale, mobilizing on a large scale for anti-China war, and saying slanderously that our country has "territorial claims" on

them, that "China has enormously impaired the interests of
the socialist big family," and that "China is the enemy of socialism." It wants Soviet troops to be "in a full state of war
at all times" and to "fight the Chinese as their fathers and
grandfathers did." In terms of geographical positions, Soviet
revisionism abuts on China. From this point of view, its threat
to our country is much greater than that of the United States
and much more direct. Militarily, Soviet revisionism is
stationing 64 to 67 army divisions along the several thousand-
kilometer border between China and the Soviet Union and between China and Mongolia. These account for 40 percent of
its total of 159 divisions of ground forces. The troops at the
border possess 15,000 tanks, which account for one-third of
its total of 45,000. It has also disposed several thousand aircraft and built several dozen missile bases in the border
area — it is posturing for a large-scale war against China.
It is actively making battlefield preparations, repairing highways, railroads, fortifications, airports and sea terminals.
Industry is being moved westward. Population is being moved
from the border to the interior. Soviet revisionism frequently
carries out military maneuvers and is stepping up reconnaissance of our country. In particular, Soviet revisionism's air
force frequently conducts long-range raid and bombing exercises, assuming that it is launching a surprise attack on strategic targets in our country. At present, a noteworthy move
of the Soviet revisionist navy is its desperate expansion in the
Indian Ocean. Its intention is to use the Indian Ocean as the
"connecting point" and to have two prongs of a naval pincer
form an arc-shaped sea-lane connecting the three continents
of Europe, Africa, and Asia. In the half-arc in the Eastern
Hemisphere, the Pacific fleet based in Vladivostok will be
despatched to the Indian Ocean via the Sea of Japan, the West
Pacific Ocean, and the Malacca Strait. In the half-arc in the
Western Hemisphere, the Black Sea fleet will be despatched
to enter the Indian Ocean via the Mediterranean Sea. (Because
the Suez Canal is not open at present, this fleet will have to
sail around the Cape of Good Hope.) In this way, Soviet revision-

ism will be able not only to have supremacy in the ocean but
also to effect complete strategic naval encirclement of our
country. Hence, we must be ready not only for a Soviet revisionist invasion from the air and by land but also for invasion
from three points in the north and for invasion both from the
three points in the north and along the coast. Soviet revisionism is continuously despatching secret agents into our country
to collect military and political intelligence and develop spy
networks under deep cover. In foreign policy, Soviet revisionism is playing double-dealing tricks. While talking with us, it
actively makes counterrevolutionary deals with U.S. imperialism and other Western countries. With the United States, it
not only holds SALT talks but actively plans the "European
Security Conference." It both seeks the goodwill of and oppresses the small revisionisms of East Europe. In all this,
its intention is to relax the situation in Europe and to stabilize
the Western front so that it may spare both hands for fully
opposing China.

  We can see from the above that Soviet revisionism, by stepping up anti-China war preparation activities, constitutes a
huge threat to us. Some comrades wrongly think that the situation is relaxed, that hostility has decreased, and that they can
take things easy in war preparation. This is very dangerous.
We should soberly realize that Soviet revisionist naval ships
are sailing in the seas around us and that Soviet revisionist
strategic reconnaissance planes are continuously conducting
electronic reconnaissance missions against us in the air above
the international waters east of Shanghai. This is the surest
proof of hostility. We must overcome ideas resulting from
benumbing by peace and make ourselves a hundred times more
vigilant. Under this excellent situation, we must deeply develop
the campaign to criticize revisionism and rectify the style of
work and carry out military and political training well. We
must continuously raise the political level and military level
of the troops and fully complete preparations against aggressive
war ideologically, materially, tactically and technically. We
must shatter with concrete actions the counterrevolutionary

plots of Soviet revisionism and support with concrete actions
the revolutionary struggles of the people of all countries in
the world.

Topics for discussion

Why is it said that Soviet revisionism is our country's most
dangerous and most important enemy?

Outline of Education on Situation for Companies

(Lesson Three)

The Great Victory of Chairman Mao's
Revolutionary Diplomatic Line

The great leader Chairman Mao teaches us: "What determines everything is whether the ideological and political line
is correct or not." In all these years, the revolutionary diplomatic line of Chairman Mao, guided by the correct leadership
of Chairman Mao himself and the Party's Central Committee,
has prevailed over Liu Shao-ch'i's line of "three reconciliations
and one reduction" [The reconciliation in our relations with
imperialism, the reactionaries, and modern revisionism, and
reduction of assistance and support to the revolutionary struggle of other peoples] and "three capitulations and one elimination" [capitulating to the imperialists, to the Soviet revisionists, and to foreign reactionaries and abolishing the anti-imperialist struggle of the suppressed people of the world] and
over Lin Piao's line of "isolationism" and "great-nation chauvinism," which were aimed at capitulating to Soviet revisionism
and betraying the country. After the elimination of this interference, we have carried into effect Chairman Mao's line and
won great victories in the international arena.

The great victories are manifested prominently in: (1) the
restoration of our country's legitimate rights of representation
at the United Nations; (2) the visit of Nixon to China; and (3) the

establishment of China-Japan and China-West Germany diplomatic relations. The attainment of these victories has greatly elevated the international prestige of our country, shattered the schemes of U.S. imperialism and Soviet revisionism to isolate and encircle our country, and has propelled and supported the development of the revolutionary struggle of all countries in the world. Revolutionary people throughout the world are hailing and applauding the victories of our country.

Nevertheless, the reactionaries at home and abroad have left no stone unturned in their efforts to slander and vilify us, saying that our talks with the United States meant a "collusion between China and the United States," an "alliance with the United States against the Soviet Union," etc. It is not surprising at all that the class enemies have made such condemnations of us. For their class nature tells them to do so. The problem is that some comrades within our own ranks, owing to their lack of a high consciousness in regard to the struggle between lines and because of their low ability to make distinctions, are being plagued by an erroneous cognizance. For example, there are some comrades who say that in the past we interpreted negotiations between the United States and the Soviet Union as U.S.-Soviet collusion, but now we too are negotiating with the United States. Hence, they asked whether we have changed our policy. There are still other comrades who are of the opinion that we and the United States have seemingly taken the same viewpoint because both the United States and our country took Soviet revisionism to task for its backing India's aggression against Pakistan the year before. All these points of view are wrong and erroneous. The implementation of Chairman Mao's revolutionary diplomatic line will inevitably be affected as long as these problems remain unsolved. To this end, we must study Chairman Mao's revolutionary diplomatic line in the light of two events of paramount importance, the visit of Nixon to China and the visit of Tanaka to China, so that the erroneous thinking which has cropped up among comrades may be clarified.

To Settle Problems with Nixon, Temporarily

   The Sino-U.S. talks and the U.S.-Soviet talks are alike in
form but different in essence. Chairman Mao has taught us
time and again, "We must look into the essence of a matter,
using its superficial phenomenon as a guide for taking us into
the house, but laying a firm hold on its essence the moment
you have stepped into the house." It was primarily for the
sake of the people that Chairman Mao invited Nixon to visit
China. Chairman Mao pointed out that we established diplomatic relations with many countries "basically by relying on the
people of these countries, rather than by relying on the govern
ments of these countries." In our diplomatic work and in our
activities in foreign countries, we consider the people as a
major target. It is for the sake of making the people of the
United States a major target of ours that we invited Nixon to
visit China.
   Some people may ask: Since it is all for the sake of the people, why then should Nixon be allowed to come for a visit? This
question was already answered clearly by Chairman Mao while
talking to Edgar Snow. Chairman Mao said, "The people of
the United States — the Leftists, the intermediate elements,
the Rightists — must all be permitted to come." He added,
"In seeking a solution of problems, the intermediate elements
and the Leftists can do nothing. It is necessary to have problems settled with Nixon, temporarily." By "temporarily," we
mean making a transitional solution with a transitional person-
age. Nixon holds the baton of power. To solve problems, we
must have talks with him. Nixon is a man of transition, through
whom we settle the Sino-U.S. relations and get in touch with the
people of the United States. If you do not talk to him, it is impossible for you to get in; nor is it possible to have your influences
brought into the United States; much less is there the possibility of doing a good job in the work with the people and in publicizing Marxism-Leninism.
   Chairman Mao's wise decision to invite Nixon to visit China
has thrown open the gate of contacts between us and the people

of the United States. It has had an influence on the people of
the United States In the past, U.S. imperialism had adopted
a policy of isolating, blockading, and containing our country,
thus isolating us from the American people for over twenty
years. There were very few contacts between people of the
two countries, and the U.S. government described us as being
very bad. Nixon's seven-day visit to China was made known
to the world through the media's use of satellites. Originally
he [Nixon] was attempting to make publicity for himself,
without noticing that the true state of affairs in China was
thus made known to people of all countries in the world. Especially noteworthy was the tremendous impact resulting there-
from when people in the United States, West Europe, and North
America saw the spiritual aspects and the actual situation of
the people of our country. Thus, the past U.S. lies slandering
China were all shattered by facts, and our international influence was expanded.

Before and after Nixon's visit to China, newspapers and
journals in the United States devoted whole pages to introduc-
tions of the situation in China, specifically publicizing Chairman Mao, reprinting Chairman Mao's poems and "Quotations
from Chairman Mao," and reporting how the Chinese books
were warmly welcomed. In many bookstores and libraries,
the books concerning China were either bought up or loaned
out at once. The number of students studying the Chinese
language in various universities of the United States increased
rapidly and tremendously. In some universities, the number
of students studying the Chinese language increased by three
to four times. This explains that China and Chairman Mao
have had an influence on the people of the United States.

The visit of Nixon to China led to the announcing of a Sino-
U.S. joint communiqué, in which both sides agreed to expand
understanding between the two countries, to establish people-
to-people contacts and exchanges in science, technology, culture, sports, and the press. This is a matter of profound significance in going one step further to open up the gate of contacts between the people of China and the United States. In the

days to come, the people of the United States may come to our
country, and we may also go to the United States. Since the
visit of Nixon to China, many American people have come to
China. These people have had a deep impression of China.
They went back to write articles making publicity for China.
Didn't the American columnist Alsop visit Yunnan not long
ago? He went home and wrote many good articles on the
changes in Yunnan and Kunming, saying that the city of Kunming
was neat and clean, that the spiritual aspect of the people was
excellent. By making use of the established channels of friendly contacts with the American people, our country has sent out
to the United States ping-pong teams, acrobatic troupes, and
delegations of scientific workers to show our work methods
to the American people and to promote understanding and
friendship between the people of China and the United States.
Chairman Mao once said, "The salvoes of the October Revolution brought us Marxism-Leninism." When Marxism-Leninism
is integrated with the revolutionary practices of China, the
Chinese revolution puts on a new look. Now our influences
have reached the United States. If only we work with patience
and enthusiasm, Marxism-Leninism-Mao Tse-tung Thought
will definitely be integrated with the practices of the revolutionary movement in the United States, thereby speeding
up the process of revolution in the United States. Chairman
Mao also said, "Hope is pinned on the people of the United
States." Revolution has already triumphed in China. If revolution triumphs also in the United States, it will create a tremendous impact on the whole world.

To Exploit Soviet and U.S. Contradictions

Furthermore, Chairman Mao invited Nixon to visit China
in order to exploit contradictions. He teaches us: "It is
necessary to pool together all struggles and gaps and contradictions which exist in the enemy camps and to use them as
a weapon of primary importance against the existing enemy."
Our invitation to Nixon to visit China proceeds precisely from

Chairman Mao's tactical thinking: "exploiting contradictions, winning over the majority, opposing the minority, and destroying them one by one." And this by no means indicates a change in our diplomatic line.

The two archenemies facing us are U.S. imperialism and Soviet revisionism. We are to fight for the overthrow of these two enemies. This has already been written into the new Party constitution. Nevertheless, are we to fight these two enemies simultaneously, using the same might? No. Are we to ally ourselves with one against the other? Definitely not. We act in the light of changes in situations, tipping the scale diversely at different times. But where is our main point of attack, and how are we to exploit their contradictions? This involves a high level of tactics. Whether or not these tactics are applied properly is a question of paramount importance that determines the fate of the world. Standing at a tower overlooking the general situation of the world, having farsightedness and a correct recognition of questions, and correctly laying a firm hold on contradictions, our great leader Chairman Mao sent out all at once our ping-pong teams and invited Nixon to visit China. This wise strategic decision of Chairman Mao is significant in the following ways:

1. First, it frustrates the strategic deployment of the Soviet revisionists, making them panic-stricken and plunging them into convulsions. Strategically, the Soviet revisionists have cherished the hope of putting us at loggerheads with the United States on a long-term basis, counting on a fight between us and the United States, so that they may fish in the troubled waters. Chairman Mao's invitation to Nixon to visit China alleviates Sino-U.S. relations. Soviet revisionists are very much afraid of this. They, therefore, switch on all their propaganda machines to whip up a new anti-China chorus. The chieftains of Soviet revisionism — Leonid J. Brezhnev, Aleksei N. Kosygin, Nikolai V. Podgorny — were thus out performing a so-called "visiting diplomacy." They called a black meeting in the Crimea of the petty revisionists to engineer anti-China and counterrevolutionary schemes. They signed with India a

so-called treaty of friendship, yet pointed the spearhead at
our country. They even colluded with the Chiang gang and
agreed to Nixon's tour of the Soviet Union. All this was a vain
attempt to cope with our diplomatic offensive. Why is Soviet
revisionism so deadly opposed to the talks of our country with
Nixon? Chairman Mao teaches us: "It is a good thing, rather
than a bad thing, to be opposed by the enemy. . . . If the enemy
energetically opposes us, saying that we are all in a mess and
are good for nothing, that is all the better for us. For it shows
that we have drawn a clear line of demarcation between the
enemy and us, that our work has produced fruitful results."
The energetic attack of Soviet revisionism on us explains that
in carrying out Chairman Mao's revolutionary diplomatic line,
we have won outstanding achievements and hit right at their
vital part.

2. Second, it aggravates the contradictions between the
United States and the Soviet Union. Strategically, the Soviet
revisionists are plotting to plunge U.S. imperialism into the
mire of Asia, of Vietnam, so that the hands of U.S. imperialism
are tied up there and cannot move more of its forces to Europe,
the Middle East, and other areas to rival Soviet revisionism.
Favorable conditions are thus created for Soviet revisionism
to impose a hegemony of its own in those areas. We agreed
to Nixon's tour of China in order that, on the one hand, we
could curb the collusion between the United States and the
Soviet Union, weaken their strength, and keep them from taking
reckless and impetuous actions to start a war. On the other
hand, we use the peace talks as a means of forcing U.S. imperialism, now beset with difficulties at home and abroad, to
withdraw its forces from Indochina, Taiwan, the Taiwan Strait,
of propelling a peaceful settlement of the questions of Taiwan,
Indochina, Vietnam, and of alleviating the tension in Asia and
other parts of the world. For over a year now, the war in
Vietnam has come to an end as a result of the struggle of the
Vietnamese people and of the work we did there. And U.S.
imperialism is kicked out of the area. From Asia and Vietnam,
U.S. imperialism has moved its forces over to Europe and the

Middle East. This has greatly aggravated the contradictions between the United States and the Soviet Union, putting the two dogs at loggerheads. This struggle of theirs is advantageous to the revolution of ours and the world's people.

3. Third, it aggravates the contradictions between U.S. imperialism and its lackeys. The visit of Nixon to China was bitterly condemned by the Chiang gang as a "perfidious and unrighteous act" of U.S. imperialism. A meeting was held to discuss the question of neutralization of Southeast Asia by the foreign ministers of Malaysia, Indonesia, the Philippines, Singapore, and Thailand. Eisaku Sato, the former prime minister of Japan, condemned the United States for "lack of uprightness and friendship." He also talked about giving up the policy of following the footsteps of the United States and of adopting a policy of independence. Contradictions between Japan and the United States were unprecedentedly sharpened. In this situation, we may see that the enemy camp is in chaos, that the morale of the enemy camp is falling and crumbling, and that a contrifugal tendency is getting more and more serious with the passage of each day. This state of affairs benefits our work and the people's revolution.

4. Fourth, it benefits our liberation of Taiwan. After its failure on the mainland, the Chiang gang fled to Taiwan. For over twenty years, the gang has relied on U.S. imperialism and signed all sorts of military and economic treaties with it. The gang depends entirely on "U.S. aid" as a means of survival. Taiwan is in reality forcibly occupied by U.S. imperialism. Taiwan is the territory of our country, and liberation of Taiwan is an internal question of ours. Because of the forcible occupation of Taiwan by U.S. imperialism, the Taiwan question has become a question of international dimensions. The Shanghai Communiqué released during the visit of Nixon to China has forced U.S. imperialism to take cognizance of the fact that Taiwan is a part of Chinese territory and that the ultimate objective is the withdrawal of all U.S. forces and military installations from Taiwan. This keeps U.S. imperialism from making a further intervention in Taiwan. Simultaneously with

the improvement in the Sino-U.S. relations, there will arise a
gradual alienation in the relations between the United States
and the Chiang gang. This is beneficial to our settlement of
the Taiwan question without foreign intervention. Meanwhile,
the Chiang gang, when formerly banking on the support of U.S.
imperialism, appeared to be quite tough. Now, in the wake of
the improvement in relations between China and the United
States, with the U.S. Army to be withdrawn from Taiwan, the
Chiang gang is no longer able to get tough. We can exploit
this by urging them to come over for talks in order to strive
for the liberation of Taiwan and the unification of the fatherland by peaceful means.

Comrades, the present improvement in the Sino-U.S. relations does not mean that the Taiwan question can be settled
immediately. We must see that the liberation of Taiwan is a
complex struggle. On the question of liberating Taiwan, there
exist two possibilities: liberation by peaceful means and liberation by force of arms. At present, U.S. imperialism has
not yet withdrawn its forces from Taiwan and the Taiwan Strait,
and the Chiang gang is still doing its utmost to repress the demands of those advocating peace talks with us. We definitely
must not pin our hope on a peaceful liberation. Our Army
must particularly step up preparedness for war and be ready
at all times to liberate Taiwan by force of arms.

To Exploit Japan's International Contradictions

The invitation for Kakuei Tanaka to visit China, like the
invitation for Nixon to visit China, is primarily for the sake
of the people. Through contacts with the upper strata of Japan,
we open up a road for doing revolutionary work among the
Japanese people and for supporting the Japanese people to
rise up and make revolution. The second purpose is to exploit
contradictions, or, more specifically, to exploit Japanese-
Soviet and Japanese-U.S. contradictions. Why is it that there
are Japanese-Soviet and Japanese-U.S. contradictions for us
to exploit? After World War II, the United States was the only

country occupying and controlling Japan. Diplomatically,
Japan was entirely dependent on the United States. Yet in
recent years, owing to the great changes in the international
situation and because of the need to accommodate itself to the
changing situation, Japan has attempted to make a gradual revision of her diplomacy of "leaning one-sidedly to the United
States" in order to carry into effect a "free and multilateral"
diplomatic line.

In connection with the relations between Japan and the
Soviet Union, the Japanese have persistently demanded that
the Russians return to them the four islands of Habomai,
Shikotan, Kunashiri, and Etorofu. They are bargaining with
Soviet revisionism for the return of the islands. Now that
Japan is attempting to reduce its reliance on the United States
and, at the same time, to secure more leverage in negotiating
with Soviet revisionism for return of the four northern islands,
she inevitably has to do something as a manifestation of her
attitude toward us. We, therefore, lay a firm hold on Japan's
contradictions with the United States and the Soviet Union and
step up our task in this aspect. Doing a good job in this task
is of great advantage to us, and it constitutes a heavy blow to
U.S. imperialism and Soviet revisionism. Because of the important strategic position of Japan, should a war of aggression
against China be started either by U.S. imperialism or by
Soviet revisionism, the two robbers, they must necessarily
use Japan as a vanguard to fight in the battle. The United States
wants to make Japan a springboard for invading China. Japan
is an important link in the U.S. imperialist crescent encirclement of China. Soviet revisionism too is attempting to make
Japan a bridgehead for starting a war of aggression against
our country. It has done its utmost to drag Japan into its Asian
Collective Security System, which aims at achieving an all-
round strategic encirclement of our country. In addition,
Japan has maintained very intimate relations with Taiwan and
has a definite influence on some of the lackeys of U.S. imperialism in Asia. Our great leader Chairman Mao foresees the
future wisely. His decision to invite Prime Minister Tanaka

to visit China and to establish diplomatic relations with Japan
has alleviated the relations between China and Japan. This
step of Chairman Mao has shattered the plot of U.S. imperialism and Soviet revisionism to achieve a strategic encirclement
of our country, has benefited our peaceful liberation of Taiwan
and our improvement of relations with the Southeast Asian
countries, and has alleviated the tense Asian and international
situation. As a result of our improvement of relations with
Japan, the Japanese are now in possession of the means of
bargaining with the United States and the Soviet Union. They
have become all the more daring and brave. Thus, the
Japanese-U.S. and the Japanese-Soviet contradictions will be
further aggravated. And we can continue exploiting their contradictions and have our work done better.

The revolutionary diplomatic line of Chairman Mao enjoys
the support of the revolutionary people of the world. We have
friends all over the world. The people of our country, under
the leadership of Chairman Mao, are holding aloft the banner
of proletarian internationalism, persistently standing side by
side with the oppressed people and nations of the whole world,
firmly supporting the revolutionary struggles of the people of
all countries, and resolutely combating the hegemonism and
power politics of the two superpowers — the United States and
the Soviet Union. This is recognized and acknowledged openly
by the revolutionary people of the whole world. The slanderous
attack of Soviet revisionism does not harm us a bit; nor does
it weaken the faith in us of the people of all countries. The
Marxist-Leninist political parties throughout the world and
the people of the third world have made a high appraisal of
and voiced support for Chairman Mao's invitation of Nixon to
visit China and Chairman Mao's revolutionary diplomatic line.
Presented in the following are comments by the leaders of the
Marxist-Leninist political parties of the world and the people
of the Third World.

Kim Il-song, premier of the Democratic People's Republic
of Korea, pointed out that Nixon "advances not as a victor but
as a defeated man." As in the earlier negotiations in Korea,

he "carries a white flag to Peking." Naldeck Rochet, a leader
of the Communist Party of France (Marxist-Leninist), said,
"This is a very great victory of the Communist Party of China
led by Comrade Mao Tse-tung in the struggle against U.S. imperialism. This, too, is a wise decision of Comrade Mao Tse-
tung." Commenting on the Sino-U.S. joint communiqué, Secretary-general of the Communist Party of New Zealand Victor
George Wilcox said: "China has firmly stood on the side of
the people in combating the archenemy of the whole world....
Nixon's visit to China shows that China is correct in adhering
unwaveringly to the Leninist concept of 'peaceful coexistence'
and in opposing the Soviet leadership's power politics and its
advocacy of demarcating spheres of interests in the world."
The Daily News of Sudan, while commenting on the Sino-U.S.
joint communiqué, stated: "China has not made a change in
her announced policy and stand, whereas the United States has
made a lot of concessions." There were also some newspapers
and journals that refuted the slanderous attacks of Soviet revisionism on us. The Information Daily of Iran said: There
are some people who pay lip service to peace but are haunted
with "anxiety and uneasiness" at Nixon's visit to China, and
they "slander that China is making a compromise, that China
is attempting to turn Vietnam over to the United States.... All
this is done for the purpose of hoodwinking the public's opinions."

Moreover, the restoration of our country's legitimate seat
of representation at the United Nations, endorsed by 76 votes
of the U. N. General Assembly, shows convincingly that the
foreign policy of our country has won the support of the people
of the world, that the international prestige of our country has
been unprecedentedly elevated, and that we have more and more
friends. At present, 90 countries have established diplomatic
relations with our country. With the exception of Portugal and
Ireland, all the European countries have established diplomatic
relations with us. And to this must be added the big increase
in the number of people coming to visit our country in recent
years. We are now trading with 132 countries and areas. The
two trade fairs in Canton last year were visited by some 8,600

people. The volume of last year's foreign trade registered a tremendous increase, an increase of 28 percent as compared with the foreign trade volume the year before. In the light of the three aforementioned questions, we can see that what renders possible an elevation of the international prestige and influence of our country with friends all over the world is the result of a thorough implementation of Chairman Mao's revolutionary diplomatic line and the great victory of Chairman Mao's revolutionary diplomatic line.

The victory of Chairman Mao's revolutionary diplomatic line delays a world war and gains time for us to step up domestic construction and to make good preparations for a world war. We must make use of this valuable time, by seriously doing a good job in the campaign to criticize Lin Piao and rectify the style of work, by earnestly carrying into effect Chairman Mao's great strategic measures, "Dig tunnels deep, store grains everywhere, and never seek hegemony," and by conducting well the military training, so as to be basically well prepared against a war of aggression, to aid and support with concrete actions the revolutionary struggle of the people of the world.

Topics for discussion

1. By integrating ideology and practice, illustrate what you have comprehended about the basic spirit of Chairman Mao's revolutionary diplomatic line.

2. By correlating the great victory of Chairman Mao's revolutionary diplomatic line, criticize and repudiate Soviet revisionism's and Lin Piao's slanders and attacks.

NECESSARY COMPROMISES (Excerpts)*

4

Chou En-lai

Chairman Mao has often taught us: We are still in the era of imperialism and the proletarian revolution. On the basis of fundamental Marxist principle, Lenin made a scientific analysis of imperialism and defined "imperialism as the highest stage of capitalism." Lenin pointed out that imperialism is monopolistic capitalism, parasitic or decaying capitalism, moribund capitalism. He also said that imperialism intensifies all the contradictions of capitalism to the extreme. He therefore concluded that "imperialism is the eve of the social revolution of the proletariat" and put forward the theories and tactics of the proletarian revolution in the era of imperialism. Stalin said, "Leninism is Marxism of the era of imperialism and the proletarian revolution." This is entirely correct. Since Lenin's death, the world situation has undergone great changes. But the era has not changed. The fundamental principles of Leninism are not outdated; they remain the theoretical basis guiding our thinking today.

---

*From Chou En-lai's "Report to the Tenth National Congress of the Communist Party of China." Peking Review, Nos. 35-36 (September 7, 1973), 22-24. The Chinese version can be found in Hung-ch'i [Red Flag], No. 9 (September 3, 1973). The title and subtitles are the Editor's.

Great Disorder on the Earth

The present international situation is one characterized by
great disorder on the earth. "The wind sweeping through the
tower heralds a rising storm in the mountains." This aptly
depicts how the basic world contradictions as analyzed by Lenin
show themselves today. Relaxation is a temporary and superficial phenomenon, and great disorder will continue. Such
great disorder is a good thing for the people, not a bad thing.
It throws the enemies into confusion and causes division among
them, while it arouses and tempers the people, thus helping
the international situation develop further in the direction favorable to the people and unfavorable to imperialism, modern
revisionism, and all reaction.

The awakening and growth of the Third World is a major
event in contemporary international relations. The Third
World has strengthened its unity in the struggle against hegemonism and power politics of the superpowers and is playing
an ever more significant role in international affairs. The
great victories won by the people of Vietnam, Laos and Cambodia in their war against U.S. aggression and for national
salvation have strongly encouraged the people of the world in
their revolutionary struggles against imperialism and colonialism. A new situation has emerged in the Korean people's
struggle for the independent and peaceful reunification of their
fatherland. The struggles of the Palestinian and other Arab
peoples against aggression by Israeli Zionism, the African
peoples' struggles against colonialism and racial discrimination, and the Latin American peoples' struggles for maintaining
200-nautical-mile territorial waters or economic zones all
continue to forge ahead. The struggles of the Asian, African,
and Latin American peoples to win and defend national independence and safeguard state sovereignty and national resources
have further deepened and broadened. The just struggles of
the Third World as well as of the people of Europe, North
America, and Oceania support and encourage each other.
Countries want independence, nations want liberation, and the

people want revolution — this has become an irresistible
historical trend.

Lenin said that "an essential feature of imperialism is the
rivalry between several great powers in the striving for hegemony." Today, it is mainly the two nuclear superpowers —
the U.S. and the USSR — that are contending for hegemony.
While hawking disarmament, they are actually expanding their
armaments every day. Their purpose is to contend for world
hegemony. They contend as well as collude with each other.
Their collusion serves the purpose of more intensified contention. Contention is absolute and protracted, whereas collusion is relative and temporary. The declaration of this year
as the "year of Europe" and the convocation of the European
Security Conference indicate that strategically the key point
of their contention is Europe. The West always wants to urge
the Soviet revisionists eastward to divert the peril toward
China, and it would be fine so long as all is quiet in the West.
China is an attractive piece of meat coveted by all. But this
piece of meat is very tough, and for years no one has been able
to bite into it. It is even more difficult now that Lin Piao the
"superspy" has fallen. At present, the Soviet revisionists are
"making a feint to the east while attacking in the west" and
stepping up their contention in Europe and their expansion in
the Mediterranean, the Indian Ocean, and every place their
hands can reach. The U.S.-Soviet contention for hegemony
is the cause of world intranquillity. It cannot be covered up
by any false appearances they create and is already perceived
by an increasing number of people and countries. It has met
with strong resistance from the Third World and has caused
resentment on the part of Japan and West European countries.
Beset with troubles internally and externally, the two hegemonic powers — the U.S. and the USSR — find the going
tougher and tougher. As the verse goes, "Flowers fall off
do what one may"; they are in a sorry plight indeed. This has
been further proved by the U.S.-Soviet talks last June and the
subsequent course of events.

"The people, and the people alone, are the motive force in

the making of world history." The ambitions of the two hegemonic powers — the U.S. and the USSR — are one thing, but
whether they can achieve them is quite another. They want to
devour China but find it too tough even to bite. Europe and
Japan are also hard to bite, not to speak of the vast Third
World. U.S. imperialism started to go downhill after its defeat
in the war of aggression against Korea. It has openly admitted
that it is increasingly on the decline; it could not but pull out
of Vietnam. Over the last two decades, the Soviet revisionist
ruling clique, from Khrushchev to Brezhnev, has made a socialist country degenerate into a social-imperialist country.
Internally, it has restored capitalism, enforced a fascist dictatorship, and enslaved the people of all nationalities, thus
deepening the political and economic contradictions as well
as contradictions among nationalities. Externally, it has invaded and occupied Czechoslovakia, massed its troops along
the Chinese border, sent troops into the People's Republic of
Mongolia, supported the traitorous Lon Nol clique, suppressed
the Polish workers' rebellion, intervened in Egypt causing the
expulsion of the Soviet experts, dismembered Pakistan, and
carried out subversive activities in many Asian and African
countries. This series of facts has profoundly exposed its
ugly features as the new czar and its reactionary nature,
namely, "socialism in words, imperialism in deeds." The
more evil and foul things it does, the sooner the time when
Soviet revisionism will be relegated to the historical museum
by the people of the Soviet Union and the rest of the world.

Recently, the Brezhnev renegade clique has talked a lot of
nonsense on Sino-Soviet relations. It alleges that China is
against relaxation of world tension and unwilling to improve
Sino-Soviet relations, etc. These words are directed to the
Soviet people and the people of other countries in a vain attempt to alienate their friendly feelings for the Chinese people and disguise the true features of the new czar. These
words are above all meant for the monopoly capitalists in the
hope of getting more money in reward for services in opposing
China and communism. This was an old trick of Hitler's, only
Brezhnev is playing it more clumsily. If you are so anxious

to relax world tension, why don't you show your good faith by doing a thing or two — for instance, withdraw your armed forces from Czechoslovakia or the People's Republic of Mongolia and return the four northern islands to Japan? China has not occupied any foreign countries' territory. Must China give away all the territory north of the Great Wall to the Soviet revisionists in order to show that we favor relaxation of world tension and are willing to improve Sino-Soviet relations? The Chinese people are not to be deceived or cowed. The Sino-Soviet controversy on matters of principle should not hinder the normalization of relations between the two states on the basis of the Five Principles of Peaceful Coexistence. The Sino-Soviet boundary question should be settled peacefully through negotiations free from any threat. "We will not attack unless we are attacked; if we are attacked, we will certainly counterattack" — this is our consistent principle. And we mean what we say.

Necessary Compromises

We should point out here that necessary compromises between revolutionary countries and imperialist countries must be distinguished from collusion and compromise between Soviet revisionism and U.S. imperialism. Lenin put it well: "There are compromises and compromises. One must be able to analyze the situation and the concrete conditions of each compromise or of each variety of compromise. One must learn to distinguish between a man who gave the bandits money and firearms in order to lessen the damage they can do and facilitate their capture and execution and a man who gives bandits money and firearms in order to share in the loot" ("Left-Wing" Communism, an Infantile Disorder). The Brest-Litovsk Treaty concluded by Lenin with German imperialism comes under the former category; and the doings of Khrushchev and Brezhnev, both betrayers of Lenin, fall under the latter.

Lenin pointed out repeatedly that imperialism means aggression and war. Chairman Mao pointed out in his statement of May 20, 1970: "The danger of a new world war still exists, and the people of all countries must get prepared. But revolution is the main trend in the world today." It will be possible to prevent such a war so long as the peoples, who are becoming more and more awakened, keep the orientation clearly in sight, heighten their vigilance, strengthen unity, and persevere in struggle. Should the imperialists be bent on unleashing such a war, it will inevitably give rise to greater revolutions on a worldwide scale and hasten their doom.

In the excellent situation now prevailing at home and abroad, it is most important for us to run China's affairs well. Therefore, on the international front, our Party must uphold proletarian internationalism, uphold the Party's consistent policies, strengthen our unity with the proletariat and the oppressed people and nations of the whole world and with all countries subjected to imperialist aggression, subversion, interference, control, or bullying, and form the broadest united front against imperialism, colonialism, and neocolonialism, and in particular, against the hegemonism of the two superpowers — the U.S. and the USSR. We must unite with all genuine Marxist-Leninist Parties and organizations the world over and carry the struggle against modern revisionism through to the end. On the domestic front, we must pursue our Party's basic line and policies for the entire historical period of socialism, persevere in continuing the revolution under the dictatorship of the proletariat, unite with all the forces that can be united, and work hard to build our country into a powerful socialist state so as to make a greater contribution to mankind.

We must uphold Chairman Mao's teachings that we should "be prepared against war, be prepared against natural disasters, and do everything for the people" and should "dig tunnels deep, store grain everywhere, and never seek hegemony," maintain high vigilance, and be fully prepared against any war of aggression that imperialism may launch and particularly against surprise attack on our country by Soviet revisionist social-imperialism. Our heroic People's Liberation Army and our vast militia must be prepared at all times to wipe out any enemy that may invade....

International opposition to the superpowers' hegemonism

Documentary Introduction

There are thirteen selections in this chapter. With the central thesis of opposition to the superpowers' hegemonism, especially that of the Soviet Union, these documents demonstrate a global dimension in their interpretations and arguments. They run from general theory to specific geographic areas throughout the world.

The first selection is a speech delivered by Chou En-lai after the signing of the Vietnam cease-fire in 1973, stressing China's "basic strategy" of opposing the superpowers. The term "hegemonism" was not yet publicly used at that time.

The second, third, and fourth selections concern European and other Second World countries. They criticize the Soviet Union for making the Warsaw Treaty Organization a tool of aggression to threaten the security of Western Europe. They accuse the Soviet Union of actually utilizing the Helsinki Conference to promote a "new stage" of her expansion in Europe and argue that the focus of the Soviet-U.S. contention for world domination is in Europe; European nations, along with Canada, Japan, and other Second World countries, should protect their independence and security by preparing for a war stemming from the superpowers' aggression.

The fifth selection attacks the Soviet proposal for an "Asian Collective Security System" as a pretext for her expansion in

Asia, and the sixth selection accuses the superpowers of making deals with each other concerning the balance of their military power in the Indian Ocean.

The seventh document criticizes the U.S. and the Soviet Union for contending for a sphere of influence in the Middle East in 1975 rather than working for peace, and the eighth selection demonstrates Soviet annoyance and vexation in the same area in face of President Sadat's peace move.

The ninth and tenth selections condemn Soviet military interventions in Angola and the Horn of Africa as having provoked world indignation and having further proven the "imperialist" nature of Soviet Africa policy.

The eleventh and twelfth selections discuss Soviet infiltration and expansion in Latin America, a traditional area of United States domination. Meanwhile, Peking has encouraged Latin America's struggle for maritime rights, independence, and a new international economic order for the entire Third World.

The final selection specifically attacks the imperialist and war policies of the Soviet Union. It urges the peoples in the Second and Third worlds, particularly those in Europe, to combat Soviet social-imperialism.

OPPOSE THE TWO SUPERPOWERS

1

Chou En-lai's Internal Report to the Party on the
Problem of the Current International Situation,
March 1973 (Excerpts)*

A. The Situation Concerning the Two Superpowers

The global struggle between the two superpowers, the U.S.
and USSR, continues to be heated. Western Europe is a juicy
piece of meat and Japan is a juicy piece of meat; they [the U.S.
and USSR] are both striving for them. China is a piece of meat
which is both large and juicy which they are attempting to acquire. However, this piece of meat is too large for them to
swallow.

In Europe, the USSR intends to keep the current border
line (Eastern Europe); it is "hammering in a nail" among
Western European countries (the nail is France); and it is
"neutralizing" Western Europe after expelling U.S. influence.
Soviet power has expanded to the point where they can do whatever they want. Japan relies on the U.S., is luring China toward herself and is also improving her relations with the
USSR. The emphasis of our policy toward Japan lies in the
broad masses of the Japanese people while the USSR and U.S.

*"Chou En-lai tsai i-chiu-ch'i-san nien san-yüeh tui tang-
nei so-tso ti kuan-yü mu-ch'ien kuo-chi chü-shih wen-t'i ti
chiang hua." Fei-ch'ing yüeh-pao [Chinese Communist Affairs
Monthly], XIX: 6 (December 1976), 93-96. This translation is
adapted with permission from Issues & Studies, XIII: 1 (January 1977), 120-127. The title is adopted by the Editor.

maintain relations with her for the sake of their own strategic
and economic advantage.

Is the strategic deployment of the USSR now directed eastward or westward? Chairman Mao has developed the following
assessment of the current military deployment of the Soviet
revisionists: for the time being, the Soviet revisionists have
deployed 111 divisions in the West, 20 divisions in Central
Asia, and 40 divisions in the vicinity of China's frontier. As
viewed from the dispersal of troops, the primary strategic deployment of the Soviet revisionists is directed westward —
toward Europe.

At present, the Soviet revisionists are chiefly contending
with the U.S. for Europe. To "concentrate troops on the frontier" of China is just fanfare and intimidation. We must not
fall for their ploy. It seems likely that, for a comparatively
long period, the Soviet revisionists will not dare have a big
fight with us except for provoking a few skirmishes along the
frontier. They all have the figures on their minds, since they
understand that we are prepared to fight a big battle.

The European countries all take different views on the wild
ambitions of the Soviet revisionists. Chairman Mao holds that
the Conservative government of Britain is relatively sober-
minded because it perceives more clearly the ambition of the
USSR. When Chairman Mao met the Foreign Minister of France,
Maurice Schumann, he said to him: "We are very clear on the
fact that the USSR is trying to lure you over and that you will
be taken in. For is it possible for France to stand by the side
of the USSR in case a world war arises? No, you French will
still side with the U.S." According to what we know, Schumann
immediately conveyed this remark to Minister of National Defense Michel Debré after his return to France.

In the areas of Asia, Africa, and Latin America as a whole,
the two superpowers, the U.S. and USSR, are intensifying their
struggle. Once the Vietnam war is concluded, the problem of
the Middle East will be given priority. The two tyrants are
still engaged in both collusion and contention, dividing the
spheres of influence and obstructing each other. There is a

piece of news that has not been announced publicly: When Nixon paid a visit to Moscow in 1972, he reached a secret agreement with the Soviet revisionists: the U.S. agreed that the USSR would allow 35,000 Jews to go to Israel annually in exchange for a U.S.-Soviet agreement which would favor the trading and economy of the USSR. Now Israel is supplied with military equipment by the U.S. The latest news is that the U.S. will furnish Israel with forty Phantom Fighters and eighty Eagle Fighters while the USSR will provide her with manpower to carry on war with the Arab countries. In the midst of competition between the U.S. and USSR, the Arab countries are disintegrating and are incapable of uniting, this being the most disadvantageous thing in their combat against Israel. Recently, Sudan's relations with Egypt have further deteriorated while there are other dangerous enemies ahead such as Algeria, Syria, Iraq, Libya, Jordan, Lebanon, They are fighting each other and creating contradictions among themselves day in and day out.

In the Middle East, the U.S. intends to take hold of two "bridgeheads"; one is Iran and the other is Saudi Arabia.

The struggle of the Palestinian guerrillas is beset by pressures and difficulties. This is induced by the disunity of the Arab countries. In an attempt to broaden their influence in the Middle East, the Soviet revisionists have made some changes in their attitude toward the Palestinian guerrillas by publishing a few statements of support.

Since the deterioration of relations between the USSR and Egypt, the Middle East policy of the Soviet revisionists has shifted from the management of key points to diversified management. Lately they have vigorously aided Syria and Iraq and offered to extract a rather large quantity of natural gas for Algeria after which a contract was signed. Egypt has two facets. On the one hand, she cannot completely get out of the control of the Soviet revisionists, exemplified by their driving away the Soviet specialists in July and requesting them to return in October; she still cannot do without the USSR. On the other hand, that she dared oust the Soviet specialists is an outgrowth of the deep development of the struggle against the two superpowers by the people of the Middle East.

Our attitude toward the Middle East has always been clear. We oppose the practice of both struggle and collusion by the two superpowers in the Middle East and the betrayal of the Arabian people by the Soviet revisionists. We support the struggle of the Palestinian guerrillas against Israel.

B. Questions Concerning the Vietnam Peace Agreement

1. After years of hard-fought battles, the Vietnamese people have finally won a basic victory. The ultimate goal of the Vietnamese people's struggle was to expel U.S. troops. Now that the U.S. troops have withdrawn, the victory is extremely clear. Nevertheless, the struggle is still very complicated. We have told the Vietnamese comrades: we must be practical and realistic. The U.S. herself knows that to continue fighting means to drag things out without knowing how long. Therefore, she will make an "honorable withdrawal" following negotiation. Besides, having fought for so many years, the Vietnamese people have suffered great losses. To continue fighting would not produce instant results [for them] either. But to compel the Americans to withdraw through negotiation will leave you yourselves [the Vietnamese] a half to one year for rest and consolidation. You can consider the problem of liberating South Vietnam later. The Vietnamese comrades have received our suggestion.

2. Upon the signing of the Paris Agreement, we differed from the Vietnamese comrades on a couple of issues: (a) On the matter of the U.S. military bases in South Vietnam, the U.S. said that she had dismantled her military bases in South Vietnam in the wake of each successive troop withdrawal. This is not true. But the Vietnamese comrades did not resolutely refute this. (b) On the question of holding democratic elections among "three political forces" in Vietnam in the future, there are no concrete provisions but only empty talk. This is disadvantageous to the leftist forces in South Vietnam. (c) We exhorted the Vietnamese comrades to persist in preventing the United Nations from taking a hand in the Paris Conference. [We felt that] the chairmanship of the Conference should be

assumed by the U.S. and Vietnam representatives in rotation,
and not by the Secretary-General of the U.N. because, once
the U.N. stepped in, all problems concerning Vietnam after-
wards would have to be handled through the U.N. and things
would become complex. Later the problem was handled through
a compromise with the U.N. Secretary-General being "seated
as an observer" and not as the Conference chairman. (d) [We
felt that] in the Paris Agreements, only the Vietnam issue should
be discussed; the problems of Cambodia and Laos should not
be dragged in. Yet, the problems of the two countries [Cam-
bodia and Laos] were still mentioned in the Agreements. This
was not good because we cannot impose the Vietnam issue on
these two countries.

3. The Soviet revisionists will intensify economic aid to the
Vietnamese people after the Vietnam war comes to an end to
balance out our influence in Vietnam. The struggle from now
on will become complicated and acute.

C. The World Situation after Vietnam Signed the Peace Agreement and Our Assessment of the Strategic Position of Countries Concerned

1. The Indochina region:
With the truce in Vietnam, the people of North Vietnam will
acquire rest and consolidation and achieve economic reconstruction within a short period. Their chief means will be
self-reliance, but, without international support, there will be
difficulties. The U.S. planes bombarded Vietnam too extensively and destroyed too much. Reconstruction will require
some international support. The Chinese people will provide
the Vietnamese comrades with necessary aid. The Soviet revisionists will also offer them rather considerable economic
assistance. They contend with us on this point, mainly vying
with us to exert influence over Vietnam.

The Vietnamese comrades will continue to work out a "Sino-
Soviet balance." This depends on how good a job we do. Of
course, our aid is devoid of any conditions and is sincere and
selfless.

At the Paris Conference, the Vietnamese comrades did not take our advice regarding the question of inviting the U.N. Secretary-General to the Conference. The reason is that the Vietnamese comrades maintained an illusion about the U.N., hoping to obtain economic aid from the U.N. and gain an opportunity to join the U.N. faster.

We advise the Vietnamese comrades to heighten their vigilance a hundred-fold during the period of rest and consolidation because the U.S. left 10,000 armed military personnel dressed in civilian clothes and appearing in the form of technical specialists and because U.S. military equipment was handed over to Nguyen Van Thieu in large quantities. Nguyen Van Thieu now maintains 800,000 troops. The Paris Ceasefire Agreement contains only a few empty phrases on the problem of holding democratic free elections among the three political powers in South Vietnam. These empty phrases are useless.

If war breaks out again in Vietnam, would the U.S. Army send hundreds of thousands of men to Vietnam as they did before? It seems unlikely. The Americans oppose this war and the U.S. government does not want to get deeper into an awkward situation because there are many problems facing the U.S. in Europe, the Middle East, and all areas where the Soviet revisionists are expanding their influence. The Vietnamese people can crush Nguyen Van Thieu politically and militarily, but they need a period of time as well as correct political [analysis] and high sensitivity to the "false support and real betrayal" of the Soviet revisionists.

The political status of Laos is favorable to her people and the signing of the Laotian armistice agreement is advantageous to the leftist forces. Future changes are dependent on a correct political line. The current situation in Cambodia is also good. The Lon Nol regime now controls only a small piece of land, and moreover, it seems that the Americans do not respect this president very much. Lately the attitude of Prince Sihanouk has been tough and resolute. Men are always subject to change and a change in the direction of progress is good.

The peace in Indochina is temporary; no one is sleeping. Our basic policy is to support all revolutionary progressive forces in overthrowing all reactionary forces and to support the struggles of the Vietnamese, Cambodian, and Laotian people just as we have always been doing.

2. Assessment of the strategic deployment of the Soviet revisionists: Since the cease-fire in Vietnam, the key strategic points of the Soviet revisionists have become, first, Europe and, second, the Middle East. Of course, sometimes it is very hard to discriminate between the first and the second.

As I have said before, their European policy is primarily a policy of polarization, a policy of compelling Western Europe to "neutralize," and a policy of going a step further to control the whole Europe. In the Middle East, they both struggle and collude with the U.S., dividing equally the spheres of influence. Their contention with the U.S. will get more intense, but they avoid face-to-face military clashes with the U.S. Lifting high the signboard of the October Revolution and the homeland of Lenin, the Soviet revisionists still maintain their global deceptiveness. Many countries become aware of this only after they have suffered bad losses.

In Asia as a whole, the Soviet revisionists are intensifying the adoption of a policy of subversion and ingratiation and will take advantage of the U.S. withdrawal of troops from Asia by attempting to "fill the vacuum." Will the U.S. give up Asia? Impossible! The U.S. will not relinquish its advantage in Asia. The U.S. has simply placed herself on the second line, but in some other places she is still on the first line. It will not be as easy as the Soviet revisionists figured to turn a profit in the future Asia, for there stands China!

On the South Asian subcontinent, the Soviet revisionists will foster "détente" among "India, Pakistan and Bangladesh" and improve and mend their relations with Pakistan in order to place India, Pakistan and Bangladesh within their "Asian Collective Security Treaty" sphere of influence.

Toward Japan, the Soviet revisionists use the exploitation of the Tyumen oil fields as a lure to improve relations with

her. However, Japan will not abandon its demand for the return of the four islands north of Japan. Under Japan's strategy
of "separation of politics and economics," it is impossible for
relations between Japan and the USSR to make any progress.
The Soviet revisionists are also attempting to lure the U.S.
into opening up the Tyumen oil fields, but the U.S. capitalists
have not shown great interest. First, the USSR uses U.S. capital to promote construction and her own capital to amplify her
armaments. Second, it will require five years after the initial
investment to produce petroleum products and who knows what
will happen in the world in those five years.

In the future, the entire strategic deployment of the Soviet
revisionists is global, confronting not only the U.S. but also us.
While they simultaneously struggle against and collude with the
U.S., they maintain completely antagonistic relations with us.
This is the essence of the problem.

Our opposing the two superpowers is a slogan. Its essence
lies principally in opposition against this most realistic enemy,
Soviet revisionist social-imperialism, and the main thing is to
combat this social-imperialism. We have a clear understanding of this problem and so does the U.S.

Last year we made comparatively good progress in our diplomatic work in Southeast Asian countries. Several countries
will probably establish relations with us this year and those
who do not entertain relations with us will develop closer contacts [with us]. The situation in the South Asian subcontinent
is, in contrast, relatively complicated; the Soviet revisionists
have a tight grip on it. Nevertheless, India's attitude toward
us has changed.

We support the European Common Market because it is a
kind of force which resists the USSR and the U.S. Among the
three principal countries in Europe, Britain, France and West
Germany, Britain has maintained rather positive relations with
us over the past year or more, for the British have accurately
sensed the trend.

The Middle East is still in a phase of neither war nor peace;
neither the U.S. nor the USSR desire a face-to-face conflict.

However, the possibility of a partial solution also exists. We have always backed the Arab countries and the struggle of the Palestinian guerrillas but have never actually meddled.

It is all right to uphold people's struggles but not adventurist actions. The foreign minister of the Malagasy Republic told me: "There are also "ultraleftist" elements in the Malagasy Republic who hope to drive away all the French." I told him: "That isn't strange, for China has those kinds of people and so do the Soviet revisionists; they pressure us to recapture Hong Kong and Macao." We said that Macao cannot be recovered, not to mention Hong Kong. To take it back would shock the British in Hong Kong and cause Britain and the U.S. to unite together; we cannot do that. There is still the Taiwan [problem]. The work [of solving it] will also require some time. It will not do to be impetuous. We must take all sides of the issue into account. Hong Kong and Macao and Taiwan are two different matters and must be handled in different ways.

We are now promoting criticism of Lin Piao and rectification with emphasis placed on the criticism of Lin on the one hand, and are driving all kinds of construction and all kinds of [other] work by criticizing Lin on the other. The most important kind of strategic deployment is to have a great leap forward in all areas, such as industry, agriculture, and technology, by adopting the advanced techniques of other countries.

3. Assessment of the strategic deployment of the U.S.:

With the truce in Vietnam, U.S. military forces will be deployed as follows:

a) The key strategic focus point will shift to Europe and Middle East;

b) Japan will be placed on the first line in Asia;

c) Construction of military bases on the Mariana Islands will be stepped up as a defensive measure on the second line against the USSR;

d) Building up the navy in the Pacific Ocean and the two wings of the West, South, and North Indian Ocean will be stepped up to block the expansion of Soviet maritime strength.

4. Evaluation of Japan's future orientation:

Japan is now standing at a crossroads.

There are two reasons which account for Japan's becoming an aggressive country since the nineteenth century: First, Japan has neither [internal] resources nor markets; second, the national economic budget of Japan is small, [thus] she has to expand outward when her domestic economic development reaches the saturation point.

The strategy of Japan after the Vietnam war has been discussed before. Of course, the pivotal point rests with her attitude toward the USSR. Ostensibly, she applies a strategy of "détente," but in essence she has adopted, politically and militarily, a policy of "resisting the USSR."

Japan has expressed some apprehension about the military threat of the USSR. Previously she relied on the protection of the U.S. nuclear umbrella, but what will she do now? Japan understands clearly that if she depends entirely on U.S. military protection, the U.S. will squeeze her neck economically. Therefore, Japan cannot help but develop her own military power. Yet would the development of military power lead her back on the old road of militarism? This is what troubles her.

Japan's Nakasone drew a "picture of displaying the armies" on his visit to China. He told us of the current military deployment of Japan, saying that Japan has only nine land divisions concentrated mostly in Hokkaido to guard against the USSR. Japan's navy is now also very small, a fleet of small vessels. What Nakasone meant is that (a) the important thing is for Japan to take military precautions against the USSR in the future, but her military strength is small and needs development; (b) as Japan's military strength is now so small, it is wrong to call her "militarist." The situation described by Nakasone is basically true.

Japan plans to expand economically to a larger area of Asia; one is Southeast Asia and the other is postwar Vietnam. She now shows deep interest, engaging in positive activities. Is Japan's future in the direction of "democracy, neutralization, independence and peace"? Or is it a return to the old road of militarism? We must carry out our work as we wait to see.

5. Our basic strategy:

It is to oppose the two superpowers, chiefly the most direct, the most perilous and the most real enemy, Soviet revisionist social-imperialism. This strategy was laid down by Chairman Mao. Chairman Mao said: "We must not fight on two fronts; it is better to fight on one front."

Should we now declare war on the Soviet revisionists? Not necessarily. The current strategy of the USSR is directed at the West, Europe and the Middle East. Toward us, she makes a lot of noise but also knows that we have been prepared for a long time. So, for a time, the situation will remain a "cold war," a diplomatic "bull fight," a "baring of teeth." But it is still necessary to guard against her taking a great risk.

We must still condemn the U.S. for whatever is reprehensible. When she oppresses the small and medium-sized countries, we must reprimand her. Of the two world superpowers, one is the most direct enemy. Now the U.S. retires to the second position. We cannot propose "uniting with the U.S. to oppose the USSR" though we have points in common with the U.S. on certain issues. Furthermore, there is the Pentagon, a den of warmongering elements, supported by the great arms manufacturers. We must maintain our vigilance against the U.S. all the same; we cannot lose it.

We are in the midst of working on Japan, sending many delegations, including political, economic and cultural ones as well as people to people friendship groups. The problem of Japan is a serious one. She is now standing at a crossroads and still has ambitions.

THE WARSAW TREATY ORGANIZATION: SOVIET SOCIAL-IMPERIALISM'S TOOL FOR AGGRESSION*

2

Ming Sung

Europe has become the strategic focus of intense contention for world hegemony between Soviet revisionist social-imperialism and U.S. imperialism. The Moscow-controlled Warsaw Treaty Organization has a special role to play in this rivalry.

Since Soviet revisionism embarked on the road of social-imperialism, the Warsaw Treaty Organization, founded in 1955, has become more and more a tool of the Soviet Union to go the United States one better in Europe and further its ends, expansion and aggression, there.

I

Under the "socialist community" signboard, the Brezhnev clique has reduced a number of East European countries to Soviet satellites and colonies and has made the organization a tool to prop up its colonial rule by subjecting these countries to military control and occupation.

The joint command of the Warsaw Pact armed forces has all along been kept in the hands of Soviet revisionism; a Soviet deputy defense minister unfailingly is concurrent commander in

---

*From <u>Peking Review</u>, No. 8 (February 21, 1975), 17-19.

chief and a Soviet brass-hat chief of the general staff, while representatives of other member states can only act as deputies. Within the command, it is only the Soviet military chiefs' words that count, while other member states' representatives are at the former's beck and call. A former Czechoslovak minister of security once complained that the defense ministers of the Warsaw Pact countries did not have equal footing with their Soviet partner in the joint command and were actually deprived of their rights there. With the power of the joint command vested in the hands of the Soviet Union, Moscow in fact has the armed forces of a number of East European countries under its thumb.

Soviet representatives are permanently stationed in other Warsaw Pact countries as "representatives of the joint command" to discharge the function of "relaying" the "directives" of the commander in chief to the defense ministers of the countries they are stationed in, to take part in various activities of the armed forces of these countries and directly interfere in the internal affairs of these armed forces. In addition, large numbers of Soviet military "advisers" and "experts" are assigned to these forces to keep them under strict surveillance.

With a view to tightening its grip on the armed forces of these countries, Soviet revisionism has pressed for "military integration," demanding that they operate under the same command, training, and formation as the Soviet armed forces.

Using the pretext of "international division of labor" and "coordination" of military economic plans, the Soviet Union also controls arms production in a number of Warsaw Pact countries, incorporating their economies into its own militarized economy. The upshot is that these countries can only manufacture weapons according to the "standard" and "specifications" provided by Moscow and they have no independent and comprehensive defense industry of their own.

According to Western news reports, the Soviet Union at present has thirty-one divisions in Eastern Europe — twenty of them are stationed in the German Democratic Republic, two in Poland, four in Hungary, and five in Czechoslovakia — where they enjoy extraterritorial rights. A Soviet-Czechoslovak treaty, for instance, stipulates that Soviet military personnel who commit offenses when carrying out duty in areas in their charge shall be under the jurisdiction of Soviet law courts, procuratorial organs, and other institutions functioning under Soviet law and that the country where Soviet troops are stationed does not have the right to intervene.

By conducting military exercises, Soviet revisionism often threatens the people of some East European countries who are resentful of its control. On many occasions it has marshaled troops on the Balkan Peninsula through the Warsaw Treaty Organization, carrying out military exercises to apply open pressure on some Balkan states. These moves have seriously threatened the independence and sovereignty of these countries.

To maintain its colonial rule in Eastern Europe, Soviet revisionism even went to the length of resorting to force through the Warsaw Treaty Organization and launching undisguised military aggression against a member state. The salient case is the armed occupation of Czechoslovakia in August 1968. The incident thoroughly exposed the aggressive and reactionary nature of the Warsaw Treaty Organization and also bared the sinister motives of Soviet revisionist social-imperialism in manipulating the organization.

II

The organization at the same time serves Soviet revisionism as a tool for threatening Western Europe, carrying out expansion and contending with U.S. imperialism for hegemony in this area.

It is well known that Soviet revisionism has always deployed most of its armed forces against Western Europe. According to Western press reports, the Soviet Union now has three-fifths of its ground forces and over three-fourths of its air force in Eastern Europe and the Soviet Union proper in Europe. Over three-fourths of its intermediate-range missiles are directed against Western Europe; three-fourths of its surface naval ships and over half its submarines are in waters around Europe. By controlling the Warsaw Treaty Organization, Soviet revisionism sees to it that the armed forces in some East European countries are attached to those of its own in Europe to form a military bloc, thus tying them to its war chariot to work for its aggression and expansion in Western Europe.

In recent years, the Warsaw Treaty Organization has continuously held joint military exercises aimed at Western Europe. According to Western military experts' analyses, these exercises usually took place with an "overall offensive" as the main theme. Through these, Soviet revisionism hopes to show the West European countries its military strength and blackmail them. Simultaneously, these exercises are designed to improve the capability of the Warsaw Pact armed forces in coordinated fighting and its command and to step up war preparations.

While exploiting the Warsaw Treaty Organization to facilitate its arms expansion and war preparations, the Soviet Union also uses it as a means to back up its position of strength and as a counterweight in diplomatic negotiations with the United States and other NATO countries for a so-called European "détente," which is a political fraud.

Through the summit and foreign ministers' conferences of the Warsaw Pact countries, the Soviet Union has published "communiqués," "declarations," "statements," "memoranda," and "proposals" on the convocation of the "European security conference." After it was convened, it took further steps to "coordinate" the "joint actions" of the Warsaw Pact countries inside and outside the conference. It also tries to manipulate the Warsaw Treaty Organization and negotiate with the Western countries through the "European security conference" to consolidate its hegemonic status in Eastern Europe and lull and divide the West European countries and squeeze out the United States so as to make way for its expansion and infiltration into Western Europe.

As to the so-called Central European "force reduction" conference, it was convened between two blocs — the Warsaw Pact countries and the NATO countries. Through these negotiations, the Brezhnev clique hopes to maintain the Warsaw bloc's superiority in conventional military strength and weaken the military strength of the United States and other Western countries. At the same time, it tries to use these negotiations to cover up its military reinforcements in Eastern Europe and its renewing of its weapons and equipment there. What the clique did both at the "European security conference" and the Central European "force reduction" conference fully exposed its ugly features of promoting sham détente and working for actual expansion in Europe.

* * *

The use of the Warsaw Treaty Organization to carry out aggression and expansion in Europe by the Soviet revisionist renegade clique has aroused increasingly strong opposition among the people of various European countries. Immediately following the Soviet revisionists' armed invasion of Czechoslovakia, Albania announced its withdrawal from the organization, dealing the Soviet revisionist renegade clique a head-on blow. The Czechoslovak people's angry tide against Soviet revisionism's colonial rule is rising unabated. Again and again, some East European countries have expressed their determination to uphold their independence and sovereignty and have taken concomitant measures. Meanwhile, the West European countries have come to see more clearly the expansionist policy being pushed by Soviet revisionism behind the smokescreen of "détente." They are heightening their vigilance against it. The tendency is that their unity in opposition to the Soviet revisionists' hegemonism is being continuously enhanced.

WHAT DOES THE SITUATION SHOW ONE YEAR AFTER THE EUROPEAN SECURITY CONFERENCE?* 3

Jen Ku-ping

It is a year since the European Security Conference closed. What changes have taken place in the entire European situation and what do these changes signify?

The stark facts of the situation point to only one conclusion: with contention between the two superpowers in Europe growing fiercer and Soviet social-imperialism stepping up its arms expansion and war preparations, Europe has become more unstable, and the threat facing the West European countries more serious. This shows that the Final Act cooked up at the European Security Conference in Helsinki a year ago is a mere scrap of paper and the so-called European security conference is in reality a European insecurity conference. Today, dark clouds of war hang over the countries in Europe. To oppose hegemonism and safeguard their independence and security remains their grave task.

Mounting Threat to West European Countries

It is still fresh in people's minds that the Soviet revisionists made a great fuss to boost the European Security Conference in the days immediately preceding its convocation and following its conclusion last year. They gave free play to the value of the Helsinki conference, holding it up as "a new stage

*From Peking Review, Nos. 32-33 (August 9, 1976), 11-13.

199

of détente" and "the dawn of peace and cooperation" in Europe.
As an earnest of their bona fide intentions they vigorously asserted that they would "steadfastly set an example to others in
realizing the agreements of the all-European conference."
However, their actions belie their words.

It was in the twelve months following the European Security
Conference that the Soviet Union continued to mass troops in
Central Europe and exert pressure at every turn. Preparing
for an "offensive war," it has beefed up the Soviet forces in
the region, streamlined their military setup, strengthened
their logistics, equipped them with sophisticated weapons and
greatly increased the amount of conventional and nuclear arms.
Maneuvers with the occupation of Europe as the goal have been
frequently held to gain "the necessary experience" for over-
running Europe when the day comes.

Whether it is military confrontation all along the front or in
the battle of words at the negotiation table, the Soviet revisionists are consumed with a desire to maintain or sharpen their
military edge over the West. The din of the European Security
Conference had yet to fade away when Moscow signed with un-
due haste a new treaty with the German Democratic Republic
to replace the treaty of "friendship and mutual assistance."
This is an important measure taken by Moscow to accelerate
its war preparations in Europe.

It was in the space of these twelve months that the Soviet
Union steadily stepped up its military pressure in Northern
Europe. In areas adjacent to Northern Europe, military de-
ployments were intensified; strategic highways were built and
double-track railways laid; a canal to the sea was expanded;
military exercises with North European countries as the
hypothetical enemy took place one after another, and the sphere
of military activities of every description was constantly wi-
dened. The airspace and territorial waters of the North European countries were time and again violated by Soviet aircraft
and warships. For the first time, a special naval task force
was sent to the North Sea with a view to controlling the sea
lanes stretching from the Baltic and Barents seas to the

Atlantic Ocean. By virtue of Soviet military superiority on the
northern flank of Europe, the masters sitting in the Kremlin
set their minds on "striking at the heart of the West European
defenses from the far north."

It was also in the space of these twelve months that the Soviet Union showed its teeth and braced up its aggressive posture menacingly in Southern Europe and the Mediterranean. A
Southern Europe command was added to the Warsaw Pact head-
quarters. The Soviet naval presence in the Mediterranean was
swollen to more than seventy ships. Its first aircraft carrier,
the Kiev, sailed into the Mediterranean in a show of force, a
move to use military blackmail against the coastal countries.
Full advantage was taken of the political turmoil and national
feuds in certain South European countries where Moscow tried
its utmost to have a finger in the pie and fish in troubled waters. The aim could only be to put a knife into the "soft under-
belly" and act in concert with operations in Northern Europe
so as to hem Western Europe in from north and south.

Again it was in the space of these twelve months that the
Soviet Union bestirred itself more actively than ever to grab
strategic points in the Middle East, which flanks Europe, and
in Africa. Only a few months after the European Security Conference, the Soviet revisionists unsheathed their butcher's
knife in Angola in a bid to entrench themselves in that country
and thus threaten the sea lanes between Western Europe and
the United States and establish control over the South Atlantic.
In recent weeks, the Soviet Union has been busy exerting its
influence in some Middle East countries and trying to cash in
on the turbulent situation in Lebanon and expand its sphere of
influence in the Middle East region.

In short, in the year following the European Security Conference, Soviet social-imperialism's threat to West European
countries has grown unmistakably. Not only has it carried out
infiltration in these countries and squeezed them on all sides,
but it has also steadily thrown a strategic encirclement around
them on the exterior lines. A glance at Europe today, whether
from the north, east, south or west, and whether in regard to

air, land or naval forces, shows that the Soviet Union is all too
ready to pounce on the victim. Never in the postwar years
have the West European countries been confronted with such a
grave threat. The so-called "new stage of détente" in Europe
is nothing but a "new stage" of expansion by Soviet social-
imperialism. The acts of the Soviet revisionists have given
the lie to their spurious rhetoric. If the European Security
Conference has brought "détente" to Europe, then why are
they so frantically engaged in arms expansion and war preparations after the conference? Since they are so blatantly carrying out infiltration and expansion, then what European "détente"
and "security" is there to talk about?

"Détente" Cannot Cover Up Expansionist Designs

The Soviet Union has been loudly singing a "détente" lullaby
while posing its threat of expansion to Western Europe over
the past year. This has not escaped people's attention. Facts
prove that the "détente" touted by the Kremlin is nothing but a
move to cover up the traces of its arms drive and war preparations, its expansionist activities against Western Europe and
contention with the United States for hegemony. It is precisely
because of this that the "détente" offensive mounted by the
Soviet Union is a real threat to Western Europe indeed.

To push its expansion behind the smoke screen of "détente,"
Moscow has tirelessly harped on the theme that "détente" benefits both sides, that "détente" is not one-way traffic," that
"there are no winners or losers." But what are the facts?

Behind a heavy smoke screen of "détente" to cover up its
arms expansion and war preparations, the Soviet Union in the
past year has made a big effort to get the West European countries to drop their guard, hoping that they would entertain illusions and lower their vigilance. It has openly preached the
nonsense that while it is "right" for the Soviet Union to increase its armed strength it is "wrong" for others to look to
their defense. As West European public opinion has pointed
out, the Kremlin aims to "gradually disarm the West" politi-

cally, and psychologically, under the signboard of détente so
as to accomplish its "task of achieving military superiority."

Under the pretext of "détente" the Soviet Union has blatantly
plotted and schemed to sow discord and divide the West European countries in an attempt to weaken and wreck their trend
toward union. Moreover, it has openly attacked the proposal
of the West European countries to form a union as running
"counter to the Helsinki spirit." Unfurling the banner of "all-
European cooperation," it has tried to cotton up to Western
Europe and infiltrate it in all spheres while doing its utmost
to squeeze out U.S. influence there. The aim is to establish
exclusive Soviet hegemony over the whole of Europe.

In hawking its shoddy ware of "materialization of détente,"
the Soviet Union has left no stone unturned to get large sums
of capital, laons, technical know-how and equipment from
Western Europe through so-called "trade exchanges" and "mutual benefit and cooperation" so that it can ease its economic
difficulties, speed up its arms expansion and war preparations,
and beef up its military setup.

For the Soviet Union, "détente" is clearly a means of attack,
a lethal instrument that kills insidiously. It is fraught with
danger for Western Europe. "Détente" has not gotten the
Soviet Union to withdraw a single soldier from the European
region, still less stopped the Soviet war chariot of aggression
and expansion in its tracks. "Détente" has not prevented the
Soviet Union from extending its sinister tentacles to Portugal;
nor has it stayed Moscow's butcher's knife in Angola. "Détente" can in no way check Soviet expansionist acts, much less
get the Soviet revisionists to give up their wild ambition of
European hegemony. The attempt to use "détente" to keep
Soviet expansionism in check, the belief that the Soviet Union,
as the "Sonnenfeldt Doctrine" makes out, would be satisfied
with its so-called "organic relationship" with Eastern Europe
and would not attack Western Europe, are policies of appeasement which Soviet expansionist activities over the past year
have proved illusory. The Soviet revisionists have repeatedly
clamored since the Angolan incident that "détente" does not

mean "freezing the status quo"; nor does it mean that "every corner of the globe" is beyond their "consideration." This makes it crystal clear that the Soviet Union's global strategic offensive would not slacken, let alone stop. It has been this way in the past, and so it will be in the future. In these circumstances, can Europe have security? So long as the Kremlin's rulers do not give up the desire to lord it over Europe, Europe cannot hope to have even a day of tranquillity.

Irresistible Trend to Unite against Hegemony

In the face of the sharpening contention between the two superpowers in Europe and the threat of Soviet expansion, what are the European countries to do to safeguard their independence and security — strive for security through struggle, or reach a compromise and get a temporary respite? Serious thought and attention ought to be given to this question on which a decision of historic importance must be made today.

The people of the European countries, which have experienced two world wars, are most concerned about peace and security on the continent. That is only natural. But hopes cannot take the place of reality. Unless properly handled, things may turn out to be just the opposite of one's hopes. Such instances can be found in Europe's history. Before World War II the fervent aspirations of the people of the European countries were to oppose wars of aggression and maintain security. But Chamberlain and his like carried out a policy of compromise and appeasement and sought accommodation with the international outlaws. The result was that the Hitlerite aggressors were allowed to nurture insatiable appetites, and for this the people of Europe had to pay dearly.

Today, the Soviet social-imperialists are following in the footsteps of Nazi Germany. The Brezhnev clique's greed and ambition far surpass Hitler's. It is noteworthy that in recent years some political figures in the West are inclined to follow an appeasement policy. In one sense, the European Security Conference is as much an outcome of Soviet machinations as

a product of the trend of thought in the West originating from
the Munich sellout. Such a phenomenon has aroused the attention of Western public opinion which points out: "Aggressors
can never be placated. A policy of appeasement has never
succeeded in history." "It will be ridiculous to think that the
Soviet Union would alter its policy if concessions were made
to it."

People are the masters of history. Europe's destiny is in
the hands of the people of the European countries. Events in
the year following the Helsinki Conference show that the conference did not solve, nor could it solve, the question of European security and that written agreements can in no way safeguard peace and security in Europe. The only sure way to deal
with the Soviet revisionists' menacing aggression and expansion is to heighten vigilance, strengthen unity, make practical
preparations and wage resolute struggle.

Moscow's acts of aggression and expansion have taught the
people of Europe by negative example and served to show them,
little by little, where the main threat to Europe comes from.
If the "détente" peddled by the Soviet revisionists still had a
few buyers a year ago, then today the "détente" hoax is on the
verge of bankruptcy. More and more prominent figures in the
West have come to realize that Soviet military might is developing at an alarming rate and that the "real danger is a false
sense of security induced by the European Security Conference
and 'détente.'" They listed facts, weighed the pros and cons,
worked out contermeasures and spoke in favor of "drawing
lessons from events since the European Security Conference"
and taking steps in all fields to counter the threat of Soviet
expansion. For some time now countries in Western Europe
[have been] steadily strengthening their armed forces to cope
with outside aggression, reorganizing and improving their
military strategy and deployment, propelling the trend of economic and political union of West European countries and their
common struggle against hegemonism. Today, many West
European countries, including some smaller ones which have
all along taken a position of neutrality, are bolstering up their

forces to resist aggression so that they can deal with eventualities and safeguard their independence and security.

Events in the past twelve months show that the situation in Europe has not developed as Moscow wishes. Despite blustering Soviet threats of expansion, the people of the West European countries are steadily heightening their awareness to oppose Soviet aggrandizement. This struggle is growing daily, and the trend of uniting to fight hegemonism cannot be checked. Though Soviet social-imperialism is flexing its military muscles and looks powerful enough, it is actually beset with a host of difficulties. One need not be frightened, for Soviet social-imperialism is tough outside but brittle inside. By stretching its tentacles to all parts of Europe and throwing its weight about, the Soviet Union will only sow the wind and reap the whirlwind and rouse the people of the European countries to greater resistance. A year after the European Security Conference, the Kremlin was obliged recently to confess that the harder it tried to palm off the "détente" hoax in Europe, "the greater has become the resistance." This clearly shows that all is not well with the Kremlin's rulers who are pushing their policy of expansion and aggression in Europe. If the people of the European countries further heighten their awakening, strengthen their unity, and press on with their struggle, Soviet social-imperialism's wild ambition to seek hegemony in Europe is sure to end in ignominious defeat.

DEFENSE OF NATIONAL INDEPENDENCE AND SECOND WORLD COUNTRIES*

4

Sa Na, Chiu Li-pen and Shen Yung-hsing

The following is a translation of the article published in Jen-min jih-pao on January 18 entitled "The Justness of Second World Countries' Defense of National Independence as Seen from Lenin's Expositions on 'Defense of the Fatherland.'" It was written at the request of readers after the publication last November 1 of the paper's Editorial Department article on the theory of the differentiation of the three worlds (see Peking Review, No. 45, 1977). The authors of the article are historians of the Institute of World History under the Chinese Academy of Social Science. Subheads are ours. — Ed., Peking Review.

In the article "Chairman Mao's Theory of the Differentiation of the Three Worlds Is a Major Contribution to Marxism-Leninism" by the Editorial Department of Jen-min jih-pao, it was pointed out that one task facing the Second World countries today, especially the developed countries in Europe, is defense of their national independence. This is entirely correct and fully conforms with the Marxist-Leninist principle of revolutionary tactics. Here is a discussion of our approach to this topic in the light of Lenin's expositions on "defense of the fatherland."

Lenin's expositions boil down to two points: (1) World War I which broke out in 1914 was an imperialist war, and the bel-

---

*From Peking Review, No. 5 (February 3, 1978), 5-11.

ligerents on both sides were reactionary; thus the task of the
proletariat of the countries concerned was to oppose this reactionary war and turn the imperialist war into revolutionary
civil wars. (2) But this did not mean that it was impossible
for a national war to take place in Europe in the conditions obtaining at the time. On the contrary, not only were the wars
waged by the weak and small nations against aggression and
oppression just, even war waged by an imperialist country,
when it itself was an object of aggression, could also become,
under certain conditions, a just war in defense of national independence.

Imperialist Wars and Tactics of the Proletariat

In 1914, when World War I broke out, Lenin, basing himself
on the Marxist axiom that war is the continuation of politics,
comprehensively analyzed the cause of the war, showed with
penetrating insight the rapacious and reactionary nature of this
imperialist war and called on the proletariat of the countries
concerned to oppose it resolutely. He put forth the correct
tactic of "converting the imperialist war into civil war" and
causing "the defeat of one's 'own' government in the imperialist war" (Socialism and War). Lenin sternly repudiated the
opportunist leaders of the Second International when they
openly raised the slogan "defense of the fatherland" to deceive
the working class and other laboring people in the countries
concerned while doing their utmost to speak in defense of this
imperialist war. Denouncing this act of betrayal, Lenin pointed
out: "To embellish imperialist war by applying to it the concept of 'defense of the fatherland,' i.e., by presenting it as a
democratic war, is to deceive the workers and side with the
reactionary bourgeoisie" (A Caricature of Marxism and Imperialist Economism).
    Lenin denounced the Second International renegades for
their despicable attempt to whitewash their acts of betrayal
by willfully distorting, with no regard for the time or the specific historical conditions, the examples of Marx's and Engels'

tactics, namely, their energetic support for the bourgeois democratic revolution and national wars in Europe in the period of laisser-faire capitalism, and their call in 1891 on the German working class to defend the fatherland.

It is true that Marx and Engels had warmly praised and actively supported the 1848 democratic revolution in Europe, that they had called on the working class of various countries to throw themselves into the struggle against the reactionary autocratic monarchy in Europe. They had also supported and extolled the national war of 1859 led by Garibaldi in Italy against Austria as well as the 1863 Polish people's national uprising against tsarist Russia, and called on the working class of various countries to lend its support to this just national war and uprising. In 1891 when tsarist Russia threatened Germany with war, Engels issued the call to the German working class to safeguard its already gained democratic position by getting ready to "defend the fatherland" with a national war against a possible war of aggression and annexation launched by tsarist Russia.

Lenin resolutely defended these correct examples of Marx's and Engels' tactics. He pointed out that in 1891, Germany, which had not yet become an imperialist country, was the center of the workers' movement in Europe, the country where the proletarian forces were most powerful; whereas tsarist Russia, which was threatening Germany with war, was the main enemy of the democratic and progressive forces in Europe. This was why Engels' call to the working class of Germany to defend the fatherland in the event of a war of aggression by tsarist Russia was made in defense of the basic interest of the proletariat and, therefore, entirely correct. However, as Lenin pointed out, "To identify, even to compare the international situations of 1891 and 1914, is a height of unhistoricalness" (To Inessa Armand). This is because the world war that broke out in 1914 was a war between two imperialist blocs in the era of imperialism and both sides wanted to redivide colonies and enslave other nations; hence, it was a predatory war between plunderers scrambling for spoils. It got the ringleaders of the Second International nowhere to cite the example of 1891 as an apology for their opportunist slogan "defense of the fatherland" in the 1914 imperialist war.

Lenin denounced the social-chauvinists of the Second International for always trying to make Belgium a case in point to justify the stand of the Belgian Socialists and, by extension, their own, for Belgium, they said, was a neutral state under German attack. But Belgium, Lenin pointed out, went into the war also to preserve its colonial rule and exploitation; a neutral country in form, it actually belonged to the block of the Allied Powers of Britain, France and Russia. Besides, in Belgium, as in the other advanced European countries, there existed a situation of proletarian revolution. So the correct tactic for the Belgian Socialists to adopt was not the "defense of the fatherland" but the preparation and launching of a proletarian revolution to oppose and stop this imperialist war.

Lenin pointed out: "In the imperialist war of 1914-17, between two imperialist coalitions, we must be against 'defense of the fatherland,' since (1) imperialism is the eve of socialism, (2) imperialist war is a war of thieves over their booty, (3) in both coalitions there is an advanced proletariat, (4) in both a socialist revolution is ripe. Only for these reasons are we against 'defense of the fatherland,' only for these reasons!" (Ibid.).

These scientific analyses by Lenin defended and developed the Marxist principle of tactics, illustrated the proletariat's attitude and tactics in regard to war in the era of imperialism, when new changes had taken place in the international political forces and the conditions for socialist revolution were ripe. They thus repudiated the fallacies of the social-chauvinists of that time and drew a clear line of demarcation between Marxism-Leninism and revisionism of the Second International.

National Wars Still Possible in Europe
in the Era of Imperialism

While bringing to light as the main tendency the attempts of

the social-chauvinists of the Second International to justify
their treacherous activities on the plea of "defense of the fatherland," Lenin sternly criticized the "Left" opportunist views pro-
pounded by those within the Party such as G. L. Pyatakov and
N. I. Bukharin as well as certain muddled ideas found within
the ranks of the revolutionaries. At that time, Pyatakov, Bukharin and their like wanted to "go somewhat more to the Left"
on the question of defense of the fatherland. They went all out
to interfere with Lenin's correct line in regard to wars in the
era of imperialism and the tactics of proletarian struggle.
They either denied the possibility of a national war in the era
of imperialism, maintaining that under no circumstances
should the proletariat raise the slogan "defense of the fatherland," and even dismissing the examples of Marx's and Engels'
tactics as "worthless," or viewed imperialist war as something immutable, something which cannot be transformed, and
thus wrongly adopted a rigid, mechanical approach toward
Lenin's proletarian tactics in struggle.

Lenin maintained that an era is the sum total of multifarious
phenomena, both typical and atypical, big and small, including
the phenomena and wars occurring in both advanced and backward countries.

Imperialist war is a typical, but not the only, phenomenon
in the epoch of imperialism. In this epoch, wars of national
liberation fought by colonies or semicolonies are inevitable;
what is more, democratic or revolutionary national wars are
still possible in Europe. Lenin said: "This 'epoch'... by no
means precludes national wars on the part of, say, small (annexed or nationally oppressed) countries against the imperialist powers...." (The Junius Pamphlet). Lenin also believed
that under given conditions, even a highly industrialized country may fight a national war against annexation by an imperialist power, because "the characteristic feature of imperialism
is precisely that it strives to annex not only agrarian territories, but even most highly industrialized regions" (Imperialism, the Highest Stage of Capitalism). Therefore, he stated
in the strongest terms: "We are not at all against 'defense of

the fatherland' in general, not against 'defensive wars' in general. You will never find that nonsense in a single resolution (or in any of my articles). We are against defense of the fatherland and a defensive position in the imperialist war of 1914-16. ...But in the imperialist epoch there may be also 'just,' 'defensive,' revolutionary wars, namely (1) national, (2) civil, (3) socialist and such like" (To G. Y. Zinoviev).

Lenin also showed the possibility of an imperialist war being transformed into a national war under certain conditions, in the light of the law of the unity of opposites. He wrote in The Junius Pamphlet: "That all dividing lines, both in nature and society, are conventional and dynamic, and that every phenomenon might, under certain conditions, be transformed into its opposite, is, of course, a basic proposition of Marxist dialectics. A national war might be transformed into an imperialist war and vice versa."

In World War I, for instance, while pointing out that Belgium went into the war with the same imperialist aims and, therefore, showed its own imperialist rapacity, Lenin envisaged the possibility of transformation if German imperialism had occupied and annexed Belgium in that war and the Belgian people had risen in a national uprising to free themselves from German imperialist enslavement. In such a case, as far as Belgium was concerned, the imperialist war would have become a national war, and it would have been justifiable and correct for the Belgian Socialists to issue to call to "defend the fatherland." In such circumstances, the international proletariat should not refuse to support the uprising on the plea that the Belgian bourgeoisie possesses "the right to oppress foreign peoples." It must see the actual social content of the uprising as a struggle of an oppressed nation for liberation from the oppressor nation and lend support to it. "There is nothing Marxist" in any other stand the international proletariat might have taken (Lenin, The Discussion on Self-Determination Summed Up). Lenin also made another assumption: If Britain, France and other countries had declared war on Germany not for imperialist aims but for safeguarding Belgian neutrality in observance of the international treaty, then the Socialists would have been justified in siding with Belgium. As he pointed out in The Nascent Trend of Imperialist Economism, "We would be for the defense of Belgium (even by war) if this concrete war were different."

This was not all. Precisely in 1916 during World War I, Lenin, in keeping with historical dialectics and the law of uneven development of capitalism, took into full account the tortuousness and complexity of the historical course of transition from the capitalist system to socialism on a worldwide scale and predicted the possible outbreak of a great national war in Europe in the era of imperialism. He said: "If the European proletariat remains impotent, say, for twenty years; if the present war ends in victories like Napoleon's and in the subjugation of a number of viable national states; if the transition to socialism of non-European imperialism (primarily Japanese and American) is also held up for twenty years by a war between these two countries, for example, then a great national war in Europe would be possible" (The Junius Pamphlet). In his opinion, though such a thing sounded incredible at that time, if this tortuousness in history was not taken into due consideration, "it is undialectical, unscientific and theoretically wrong" (Ibid.).

The aforementioned teachings of Lenin's tell us many things. First, while opposing the opportunists' advocacy of defense of the fatherland in an imperialist war, Marxists should never hold that in the era of imperialism one can indiscriminately negate national wars and deny the justification of defense of the fatherland by the proletariat under certain conditions. On the contrary, "it is precisely in the 'era of imperialism,' which is the era of nascent social revolution, that the proletariat will today give especially vigorous support to any revolt of the annexed regions so that tomorrow, or simultaneously, it may attack the bourgeoisie of the 'great' power that is weakened by the revolt" (Lenin, The Discussion on Self-Determination Summed Up). Second, while criticizing the opportunists for distorting the examples of Marx's and Engels' tactics, Marxists must in no way consider these examples worthless in the era of imperialism. On the contrary, the proletariat, instead of throwing overboard these examples of tactics, must draw useful and most precious lessons from a concrete analysis. "Rejecting any examples of Marx's tactics" "would mean professing Marxism while abandoning it in practice" (Ibid.). Third, the proletariat should by no means stick to a hard and fast formula in regard to whether it should support wars breaking out in the era of imperialism and whether it should recognize the defense of the fatherland as justified, but should make a concrete analysis of each war, because "wars are a supremely varied, diverse, complex thing. One cannot approach them with a general pattern" (Lenin, To Inessa Armand).

During World War II, Stalin, basing himself on these principles of Lenin's, made a concrete analysis of the war and concluded that it was not a typical imperialist war like World War I; nor was it immutable and inconvertible. Before World War II broke out on the European continent, there were Japanese imperialist aggression against China, Italian imperialist aggression against Ethiopia (Abyssinia) and the German and Italian fascist war of aggression against the Spanish Republic. As far as the victims of aggression were concerned, the wars to defend their fatherland and resist Japanese, German and Italian fascist aggression were, from start to finish, just wars for national liberation. When the whole of Europe became engulfed in the war, especially after the attack on the Soviet Union by Hitlerite Germany, World War II became a war completely antifascist in nature, because the working class and patriotic forces in the countries subject to aggression took an active part in the antifascist war to defend their national independence. Stalin said: "The Second World War against the Axis powers, unlike the First World War, assumed from the very outset the character of an antifascist war, a war of liberation, one of the tasks of which was to restore democratic liberties" (Speech Delivered at an Election Meeting in the Stalin Election District, Moscow, February 9, 1946). It is evident that during

World War II the slogan "defense of the fatherland" was correct
for countries fighting against fascism. It is for this reason that
the Soviet Union formed an antifascist alliance with the United
States, Britain and France in a common effort to defeat the German, Italian and Japanese fascists in their war of aggression
to enslave the people of the whole world. The tactics and policies adopted by Stalin were undoubtedly in conformity with
Marxist-Leninist principles on tactics.

Be Well Prepared against War of Aggression

The foregoing analyses show the basic Marxist-Leninist position and approach to the question of wars between nations or
countries: we should discern the nature of a war by examining
what politics the war has continued; we should analyze the historical role of each war by examining it in the context of the
particular conditions of the time; we should decide our attitude
toward the war in a concrete way by proceeding from the general situation in the whole world and the interests of the proletariat as a whole and basing ourselves on such factors as the
balance of class forces, whether the conditions for revolution
are ripe or not and the prospects of the war and proletarian
revolution. Generally speaking, the proletariat must support
the colonies and semicolonies in their national wars against
imperialism; it must oppose imperialist wars both sides of
which are fighting over division of spoils and loot; it must aid
and support national wars waged by developed or undeveloped
countries against annexation and enslavement by imperialist
powers; it must resolutely support the socialist countries'
wars against imperialist and social-imperialist aggression
and subversion in order to defend the fruits of victory of socialism. Of course, there are many kinds of wars, and they
are extremely complicated. In dealing with a war, Marxist-
Leninists must never proceed from general principles and
draw conclusions accordingly, but should make a concrete
analysis of a specific war and, in the light of the development
and changes of the war, work out the correct tactics to follow.

Today, the world is still in the era of imperialism and proletarian revolution as Lenin observed. But great changes have
taken place in the balance of the world's political forces and
the international situation today as compared with the period
of World War I and the 1950s and 1960s after World War II.
The national-liberation movements are surging forward while
the colonial system disintegrates. As a result of the uneven
development of imperialism, the imperialist camp headed by
the United States has broken up. The Soviet Union, the world's
first socialist state, has degenerated into social-imperialism
after the usurpation of the supreme leadership of the Party
and state by the Khrushchev-Brezhnev clique, and the socialist camp is now no longer in existence. By dint of their enormously inflated economic and military strength, the Soviet
Union and the United States have become superpowers lording
it over all the other countries. The developed capitalist countries of Europe have been relegated to a position of secondary
importance. The vast upheavals and great divisions of the
1960s led to the formation of three worlds which are interconnected and mutually contradictory. Some developed countries in the Second World, though still oppressing and exploiting the Third World countries, are, in varying degrees, being
controlled, threatened and bullied by one or the other of the
two superpowers. Some East European countries have lived
under the heel of Soviet social-imperialism, which occupies
their land, tramples on their sovereign rights, and robs them
of their resources; in reality, they have become Moscow's dependencies. For these countries, the primary immediate task
at present is undoubtedly to fight for and defend national independence and free themselves from the clutches of Soviet
social-imperialism. In the case of the West European countries, they need to free themselves from the grip of the United
States and fight for "equal partnership"; at the same time,
they face the grave menace of an aggressive and expansionist
Soviet Union. Today, what bothers them is no longer the problem of redividing the world with the two superpowers but how
to safeguard their own independence and security. The same

is more or less true of Canada, Japan, Australia, New Zealand
and some other countries.

As everybody can see, the Soviet Union and the United States
are locked in a fierce struggle for world domination, and the
focus of their contention is Europe. As Soviet-U.S. rivalry
continues, a war is bound to break out some day. In fact, both
are making active preparations for a new world war. If the
war breaks out, Europe is certain to bear the brunt of the attack. Obviously, the new world war touched off by the fierce
contention between the two superpowers will take on some new
features different from those of World War I and World War II.
This world war, when it is between Soviet social-imperialism
and the Second World countries, will be a war between the aggressor and those fighting against aggression, between the an-
nexationist and those against annexation.

At present, Soviet social-imperialism, which is on the offensive in its contention with the United States, is making extensive war deployment in Europe. It keeps augmenting its military strength in Central Europe and is stepping up its pincers
drive against Western Europe from the northern and southern
flanks. The independence and security of the West European
countries are now being seriously threatened. If a new war
breaks out, they will inevitably become the first object of Soviet attack. If one looks at the way the Soviet Union pushes
around and oppresses its East European "allies," it is not difficult to imagine what things will be like once it has extended
its aggression to the West European countries. Therefore,
these countries will in fact be brought face to face with the
serious problem of defending their national independence. The
outlook is quite clear. If Soviet social-imperialism imposes a
war of aggression on the developed countries in Europe, won't
the situation be like what Lenin foresaw in 1916? Isn't it possible that many European nation-states of great vitality will
get into the clutches of the new tsars in the Kremlin and be
subjected to enslavement? Owing to, among other things, the
spread of revisionist ideas and the split within the working
class itself, the proletariat in the developed European countries

for the time being does not in fact have a revolutionary situation in which it can effect a direct seizure of political power. In these circumstances, is it not entirely conceivable and inevitable that a great national war as envisaged by Lenin will take place in Europe, a war that is progressive in nature? Don't the examples of Engels' tactics applied in 1891 still have a great immediate significance today?

Hence, it is absolutely necessary and correct for the people of the Second World countries, faced as they are today with the threat of bullying, oppression and aggression by Soviet social-imperialism, to expose thoroughly the Kremlin's war machinations, oppose appeasement and be well prepared against a war of aggression. Should the war break out, the proletarians of these countries should come to the forefront of a national war and fight for the survival and independence of their nations. This is completely in accord with the aforesaid Marxist principle of tactics advanced by Marx and Engels and developed by Lenin, Stalin and Chairman Mao. It is also in conformity with the fundamental interests of the people of both the Second World countries and the world as a whole.

SOVIET SOCIAL-IMPERIALISTS COVER SOUTHEAST ASIA: THE "ASIAN COLLECTIVE SECURITY SYSTEM" IS A PRETEXT FOR EXPANSION*   5

Hsinhua Correspondent

Moscow has been working overtime to tout its "Asian collective security system" in Southeast Asia. Now that the United States has readjusted its strategy in Asia following its defeat in, and withdrawal from, Indo-China, the Soviet Union is making a fresh attempt to step into the shoes of the United States and establish hegemony in Southeast Asia.

Soviet envoys in Southeast Asian countries have been particularly profuse these days in talking about the benefit of having an "Asian collective security system." No less enthusiastic are Soviet newspapers and Radio Moscow. This so-called "security system," which has long been rejected by the Southeast Asian countries, would, according to Soviet propaganda, turn Southeast Asia into "a region of lasting peace." A TASS commentary on July 21 had the effrontery to describe "the European security conference" as an "example for other parts of the world, including Asia." It made known Moscow's intention to cash in on the Helsinki conference to peddle so-called "collective security on the Asian continent." Particularly noteworthy is the fact that Moscow has linked the "Asian collective security system" with

---

*From Peking Review, No. 33 (August 15, 1975), 20-21.

the proposal for the neutralization of Southeast Asia put forward by the five member countries of the Association of Southeast Asian Nations (ASEAN). The attempt to confuse fish
eyes with pearls. The commentary alleged that the two
"have many points in common with regard to the objective of
safeguarding the security of Asia" and are even "consonant
with" each other. After the Indo-China war, it asserted, acceptance of the "Asian collective security system" is "particularly
realistic" and "urgent."

What "common points" and "consonance" are there between
the Soviet "Asian collective security system" and the proposal
for the neutralization of Southeast Asia? A cursory comparison
and analysis of the two will show up Moscow's sinister designs
on Southeast Asia.

As is well known, the proposal for the neutralization of Southeast Asia was formally tabled at the ASEAN foreign ministers' meeting in Kuala Lumpur in 1971. The Kuala Lumpur
Declaration signed then by the foreign ministers of Malaysia,
the Philippines, Thailand, Singapore, and Indonesia clearly
states that the five countries are determined to make Southeast
Asia "a zone of peace, freedom, and neutrality, free from any
form or manner of interference by outside powers." This has
been reaffirmed time and again by leaders of the five countries
who went on record to make the whole of Southeast Asia "a region free from the contention and conflicts of all big powers,"
to put "an end to foreign interference in our internal affairs,"
and to "establish regional cooperation and build a new Southeast
Asia free from foreign domination and influence." Over the
years, the five ASEAN countries, intent on speeding up the
neutralization of Southeast Asia, have forged closer relations
among themselves, strengthened their economic cooperation,
and actively developed relations of friendship and cooperation
with other Third World countries. With them, they pressed forward their just struggle to oppose superpower hegemonism and
power politics and safeguard their national independence, sovereignty, and economic rights and interests. This shows that
the proposal for a zone of neutrality in Southeast Asia reflects

the desire of countries and people in the region to rid themselves of superpower interference and control and thus has
won the sympathy and support of many Third World countries.

The "Asian collective security system" dished up by the Soviet social-imperialists under the signboard of "peace" and
"security" is designed to serve nothing but the Kremlin's policies of aggression and expansion. It is contrived for the purpose
of contending with the United States for hegemony in Asia, dividing the Asian countries, and bringing small and medium-
sized Asian countries into their sphere of influence. Lenin said,
"We judge a person not by what he says or thinks of himself,
but by his actions" (Materialism and Empirio-Criticism). Now
let us see some of these Soviet actions, see how the Soviet Union
has threatened and undermined the independence and sovereignty of countries in Southeast Asia.

For years, the Soviet social-imperialists have been scheming
to secure military bases in Southeast Asia. Motivated by their
quest for sea supremacy, they have sent large numbers of warships to sail between the Pacific and the Indian Ocean in a show
of force which threatens the peace and security of the Southeast
Asian countries. Back in 1969, Malaysia and Indonesia declared
a twelve-nautical-mile territorial water limit to ensure their
sovereignty over the Strait of Malacca. In 1971, the governments of Malaysia, Indonesia, and Singapore together issued a
statement declaring joint control of the Malacca and Singapore
Straits. However, ignoring the strait countries' sovereignty,
the Soviet Union obstinately insisted on the right of "free passage" for its warships through the Strait of Malacca. And on
many occasions Soviet vessels did sail through the Strait of
Malacca without prior permission, thus turning the territorial
waters of the strait countries into the high seas. This lays bare
Moscow's hegemonic stand toward these countries.

To achieve its objective of expansion and penetration, the Soviet Union has been stepping up its espionage activities in the
Southeast Asian countries too. Here it collected political, economic, and military information, groomed pro-Soviet forces,
and interfered in the internal affairs of these countries. Official

Thai sources disclosed that the number of Soviet spies in Thailand has more than trebled since the U.S. defeat in Indo-China. Soviet spy ships in various guises make a point of intruding into the territorial waters of Southeast Asian countries to gather intelligence. In the first half of this year alone, there were three illegal Soviet intrusions into Indonesian territorial waters. The military commander of the Nusatenggara Region was compelled to bar all Soviet crews from going ashore and to take measures against their illegal activities.

Moscow has all along tried to sabotage the proposal for the neutralization of Southeast Asia. In 1971, shortly after it was signed by the five ASEAN foreign ministers, the Kuala Lumpur Declaration was slandered and attacked by the Soviet Union which asserted that the proposal "provides no answer to the problem of security of that continent" and that turning this area into a zone of peace and neutrality "cannot be implemented without a reliable system of guarantees." The China Press, a Malaysian paper, pointed out penetratingly that the Soviet Union's derisive interpretation of the proposal as "a battle on paper" "shows that in the mind of the Soviet Union, there is no place for any proposal from another nation or group of nations except 'Brezhnevism.'"

But now Moscow has changed its tune, chanting that the neutralization proposal is "consonant" with its "Asian collective security system." This is really ridiculous.

The proposal for the neutralization of Southeast Asia and the "Asian collective security system" are two diametrically opposed ideas. There are no "common points" or "consonance" between them. The Soviet Union's design is, in its own words, to have the neutralization proposal "included in the framework of the idea of an Asian collective security system." In fact, it is trying to bring Southeast Asian countries into the orbit of the Soviet "Asian collective security system."

Today, the growing awakening of the Southeast Asian peoples has enabled them to see more clearly than ever that the bitter rivalry between the two superpowers, the Soviet Union and the United States, especially the intensifying Soviet expansion and penetration in Southeast Asia, is the source of turbulence in the region. In a recent issue, the Thai weekly Mahanakon wrote editorially, "The fact that Thailand demands a U.S. pull-out does not mean that she will open her door to the Soviet security system." The Brezhnev clique "really underrated the wisdom of the Asian people when it tried to use its 'Asian collective security system' as bait to lure Asian countries into the Soviet trap." A Philippine paper, The Orient News, said: "The Kremlin's sinister designs cannot be covered up for good. Public opinion in Asia has seen through ever more clearly the essence of the 'Asian collective security system.'"

A Malaysian paper, Kuang Hua Yit Pao, said editorially that the Soviet Union's real aim in trying to set up an "Asian collective security system" to "to achieve its design of contending with the other superpower for hegemony in Asia."

Countries in Southeast Asia have long discerned Soviet social-imperialism's machinations to supplant U.S. imperialism and establish hegemony in Southeast Asia. They are keeping their vigilance sharp. They are determined to prevent a situation in which the tiger is let in through the back door while the wolf is repulsed at the front gate.

SOVIET-U.S. BEHIND-THE-SCENES DEALING
OVER THE INDIAN OCEAN*

6

Hsinhua Correspondent

The Soviet Union and the United States are making a deal
on the Indian Ocean behind the backs of the countries in that
region. Twice this year they had talks, first in Moscow in
June and then in Washington in September, and now it is revealed that the two are going to have a third round of talks
this month with Berne, Switzerland, as the venue to restrict
their naval activities in that ocean.

Back in 1971, at its Twenty-sixth Session, the U.N. General
Assembly adopted a resolution called the Declaration of the
Indian Ocean as a Zone of Peace by sixty-one votes, the majority of these being cast by Third World countries. The resolution stipulated "eliminating from the Indian Ocean all bases,
military installations, logistical supply facilities, the disposition of nuclear weapons and weapons of mass destruction and
any manifestation of great-power military presence in the
Indian Ocean conceived in the context of great-power rivalry."
This resolution was submitted in view of the fact that contention between the two superpowers was sharpening in that ocean.
In August last year, the Fifth Nonaligned Summit Conference
adopted a political declaration calling on nonaligned states in
the Indian Ocean region and other littoral and hinterland states
of the ocean to convene a conference to discuss the implementation of the U.N. General Assembly resolution on the Indian
Ocean peace zone. On November 18, this year, the First Committee of the U.N. General Assembly also passed a resolution

*From Peking Review, No. 50 (December 9, 1977), 24-25.

224

urging the big powers to join the countries in the Indian Ocean region in implementing the above resolution.

However, disregarding the aspirations of the Third World countries, the two superpowers held talks on the Indian Ocean without consulting the states in the region. This new tactic employed by the Soviet and U.S. hegemonists in their intensified contention in that ocean stands in direct opposition to the U.N. resolution on the Indian Ocean as a peace zone.

It is obvious to all that the two superpowers are the main obstacle to the establishment of the peace zone. Their attitude is sharply opposed to the proposal of the Third World countries. The Soviets mouth "sympathy" for the proposal while grossly undermining it in practice. In his speech at the U.N. General Assembly on September 27, A. A. Gromyko said that the fundamental prerequisite for the declaration of the Indian Ocean as a zone of peace is dismantlement of the existing foreign military bases in the region and forbiddance to build new ones. These grandiose words do not bear careful scrutiny. First, the Soviet Union makes no mention of eliminating foreign military presence, which means that its naval squadron regularly stationed there will hang on and that its "military presence" will continue to expand and no one can check it. Second, by dismantling "existing foreign military bases" the Soviets refer only to U.S. bases and not their own de facto bases. They have all along denied their presence, and according to their logic there is no question of dismantling. Third, the so-called "no new military bases should be established" is sheer hypocrisy. If the Soviet Union really has no such intention in the Indian Ocean, why did it recently send "high-ranking diplomats," "a fishery delegation," "TASS correspondents" and a "scientific survey ship" to the Maldives and request the lease, reportedly at a huge price, of the base on Gan Island? These facts completely lay bare Moscow's hypocritical "sympathy" for setting up the Indian Ocean peace zone and show that it is the most dangerous enemy in undermining security in the region.

The U.S. formula for the December talks in Berne, as reported, is to "stabilize" the balance of naval strength of both parties in the Indian Ocean. This is part of the "package deal" the United States recently proposed to the Soviet Union. To "stabilize" the balance of military strength of the two sides in the Indian Ocean — what does it mean? It means that the United States will not demand the removal of the Soviet military presence and military bases and, of course, the United States expects it will not be asked to do so either. This is a hoax the two are playing at "balance of strength." However, no matter what the "balance of strength" between the two is, the security of the people in the Indian Ocean region will continue to be seriously menaced.

Soviet-U.S. contention for hegemony in the Indian Ocean is of major strategic significance to their overall contention for world hegemony. For either of them, the negotiations for limiting their naval strength in the Indian Ocean are merely a device to tie the other's hands and gain supremacy for itself in the Indian Ocean. This has nothing to do at all with establishing the Indian Ocean peace zone and is diametrically opposed to the security of the people living in the region.

Not long ago, the Somali government forced the Soviet Union to remove all its military installations and military experts on Somali territory and territorial waters. This is an indication of the new awakening of the people in the Indian Ocean region. The establishment of the Indian Ocean peace zone depends on the united strength of the Third World countries which have become the main force in the struggle against imperialism, colonialism and hegemonism. Gone are the days when a few imperialist powers could, behind closed doors, mark out spheres of influence, carve up weak or small countries or violate their interests. The Soviet Union and the United States, both non-Indian Ocean countries, can never fool anyone; nor can they succeed in making shady deals on the Indian Ocean behind the backs of the Third World countries in the region. As the Iranian paper Tehran Journal pointed out: "From the start, it was quite obvious to political analysts that negotiations between the two superpowers on the future of Indian Ocean security and stability would ultimately prove to be a classic case of 'preposterous diplomacy.'"

THE MIDDLE EAST: A NEW ROUND OF SOVIET-U.S. CONTENTION* 7

Peking Review

Starting anew, Washington is trying to continue its exclusive role in a "peaceful solution" to the Middle East issue. Moscow, on the other hand, has been overhauling its tactics in an effort to snatch the initiative from its opponent, once again showing its true features of sham support but real betrayal in its relations with the Arab people.

A new round of contention for hegemony in the Middle East between the two superpowers, the Soviet Union and the United States, is on.

Since the end of the October 1973 Middle East war, the two have been trying hard to seize the initiative for a so-called "peaceful solution" to the Middle East question, one seeking its "step-by-step solution" and the other favoring its Geneva Conference approach. Each has schemed to keep the other out and augment its own influence in the region.

Immediately after Kissinger's "shuttle diplomacy" flop last March, Washington made it clear that it would "reassess" its Middle East policy, which was meant, in actual fact, to urge the parties concerned to reconsider their policies, thus enabling the United States to start afresh, continue to have an exclusive

---

*From Peking Review, No. 28 (July 11, 1975), 15-16.

role in a "peaceful solution" in the Middle East, and widen its influence there.

Following its defeat in Indochina, the United States, with its hands now free, has managed to strengthen its position in its rivalry with the Soviet Union in both Europe and the Middle East. Early in June, U.S. President Ford personally held talks with Egyptian President Sadat in Salzburg, Austria. Back in Washington, Ford and Kissinger talked with Israeli Prime Minister Rabin and also Syrian Vice-Premier and Foreign Minister Khaddam. The United States, Ford announced, would oppose any stagnation or stalemate in the Middle East situation. Referring at a press conference to the chances for resumption of Egyptian-Israeli negotiations, Kissinger said, "We will support whichever approach seems most promising," and "a trip (by himself to the area) is not excluded."

The Soviet Union too has overhauled its tactics in the light of U.S. activities. On the one hand, it has launched large-scale diplomatic campaigns to try to seize the initiative for a "peaceful solution" to the Middle East question. On the other, it is energetically seeking new "footings" in Arab countries to bolster its position in the rivalry with the United States.

Since April, leaders of Iraq, Syria, Egypt, and the Palestine Liberation Organization (P.L.O.) have been invited to visit Moscow. Using both stick and carrot, Moscow has tried hard to impose its will on others so as to have more say on the Middle East question. In addition, it has hatched schemes in dealings with Israel at meetings in several places. It was reported that two Soviet "emissaries" who secretly visited Israel in April said the Soviet Union would not insist on the participation of the P.L.O. as an independent delegation at the Geneva Conference, provided Israel would agree to the inclusion of the P.L.O. representatives in the Syrian, Jordanian, or Arab League delegations. As the Times of London put it, the Soviet envoys' mission was to urge the Israeli leaders to "renounce the United States' step-by-step approach to a Middle East settlement." Moscow, moreover, repeatedly stresses the guarantee of Israel's existence and security. Arab public opinion has

pointed out that it is the Palestinian and other Arab people, not
the Israelis, whose existence and security must be guaranteed
and this can only be the result of negotiations, never the prerequisite. The treacherous nature of the Soviet statement is
all the more evident, considering the fact that large areas of
Arab territory are under Israeli occupation and the Palestinian
people are to this day still deprived of their rights. This new
disclosure of the Soviet Union's scheme of sham support but
real betrayal of the Arab people in general and the Palestinian
people in particular has opened their eyes even wider. Moscow
thus failed to achieve its anticipated objectives in the secret
talks with Israel.

The men in the Kremlin have lately stopped their high-
sounding publicity on the Geneva Conference. Earlier they
were all for the conference working out a "complete solution"
to the Middle East question as a counter to U.S. "quiet diplomacy" and the "step-by-step solution," proclaiming that the
conference was the "only way" and the "best place" for an
"overall solution" of the Middle East question. In February,
Gromyko hastened to the Middle East before Kissinger got
there, insisting on the "immediate" reopening of the Geneva
Conference "no later than the end of February or the beginning
of March in any case." But when Kissinger's "shuttle diplomacy" failed, Moscow suddenly began stressing the need for
"serious preparation" for the conference and lately has dropped
it altogether. The Western press points out that Moscow, not
wishing to shoulder "responsibility" in case of failure at the
Geneva Conference, is therefore shelving "plans for Middle
East parleys." This behavior on the part of the rulers in the
Kremlin again shows that their clamor for the Geneva Conference was aimed only at foiling Kissinger's "step-by-step solution." What they are interested in is not a "solution" to the
Middle East problem but some cheap propaganda to swindle the
Arab people.

The Soviet Union has now changed to a flank attack. This is
because it hopes to turn the tables in its rivalry with the United
States for a "peaceful settlement" of the Middle East problem

and at the same time meet the needs of its contention with the United States in Europe and the Mediterranean. Kosygin's visit to northern Africa in May was one noteworthy step to apply this strategy. A Western news agency pointed out that it represented "a major development" in Moscow's Mediterranean and Middle East policy and that it indicated the Kremlin's intention to "seek new friends among the Mediterranean and Arab countries, especially in view of Egyptian President Anwar el Sadat's evident unwillingness to be absorbed into the Soviet sphere of influence." A Malaysian paper noted that this Soviet move was an attempt to "establish a military base" in the strategic Mediterranean countries. "It not only extends the Soviet influence in the Middle East, but also is a great help to its naval tactics around the world." The same paper pointed out that another Soviet "intention" was to "sow dissension among the Arab countries."

At present, both Moscow and Washington are studying the situation closely, putting out feelers everywhere and thinking of what to do in a new and even fiercer round of contention. As a result of the intensified contention between the two superpowers, the Middle East situation has become more tense and unstable.

But the fact is that neither the "reassessment" advertised by Washington nor the Geneva Conference prated by Moscow, neither the "quiet diplomacy" and "step-by-step solution" nor the so-called "overall solution" at the Geneva Conference can really solve the Middle East problem. Soviet and U.S. aggression and contention in the Middle East have enabled the Arab people to see more clearly the real hegemonic features of the two superpowers, especially that superpower which claims to be their "natural ally." The key to the complete solution of the Middle East problem rests on the fighting unity of the Arab people. As Moscow and Washington escalate their contention in the Middle East, the Arab people will launch their struggle against hegemonism on an ever-larger scale.

THE MIDDLE EAST: SOVIET VEXATION*

8

Hsinhua Correspondent

After Egyptian President Anwar Sadat took the peace initiative last November, the Soviet Union galvanized its propaganda machine to set up a barrage against Egypt. The Kremlin has directly commanded actions to split the Arab ranks and disrupt Arab unity. Brezhnev personally came out with a statement on February 21, saying, "The imperialists strive to split the national-liberation movement, to find in its ranks conciliators and capitulators." Directing the spearhead of his attack at Egypt, he slandered the Egyptian leadership as having "embarked on the road of separate deals with Israel."

One would like to ask: When a leader of a sovereign Arab state took the initiative, approved by his people as a due move, to preserve national independence and state sovereignty and throw off foreign interference, and in the negotiations with Israel, stuck to the just stand calling for recovery of the lost Arab territories and the restoration to the Palestinian people of their national rights and for an all-round solution, how could he have offended the Soviet Union which has nothing to do with the Middle East?

To this, the Egyptian paper Al Akhbar gave the correct answer in an editorial stating, "Brezhnev's anger and criticism are understandable, for Egypt has rejected its patronage and has freed her will from Soviet domination and ambitions. It is

*From Peking Review, No. 11 (March 17, 1978), 43-44

231

quite natural that the Soviet leaders should vent their wrath on
Egypt and her policy."

This is exactly how things stand. Egypt, the Sudan and Somalia have one after another seen through Soviet ambitions
and freed their will from their influence. Especially Egypt,
having suffered with surfeit at the hands of social-imperialism,
has taken four steps against hegemonism during the past six
years. In 1972, it expelled the Soviet military personnel as the
first step to get rid of Soviet shackles. The next year, going
against the Soviet will, it launched the October War and won
an important victory over the Israeli aggressors. In 1976, it
abrogated the Egyptian-Soviet treaty of "friendship and cooperation" and denied the Soviet Union the right to use its port
facilities. Last year, President Sadat held direct negotiations
with Israel in an effort to make a comparatively thorough
break with Soviet control over the Middle East peace talks.
In a certain sense, this also weakened U.S. manipulation of the
talks. Sadat's move has aroused anxiety on the part of both
superpowers, especially the Soviet Union.

The Middle East is strategically important for Soviet contention with the other superpower for world domination. Before 1972, the Soviet Union kept a firm grip on the Arab countries while conniving at Israel in its aggression, thus exerting
an incalculable influence on war and peace in the Middle East.
But its favorable position did not last long. With the expulsion
of nearly 20,000 Soviet military personnel from Egypt, it lost
its control over the Middle East situation. And this has become a source of vexation for makers of the policy of aggression in the Kremlin. Furthermore, Moscow's worries were
increased after the October Middle East War, when the United
States assumed the role of special mediator between the Arab
states and Israel, basically excluding the Soviet Union from
the Middle East peace talks. Last October 1, the Soviet Union
and the United States made a bargain. They issued a joint
declaration on the Middle East, proposing the reconvening of
the Geneva Conference before the end of the year, with both
of them as cochairmen. The Soviet Union imagined that this

could bring to an end the days when it was barred from inter-
fering in the Middle East peace talks. It never occurred to
Soviet rulers that all their schemes would come to naught as
a result of President Sadat's move of holding direct negotiations with Israel.

Brezhnev complained that because of the Egyptian leader's
action, "the cause of the Middle East settlement has been
pushed back." He called for "return of the cause of the settlement to the channel of the Geneva Conference," saying this
would "make a big contribution to the cause of improving the
international climate."

Pravda commented: "The situation is far more complicated
than that followed publication of the joint Soviet-U.S. statement
on the Near East when real hope for a package solution within
the framework of the Geneva Conference has emerged."

An article by the editorial board of the weekly New Times
said that it is "not by a separate deal but through the Geneva
Conference" that "a just and lasting peace in the Near East"
can be reached.

In a word, what Moscow wants is to rush to Geneva. The
Soviet leadership and their publications really have a "Geneva
Conference craze." Naturally, what they are enamored with
is not a Middle East settlement but a scheme to subordinate
Middle East developments to the requirements of their contention with the United States and to go on meddling with a
free hand. That is to say, quoting Pravda, "no one can...
efface it [the Soviet Union's role] in this [Middle East] as in
any other area of the world."

That is what vexes the Soviet Union. How to reply to Soviet
fault-finding and vexation? The Egyptian paper Al Akhbar put
it well when it said: "There are sovereign nations and states
which are exclusively entitled to adopt their own policy, decide their own fate and make their own history, in spite of the
will of Moscow rulers." "Further lessons on the meaning of
independence and sovereignty will be taught to the Kremlin
leaders by nations in the area."

People's Daily

The development of the Angolan situation has drawn close attention and common concern all over the world. Current events
there, against the background of fierce rivalry between the two
superpowers, make up a serious incident unprecedented in the
African national liberation movement's postwar history. Its se-
riousness lies above all in the fact that the superpower which
flaunts the label of socialism has crossed seas and oceans and,
through naked armed intervention, has thrown a young nation in
southern Africa into a state of division and civil war immediately after it had attained independence. This is a big exposure
of the policy of colonial expansion pushed by the Soviet revisionists and new evidence of the ambitious new czars' feverish bid
for world hegemony.

In the past ten years and more, the Soviet revisionists have
assumed an offensive posture, carrying out one act of aggression and expansion abroad after another: They wormed their
way into the Middle East, invaded and occupied Czechoslovakia
in Eastern Europe by armed force, stirred up conflicts in the
South Asian subcontinent, subsequently thrust themselves into
Portugal in Southern Europe, and have now laid hands on Angola

---

*"Su-hsiu chih-min k'uo-ch'ung ti ta pao-lu." Jen-min jih-
pao [People's Daily], editorial, February 4, 1976, p. 1. This
translation is taken from Peking Review, No. 6 (February 6,
1976), 8-9.

in Africa. Facts speak louder than words. The Soviet social-imperialists have fully revealed their reactionary and aggressive nature.

The unbridled Soviet intervention and aggression in Angola is most shocking in its viciousness of tactics, sinister designs, and arrogance. What the Soviet revisionists have done in Angola greatly widens one's horizon as to what the Moscow brand of neocolonialism is.

First, under the signboard of "supporting the national liberation movement," they have sown dissension among the Angolan liberation organizations and split them in order to fish in troubled waters. They have lauded one such organization to the skies and trampled underfoot the other two. They time and again have undermined the joint agreements and ceasefire agreements among the three liberation organizations, and they alone have wrecked the transitional government which was a symbol of Angolan national unity. They have incessantly added fuel to the fratricidal civil war. The Soviet revisionists have really outdone the old-line colonialists in their vicious tactics of making Angolans fight Angolans.

Second, in the name of the "internationalist duty" of a "socialist country," the Soviet revisionists not only provide guns, but also men, to take part directly in the massacre. They have sent some 1,000 military personnel to Angola as advisers and egged on Cuba to dispatch over 10,000 troops there. They have shipped to Angola large amounts of arms, everything from rifles, rockets and armored cars to fighter planes. They have established a costly sea and airborne supply line of over 10,000 kilometers across the oceans for shipments of military personnel and arms. They have even sent warships to the West African and Angolan coasts to make armed threats. All this brings the vicious features of the Soviet revisionists as a conqueror into the broad daylight.

Third, under the cloak of a "natural ally," they issue orders to African countries, threaten and intimidate them, and unscrupulously sabotage African unity. On the Angolan question, they openly tried to coerce the Organization of African Unity into

following their baton, using power politics against the independent African states. They threw their weight about and became
overbearing. Time and again they have ordered heads of some
sovereign African states about and recriminated those who refused to obey and labeled them "imperialist lackeys." They
have inherited and developed the tyranny of the old-line colonialists who lorded it over the African people for centuries.

The Soviet social-imperialists have all along flaunted the
banner of socialism. On the pretext of opposing imperialism
and colonialism and supporting the national liberation movements and revolutionary struggles, they stretch their tentacles
into other countries to carry out colonialist domination and exploitation. By forming military blocs, concluding friendship and
cooperation treaties and making great use of economic and military "aid," they try hard to control and enslave not only the
Third World but also the Second World countries. And when
they fail to achieve their ends by "peaceful" means, they resort
to military coup d'état, subversion, and even direct armed intervention and aggression in these countries.

No excuse, however cleverly concocted, can cover up the ugly
role played by the Soviet revisionists in Angola, a role that has
both the old-line colonialists' brutality and the neocolonialists'
cunning.

Fulfillment of "internationalist duties" by a "socialist country"! When the Algerian people fought for national independence,
the Soviet revisionists stood by with folded arms, saying that
they would not interfere in another country's "internal affairs."
At the crucial juncture of the Egyptian people's war against aggression, they stopped arms supplies to get a stranglehold on
them. When the Cambodian people waged a punitive war against
the Lon Nol clique, they sided with the traitors. Is your criminal record of being betrayers of internationalism still not long
enough? Take the case of Angola. You never extended any real
support to the Angolan people during their protracted and arduous struggle to free themselves from the Portuguese colonial
yoke, but right after the collapse of the old colonial rule and the
attainment of independence by the Angolan people, you become

most "generous" by sending a great amount of lethal weapons
of the latest type to stir up and aggravate the civil war. Can a
real socialist country do a thing like this? This conduct of the
Soviet revisionists proves exactly that like Hitler years ago,
they are a gang of "brazen imperialists and arrant reactionaries" "using the flag of...'socialism' to cover up their predatory imperialist nature" (Stalin, Twenty-fourth Anniversary of
the Great October Socialist Revolution).

"Defense" of Angola's "sovereignty, independence, and territorial integrity"! It is known to all that the three Angolan liberation organizations reached an agreement in early 1975 and
forced the Portuguese authorities to recognize the Angolan people's right to independence. If there had been no meddling by
the Soviet revisionists, by last November Angola would have
become a country with "sovereignty, independence, and territorial integrity" standing erect on the African continent. Now,
styling themselves overlord in Angola, the Soviet revisionists
pay no heed to the wishes and interests of the Angolan people,
while their troops and the troops sent under their instigation
run amuck and bring disaster to the land of Angola. It is precisely the Soviet revisionist interventionists who have crudely
trampled on the sovereignty of Angola, seriously threatened its
independence and unscrupulously violated its territorial integrity. It is obviously futile for the Soviet revisionists to justify
their armed intervention in Angola by so-called opposition to
South African intrusion. It is well known that the Soviet social-
imperialist intervention antedated South African authorities'
meddling. It was the truculent Soviet intervention that provided
South Africa with the opportunity to stir up trouble in Angola.
Messrs. Soviet revisionists, as an old Russian maxim goes:
"Don't put the plough before the cow." Both you and the South
African racist regime are the deadly enemy of the Angolan and
African people.

The Soviet revisionists have repeatedly claimed they "do not
seek anything in Angola — either economic, military, or other
gain." This is a typical self-exposing lie. In fact, Soviet social-
imperialism has long coveted Angola, "the jewel of Africa," and

set its mind on awaiting an opportunity to replace Portuguese colonialist rule there. For a long time, the Soviet propaganda machine has openly talked of "the enviable natural resources in Angola" and its "extremely important strategic position." That the Soviet revisionists have got their hands on Angola regardless of all consequences is due not only to Angola's abundant mineral deposits, including both oil and diamonds, but also to the need in their counterrevolutionary global strategy of seeking world hegemony. Their attempt to seize Luanda and Lobito and other naval and air bases in Angola is to threaten from the east and the south the sea passage of the United States and West European countries for oil shipment and to dominate the Southern Atlantic. Furthermore, they also intend to make Angola a springboard for expansion in central and southern Africa and further undermine the national liberation movements in all southern Africa and grab the region's strategic resources. It is very clear that their barefaced intervention in Angola is an important move for the seizure of strategic areas and for their intensified strategic disposition in the interest of their contention with the United States for world hegemony.

True, the situation in Angola is complicated, and there are all sorts of contradictions and struggles. But once the meddling and intervention by this superpower, the Soviet Union, are done away with, it would not be difficult to bring about a proper settlement of the other contradictions, including the differences among the different factions in Angola and among the African countries. On the contrary, if the Soviet revisionists are allowed to do evil in Angola and realize their designs, it is hard to say that there will not be a second or even a third Angola. Until the Soviet revisionist intervention is done away with, there can be no peace or tranquillity in Angola and in the continent of Africa. This truth is becoming clearer and clearer.

All over the continent of Africa today, the main stream of the united struggle against imperialism, colonialism, and hegemonism is on the rise, while the wicked Soviet design to undermine Angola's national independence and Africa's militant unity is doomed to ignominious failure. The Angolan people who have just thrown off the nearly five-century-old Portuguese colonialist rule are capable of solving their own problems and building up an independent, unified, nationally united new Angola. The road to this goal is by no means smooth or easy, but its realization is inevitable and beyond doubt. Similarly, the great African people who have stood up will certainly do away with superpower aggression and interference, close their ranks, heighten their vigilance, distinguish the true from the false and friend from foe, and push the struggle against imperialism, colonialism, hegemonism, white racism, and Zionism ahead to a new stage.

SOVIET MILITARY INTERVENTION PROVOKES WORLD INDIGNATION*

10

Horn of Africa

Peking Review

Fierce contention between the two hegemonic powers, and especially Soviet intervention and instigation, has steadily aggravated the dispute between Ethiopia and Somalia over Ogaden. Lately, with a massive flow of Soviet arms and men into the Horn of Africa, the flames of war in this region are spreading, engulfing the Horn of Africa in mounting tension.

Flames of War in Ogaden

To date, Ethiopia has dispatched 40,000 men of its regular forces, plus 80,000 militiamen, to the Ogaden region, while the Somalia-backed Western Somali Liberation Front has 30,000 to 40,000 troops there. Somalia's own regular troops too have joined in the fighting. As announced on February 6 by Fikre Selassie Wogderess, Secretary General of the Ethiopian Provisional Military Administrative Council, Ethiopian troops have been closing on Ogaden in attacks from all directions. It is reported that since early February, Ethiopian troops have launched offensives and pushed their positions forward by more than 100 kilometers along the railway line linking Addis Ababa and Djibouti, right up to the town of Adi Galla on the line.

A communiqué of the Western Somali Liberation Front dated February 8 said that Soviets and Dubans had a part in the

*From <u>Peking Review</u>, No. 8 (February 24, 1978), 20-22.

240

Ethiopian counteroffensive. It has been disclosed that no less
than 3,000 Cubans and over 1,000 Soviet personnel have been
involved in both air and ground operations in the Horn of Africa.
In addition, several thousand more Cuban soldiers on board
Soviet warships cruising along the Red Sea coast are ready to
land at a moment's notice.

Historical Background

The Ogaden dispute between Ethiopia and Somalia is an issue
left over from the last century by the colonialists of the West.
Somalia stands for national self-determination by the Somalis
living in the region and gives support to the Western Somali
Liberation Front founded in Ogaden in 1963 for national self-
determination and independence. Ethiopia maintains that Ogaden is a part of Ethiopian territory.

Many African countries, as well as the Organization of African Unity [OAU], hold that the two countries concerned should
settle their dispute through peaceful negotiations or through
OAU mediation and have worked for this accordingly. Then
there is the Soviet Union, which, prompted by its hegemonic
drive for control of the strategic Horn of Africa and taking
advantage of the dispute, does its best to sow discord between
the two countries and fish in troubled waters. At first, it waved
the banner of "assistance" and "support" in an attempt to turn
Somalia into a bridgehead for expansion in the Horn of Africa
and the Indian Ocean. Later on, as U.S. military presence
there was ousted, it hurriedly elbowed its way through to Ethiopia to fill the "vacuum," while switching its "support" to the
country with still greater fervor. Its large shipments of arms
and men to the Horn of Africa have exacerbated the Ethiopian-
Somali dispute, creating a situation where both sides are using
Soviet arms in the hassle.

"Russians, Go Home!"

Massive military intervention by the Soviet Union and Cuba

in the Horn of Africa has been strongly denounced by the Somali side. On February 12, in Mogadishu, the Somali capital, 50,000 people rallied and demonstrated, shouting "Russians, Go Home!" Some of the placards carried by the demonstrators read: "Down with social-imperialism!" "Down with the Soviet Union!" and "The peace-loving people of the world must know the Soviet Union and Cuba are aggressors!"

1. THE YEMEN ARAB REPUBLIC 2. THE PEOPLE'S DEMOCRATIC REPUBLIC OF YEMEN 3. OMAN

The mass rally was held in the wake of an announcement made earlier on the morning of the same day about the decisions of the Central Committee of the Somali Revolutionary Socialist Party, which met on February 8 and 9. Somalia, the decisions said, has decided to carry out nationwide general mobilization and institute a state of emergency for resisting the naked invasion masterminded by the Soviet Union. The decisions also demanded a cease-fire and withdrawal of foreign troops from the said region to ensure a lasting peace in the Horn of Africa.

President Mohamed Siad Barre of Somalia, who addressed the rally, urged the Somali people "to be ready to defend the national independence and sovereignty of your country." "The Somali people," he declared, "will never accept domination by any country." "They will never bow to arrogance and hegemonism; they are ready to defend their national independence and sovereignty at all costs." "Somalia will never surrender to the Soviet Union."

Anxiety of Neighboring Countries

Some African and Arab countries have shown grave anxiety over the situation in the Horn of Africa brought about by the Soviet Union's pouring oil on the flames. They hold resolutely that this intervention from the outside world must be stopped.

Egyptian President Anwar Sadat expressed his worries about Soviet involvement in the Horn of Africa to U.S. Senators in Washington on February 7. One U.S. Senator quoted President Sadat as saying: "The Soviets are now moving to Berbera, which was the Soviet base in Somalia." "After the Soviets knock out Somalia, they will then turn on the Sudan and Egypt."

Sudanese President Nimeri said: "The Soviet Union is trying to exploit the situation in an attempt to establish a foothold in the Horn of Africa so as to facilitate its infiltration into the continent and occupy it bit by bit. It is also attempting to establish a base to watch over the oil states, as it will face a shortage in its oil resources toward the 1980s.

In sending large quantities of arms into the Horn of Africa, he added, "the Soviet Union wants to teach the Somalis a lesson and make them an example to other African states for expelling Soviet military experts." "The Sudan will be the next target of the Soviets," President Nimeri warned, "but it will teach them a lesson they will never forget."

In Conakry, Guinea's President Sekou Touré pointed out that "there are zones of tension, but the most dangerous zone today is the Horn of Africa where war is spreading. What we regret in the relations between Ethiopia and Somalia is the intervention of foreign powers which consider it their right to end conflicts between African states in any way they prefer."

Seyni Kountche, Niger's head of state and president of the Supreme Military Council, felt disheartened and disappointed with the big powers' attitude toward Africa. At a time when certain areas of Africa are suffering from starvation, he observed, the big powers have flooded other parts of the African continent with costly, sophisticated weapons in order to provoke fighting among Africans.

Speaking to the press in Abidjan, the capital of Ivory Coast, Zairian President Mobutu Sese Seko condemned the intervention of foreign powers in Africa. These powers, he noted, have fanned the flames of war in Africa and have tried to split Africa in order to maintain their interests on this continent.

Recently a number of African and Arab newspapers have published commentaries and articles exposing and repudiating underhanded Soviet activities in Africa.

The Zambia Daily Mail in a February 10 article entitled "Kremlin's Crime in the Horn" pointed out that, flouting public opinion of the world, Africa included, the Russians are making ready to take huge risks to enable themselves to succeed in their intervention. Such is "Russia's crime in the Horn of Africa, and those who see it for what it is have a duty to denounce Soviet military intervention just as American military intervention in Vietnam was denounced."

The Voice of Africa, a Senegalese journal, wrote: "The Soviet presence in Africa, direct or through the Cubans, poses a real problem. One wonders whether it is...a new attempt to colonize the continent." Noting that "the first exclusive concern of the USSR in our continent is military presence," the journal called on the African countries to be on guard.

In the Kuwaiti paper Al Qabas, a signed article published on February 14 said that the Soviet and Cuban troops' intervention in the issues which have arisen in the Horn of Africa directly threatens most of the Arab countries. Both the contention and collusion between the Soviet Union and the United States in this area, it said, are aimed at dividing the Arab people.

Reactions from the West

Western political circles and opinion have been worried about Soviet expansion in the Horn of Africa. French President Valery Giscard d'Estaing stressed that the big powers should discontinue their shipment of arms to the region. Italian Foreign Minister Arnaldo Forlani said: "One cannot

expect that the West will tolerate any blockade of the sea lane
which is essential and vital to the Western economy. It is
necessary to look for a settlement through negotiation. This
is why Italy is working for this end." British Foreign Secretary David Owen told reporters that "any introduction of conflict to the territory of Somalia would be a very grave event."

 UPI reported in a February 10 dispatch that "Britain and
other Western countries have already protested to Moscow
about the involvement of Cuban troops in the Horn of Africa."
The U.S. paper Chicago Tribune said editorially on February 9 that the Soviet Union has flung itself into a reckless
gamble to win control of the strategic Horn of Africa, and
has thus posed a challenge which the Carter administration
will have to face.

The West Berlin paper Der Tagesspiegel carried on February 5 an article entitled "Brezhnev's African Adventure,"
which pointed out that the outbreak of war in the Horn of
Africa "is due to the imperialist policy pursued by the Soviet
Union. Moscow desires to control the Red Sea and the Suez
Canal which is the sea route and oil transport line vital to
Western Europe." But the Africans, it added, "do not want
to see neocolonialism replacing the colonialism that has once
been overcome."

Peking Review

Contention in Latin America between the two superpowers —
the Soviet Union and the United States — has continued to intensify in the last two years. As indicated by the development
of events there, however, Soviet expansion and infiltration, in
the face of tidal waves in the Latin American countries to safeguard and consolidate national independence and fight hegemonism, is running into one kind of resistance after another. U.S.
maneuvers to maintain control over Latin America too have
suffered continued setbacks.

As in their contention in other parts of the world, the Soviet
stance on Latin America is an offensive one, with the United
States making every effort to keep it out of the Western Hemisphere while looking for a chance to strike back. The September 1973 Chilean military coup was one of the events that pointed
up the on-going U.S.-Soviet rivalry in Latin America. Since
then, Moscow has been regrouping its forces in a further effort
to secure a new foothold in South America.

Soviet Expansion and Infiltration

To achieve this, the Soviet Union has applied its same old political trick of professing itself the "ally" and "supporter" of
countries in Latin America opposed to U.S. imperialist oppression, control, and plunder, hoping to edge out U.S. influence

---

*From Peking Review, No. 29 (July 18, 1975), 12-13.

with the help of the anti-U.S. feelings in these countries. In
Latin America, it has also seized on every opportunity to make
a gesture of "supporting" such countries in their struggle
against the U.S. despotic way of doing things in the Organization
of American States and in their opposition to the transnational
corporations and the new U.S. trade act, while at the same time
harping on the idea that Latin American countries should develop their relations with the "socialist community" advertised
by Moscow. Taking advantage of the shaky position of the inter-
American system which took Washington years to build and the
Latin American countries' growing separatist tendency toward
the United States, the Soviet Union has brought the "Council for
Mutual Economic Assistance," which is a neocolonialist yoke,
into Latin America in its search for new victims. On the Panama Canal issue, the Soviet Union also has feigned "support"
for Panama's claim to sovereign rights and proposed the "internationalization" of the canal with the real intention of facili-
tating its own presence in this strategic watercourse linking the
Pacific with the Atlantic.

In the economic field, the Soviet Union has in the last two
years promised certain Latin American countries huge economic "aid" and trade and for the first time sold heavy ground
military hardware to South America. Its economic "aid" in recent years has been in the form of taking part in public works
construction on the continent. By offering low tenders, it showed
its interest in providing money, technology, and equipment for
building hydroelectric stations in some South American countries. As a country which has been expanding with a vengeance
its naval capability in recent years, the Soviet Union also has a
special interest in financing construction of fishing ports in
Latin America.

Reports from some countries reveal the Soviet Union's obvious political aims in its trade with Latin America. For instance, it managed to make its way into a central American
country through coffee purchases. It takes advantage of the
acute economic crisis in the West to push trade all the more
vigorously with the Latin American countries as a means of

infiltration. In 1974, for instance, it bought large quantities of
Latin American unsold commodities such as leather shoes,
beef, wine, and coffee. In trade with Brazil, it does not mind
registering huge trade deficits from year to year, which "is
obviously pursuing political interest," as a report by the Bra-
zilian Federal Commission for Trade Information pointed out.

In the military field, there has been a marked increase in
Soviet navy and air force activities in the Western Hemisphere.
A Soviet fleet made its thirteenth cruise in the Caribbean Sea
at the end of last February. In late September 1974, this fleet
that was making a show of force in this area included for the
first time a "Kresta class II" missile-carrying cruiser, while
Soviet "Bear D" naval reconnaissance aircraft made their six-
teenth reconnaissance and intelligence gathering flights over
the Caribbean. Such frequent Soviet naval and air force presence in this area is at once an extension of its military activities closer to the United States proper and a display of force in
its contention with the United States in Latin America.

U.S. Strengthens Countermeasures

Accordingly, the United States has strengthened its measures
to counter Soviet expansion and penetration. To counterpose
Soviet propaganda that the Latin American countries should develop relations with the "socialist community" and stymie the
Soviet attempt to win over these countries, the United States
last year twice proposed to the Latin American countries the
"establishment of a new community" in the Western Hemisphere.
It also tried to smooth over the disputes in its bilateral relations with these countries, promising concessions on the Panama Canal, the new U.S. trade act, and other issues. It again
has offered huge loans through the international financial institutions under its control to some Latin American countries re-
ceiving Soviet "aid."

Confronted by Soviet military expansion and infiltration in
Latin America, the United States has strengthened its military
deployment along its eastern and southern coasts as well as in

the Caribbean Sea and the Panama Canal Zone. Legislation has
been revised to enable the renewal of military loans and arms
shipments to Latin American countries. U.S. Defense Secretary
James Schlesinger, testifying before the House on February 26,
spoke of "a substantial flow" of Soviet arms into Latin America
and declared that his country "is prepared to take whatever actions are necessary to maintain our [U.S.] security in the Western Hemisphere."

In May, Senator George McGovern, the 1972 Democratic
presidential candidate, visited Cuba and told newsmen his view
that U.S. policy toward Cuba formulated some years ago must
be modified. Earlier, in a policy statement, Secretary of State
Henry Kissinger conceded that "we see no virtue in perpetual
antagonism between the United States and Cuba. Our concerns
relate above all to Cuba's external policies and military relationship with countries outside the hemisphere."

Latin America Opposes the Two Superpowers

The rivalry between the two superpowers in Latin America
poses a threat to the sovereignty and security of the countries
and peoples on that continent. Its people oppose U.S. imperialist domination and aggression on the one hand and Soviet social-
imperialist expansion and penetration on the other. Leaders of
a number of countries have unequivocally declared that the
Latin American countries cannot possibly get rid of their dependence on one country only to replace it by dependence on another. In the words of Peruvian President Juan Velasco, "We
are no longer a colony of anybody"; "at no price, be it gold or
force, will we allow our dignity and pride to be trampled upon."

The Soviet Union, by its persistent refusal to sign Additional
Protocol II to the Treaty for the Prohibition of Nuclear Weapons
in Latin America, by its hegemonic stand at the United Nations
Conference on the Law of the Sea and other international meetings, and by its subversive and intervention activities in Latin
America, has betrayed its social-imperialist nature to a fuller
extent before the Latin American people. Many countries there

are on guard against the Soviet effort to lure them to have closer relations with its "community." Its politically motivated offers of economic "aid" have also aroused suspicion among the Latin American countries. As to Washington's proposed "establishment of a new community," that is not plain sailing either. The third "new dialogue" scheduled to take place in Buenos Aires between the United States and the Latin American countries died aborning amidst the opposition by the latter to the new U.S. trade act.

LATIN AMERICA FORGES AHEAD
IN THE STRUGGLE AGAINST
IMPERIALISM AND HEGEMONISM*

12

Yu Ping

The Latin American countries make up an important part
of the Third World. In the struggle against imperialism, colonialism and hegemonism, these countries and their peoples
have emerged full of militancy.

The year 1977 saw their struggle in defense of national independence and state sovereignty develop in depth.

Supporting Panama's Recovery of Canal Zone

The Panamanian people won a major victory in their struggle
to recover sovereignty over the U.S.-occupied Canal Zone.
Since the outbreak of the anti-U.S. patriotic movement in January 1964, the heroic people of Panama have persisted in their
struggle. They finally forced the U.S. government to agree to
a new canal treaty with the Panamanian government and to
abrogate the "U.S.-Panama Treaty" which was forced on the
Panamanian people in 1903 at bayonet point. The new treaty
was signed in September last year.

The Panamanian people's victory in recovering sovereignty
over the Canal Zone is also a victory for Latin American solidarity. In the common struggle against imperialism and hegemonism, the peoples of Latin America have all along encouraged and supported each other. Last August, the leaders of

*From Peking Review, No. 2 (January 13, 1978), 19-21.

Colombia, Venezuela, Costa Rica, Panama, Mexico and Jamaica meeting in Bogota resolutely supported the Panamanian people's struggle and denounced U.S. imperialism's colonialist actions. Praising the anti-materialist meeting, public opinion in many countries said that it pointed out to the world that the Latin American states were at one in safeguarding their common aims.

Safeguarding Maritime Rights

The Latin American countries took the lead in the struggle to safeguard maritime rights. Twenty-five years ago Peru, Ecuador and Chile signed the Santiago Declaration which announced the three countries' establishment of a 200-nautical-mile territorial sea limit and their determination to defend their sea rights. This struggle initiated by the Latin American countries has become an irresistible world trend.

Late last September, disregarding Soviet threats and bluster, the Argentine Navy on three successive occasions arrested seven Soviet fishing vessels for intruding into Argentine territorial waters and poaching. The Argentine government also lodged strong formal protests with Moscow against its hegemonic actions. Other Latin American countries voiced their support for Argentina's just struggle to safeguard its national rights and interests. Condemning the outrageous actions of the superpowers in plundering maritime resources at will, President Perez of Venezuela pointed out that such behavior was the extension of colonialism on land to the seas and was even more harmful to humanity than the old colonialism which had already brought so much misery to the continents of Latin America, Asia and Africa. The Third World countries cannot tolerate such a situation, he declared. The leader of the Mexican fishery organization also denounced Moscow's "piratical actions" and accused Soviet and other foreign vessels of plundering each year 50 percent of the shrimp produced in the Gulf of Mexico. "These pirates," he complained, don't care if the shrimp become extinct but just grab them. The Mexican government has recently announced the purchase of a fleet of thirty-six naval vessels to protect its 200-nautical-mile exclusive economic zone.

In the struggle against big power economic hegemonism, the Latin American countries together with the other Third World countries are striving for the establishment of a new international economic order.

To make their struggle more effective, the Latin American countries are constantly coordinating their actions and positions. They have set up the Latin American Economic System, the Central American Common Market, the Andean Pact Organization, the Caribbean Community and the Latin American Energy Organization as well as some specialized bodies dealing with raw materials and commodities. All this has enabled the Latin American countries to follow a common policy toward big or strong countries.

The Latin American countries have coordinated their actions with the African, Middle Eastern and other Third World countries. Embracing many Latin American and African countries, eight associations of raw-material-producing countries, including the associations for bauxite, cocoa and bananas, met last August to study the question of setting up a council of the association of producer countries. The countries of the African, Caribbean and Pacific communities have also met to coordinate their positions on the question of maintaining the prices of sugar and bananas. Furthermore, the Latin American, African, Middle Eastern and other Third World countries time and again have fought shoulder to shoulder and have made joint efforts at the U.N. Sea Law Conference, the North-South Dialogue, the Negotiating Conference on a Common Fund for the Integrated Program for Commodities and other international conferences.

A Common Cause

While accelerating the pace of integration on their continent, the Latin American countries have come to realize that the

struggle to establish a new international economic order is not
only the affair of Latin America, but the cause of the entire
Third World. Many countries have, therefore, set up special
organizations and research bodies to strengthen their study
of Third World political and economic affairs and to give support to the struggles of the Third World countries. A statement issued by the preparatory committee of the Venezuelan
Committee of Solidarity with the Struggles of the Third World
pointed out that "the support, friendship, solidarity and joint
efforts of the countries of Asia, Africa and Latin America will
enhance the formulation by the Third World of a common policy against the hegemonist role of the superpowers in controlling the destiny of mankind."

Strengthening Links with Other Third World Countries

During the past year, the Latin American countries have by
various means strengthened mutual support and expanded
trade and cooperation with other Third World countries, thus
promoting the development of the Third World's strength in
the struggle against imperialism, colonialism and hegemonism.

The exchange of visits between state and government leaders
of Latin American, African and Middle Eastern countries increased markedly last year as compared with previous years.
For the first time, two South American countries received
heads of state of West African countries. Venezuelan President Perez paid a visit to six Middle Eastern and African countries. These state and government leaders exchanged views
on international questions of common interest to the Third
World. In their joint statements, they reaffirmed the principles of sovereign equality among states, self-determination
and nonintervention, resolutely upheld the sovereign right of
each state to control and dispose of its own natural resources,
supported the principle of nonalignment and demanded the establishment of a new international economic order. In their
speeches and joint statements, some heads of state laid special
emphasis on the need to promote understanding, solidarity

and cooperation among the Third World countries.

The Latin American countries, which suffered from colonial oppression over a long period of time, have expressed their firm support for the struggles of African and Middle Eastern countries to eliminate colonialism and racism and win national liberation and national rights. In the Mozambican-Guyanese, Mozambican-Jamaican, Venezuelan-Iranian and Venezuelan-Kuwaiti joint statements, the heads of state or government of these countries supported the Palestinian people's struggle to recover their inalienable national rights and demanded Israel's withdrawal from the Arab territories it has occupied since 1967. They also denounced all manifestations of racial discrimination, supported the resolutions of the UN General Assembly and Security Council on sanctions against the South African and Rhodesian regimes and backed the armed struggles of the people of Zimbabwe and Namibia for liberation. On their part, a number of African leaders expressed their support for the Panamanian people's struggle to recover their sovereignty over the Panama Canal and for the Latin American countries' demand for a nuclear-free zone and their right to the peaceful use of atomic energy.

The intensifying rivalry between the two superpowers, the Soviet Union and the United States, in the Middle East and Africa, especially Soviet armed intervention in Africa through Cuban mercenaries, has aroused concern in the Latin American countries and was condemned by public opinion there.

Regional economic cooperation between the Latin American countries and the African and Middle Eastern countries is on the increase. An Arab-Latin American bank was established last October. The Third Pan-American-Arab Congress met last November and approved a decision to set up the Pan-American-Arab Federation of Chambers of Commerce for the purpose of strengthening economic, trade and financial ties between the Arab and Latin American countries. The eleven member Latin American Free Trade Association and a mission of the U.N. Economic Commission for Africa met last April and exchanged experience on cooperation among the developing countries. The African, Caribbean and Pacific countries worked out specific rules concerning various action programs for broader cooperation.

The Latin American people are steadily advancing in the course of struggle. Together with the peoples of the rest of the Third World, they are valiantly playing the role assigned to them by history as the main force in the struggle against imperialism, colonialism and hegemonism.

13

SOVIET SOCIAL-IMPERIALISM: THE MOST DANGEROUS SOURCE OF WORLD WAR*

Hsinhua Correspondent

With the two superpowers, the Soviet Union and the United States, locked in ever-fiercer contention for world hegemony, the danger of a new world war is visibly growing, and it is bound to break out someday. The most dangerous source of war today is precisely the wildly ambitious Soviet social-imperialism.

Characteristics of Social-Imperialism

Engaged in unbridled aggression and expansion abroad in contending for world hegemony, Soviet social-imperialism inevitably will go to war. Above all, this is determined by its social system.

Once a socialist state, the Soviet Union has degenerated into a social-imperialist state ever since the renegade Khrushchev-Brezhnev clique usurped Party and state power, pursued a revisionist line, and restored capitalism in an all-round way. Having placed itself in the ranks of the imperialist states, it inevitably comes under the basic law of imperialism and is enmeshed in a multitude of inherent imperialist contradictions. Social-imperialism is, therefore, entirely the same as capitalist imperialism in nature. Lenin pointed out on many occasions

*From Peking Review, No. 5 (January 30, 1976), 9-13; and No. 29 (July 15, 1977), 4-10, 21.

that imperialism is war itself. Modern war is born of imperialism. Certain characteristics of the Soviet social-imperialist system, however, make it more rapacious and more truculent in its aggression and expansion abroad.

Its political system is brutal fascist dictatorship. Chairman Mao has pointed out: "The rise to power of revisionism means the rise to power of the bourgeoisie." "The Soviet Union today is under the dictatorship of the bourgeoisie, a dictatorship of the big bourgeoisie, a dictatorship of the German fascist type, a dictatorship of the Hitler type." This scientific thesis of Chairman Mao's profoundly exposes the class nature of Soviet social-imperialism and its reactionary character. The Soviet bureaucrat-monopoly bourgeoisie represented by the Khrushchev-Brezhnev clique is utterly reactionary, inveterately hostile to and morbidly afraid of the people, and it only can rely on the most barbarous fascist dictatorship to buttress up its reactionary rule. It has called out both military and police forces, supported by tanks and armored cars, in sanguinary suppression of mass strikes, demonstrations, and uprisings in many parts of the country like Tbilisi, Chimkent, Kharkov, Dnieprodzerzhinsk, Kaunas, Tallin, Minsk, Leningrad, and Novosibirsk. It has issued numerous decrees, ordinances, and decisions for the suppression of the people while setting up new repressive organs and continuing to expand existing ones. Military and police units and special agents in particular keep civilians, cadres, and servicemen throughout the country under close surveillance and persecute them whenever they see fit. Even more brutal, there is the oppression of the minority peoples by the new czars. One certainly will be persecuted in the Soviet Union today for showing any discontent with the clique's dark rule and defying it, or even if one is merely suspected. Millions have been either thrown into prison, detained in so-called psychiatric hospitals and labor camps, or exiled. As in the old days, the country has become a prison of nations. Soviet social-imperialism, which exercises fascist dictatorship at home, is pushing hegemonism abroad. The Brezhnev clique has in recent years trotted out an assortment of imperialist "theories" to facilitate its rabid drive for world hegemony, "theories" known as "limited sovereignty," "international dictatorship," "big community," "the interest involved," and so on.

The economic base of Soviet social-imperialism is state monopoly capitalism which came into existence after the revisionist renegade clique seized political power. Lenin pointed out, "The deepest economic foundation of imperialism is monopoly" (Imperialism, the Highest Stage of Capitalism). This has found the most striking manifestation in Soviet social-imperialism. In capitalist imperialist countries, "private and state monopolies are interwoven" (Ibid.), and private monopoly is the principal economic form with a number of big financial groups existing side by side. State monopoly, in essence, is an instrument which private monopoly groups use to grab maximum profits with the help of the state machine. In the case of the social-imperialist Soviet Union, state monopoly capitalism directly takes the form of ownership by the bureaucrat-monopoly capitalist class, with its members — a handful of people — represented by the Soviet revisionist leading clique running the state machine and directly controlling the entire national economy and all economic lifelines. The state under the dictatorship of the bureaucrat-monopoly capitalist class becomes "the ideal personification of the total national capital," while all monopoly capital in the Soviet Union is under the exclusive control of this center. Compared with the capitalist imperialist countries, state monopoly capitalism in the Soviet Union is more monopolistic by nature, has a higher degree of concentration, and exercises tighter state control. A handful of Soviet bureaucrat-monopoly capitalists assumes complete control of the country's economy and home market, bleeding the Soviet working people white at a rate of exploitation doubling that in czarist Russia. Hence the various sharpening contradictions in the country. Domestic monopoly will, of course, grow into international monopoly. As Lenin put it, "The capitalists divide the world, not out of any particular malice, but because the degree of concentration which has been reached forces them to adopt this method in order to obtain profits" (Ibid.). To obtain maximum profits, the

Soviet bureaucrat-monopoly capitalist class sets out to step up aggression abroad, annex new territories, expand spheres of influence, make off with other countries' raw materials at low prices, dump commodities on foreign markets, export capital, and shift its burden of crises onto others. Thus, Soviet social-imperialism has become one of the world's biggest exploiters. Although monopolistic domination has replaced free competition in the age of imperialism, competition persists and is bigger in scale, greater in depth, and fiercer in intensity and destructiveness. Lenin noted, "It is this combination of antagonistic principles, namely, competition and monopoly, that is the essence of imperialism" (Materials Relating to the Revision of the Party Program). Both superpowers' monopoly capitalist classes try their utmost to monopolize the world's resources and markets on the basis of monopoly over their domestic economies, so they are bound to compete fiercely with each other in all fields. The degree of concentration and monopoly of the domestic economy by the Soviet bureaucrat-monopoly capitalist class throws into the shade private and state monpoly capital in any capitalist imperialist country. This explains why it is trying desperately to edge out competitors everywhere in the world.

A Peculiar Form of War Economy

Owing to the uneven development of imperialism, a change has taken place in the balance of forces between the two super-powers in the last few years. With the swelling of its military strength, Soviet social-imperialism has become more unrestrained in its ambition to attain world hegemony through war.

Modern history has proven that wars among imperialist powers for world domination are closely linked with their uneven development. Lenin observed that "uneven economic and political development is an absolute law of capitalism" (On the Slogan for a United States of Europe) and that "any other basis under capitalism for the division of spheres of influence, of interests, of colonies, and so forth than a calculation of the strength of the participants in the division, their general economic,

financial, military strength, and so forth is inconceivable"
(Imperialism, the Highest Stage of Capitalism). In the stage of
imperialism, the further aggravation of uneven development of
the imperialist powers brings about rapid changes in their relative strength. This inevitably sharpens their contradictions
and causes them to scramble fiercely in order to redivide the
world. Both the First and Second World Wars broke out against
such a background.

Since World War II, U.S. imperialism has been hit hard in its
wars of aggression against Korea and Vietnam, and its political
and economic crises have steadily deepened. It no longer is in
its prime and is going downhill every day. On the other hand,
the newcomer, Soviet social-imperialism, does all it can to act
as the global overlord in place of U.S. imperialism. As it lags
behind its opponent U.S. imperialism in economic and financial
strength and other fields, it is bound to desperately increase its
military strength in a bid for world domination. The state apparatus of fascist dictatorship in the Soviet Union, combined
with highly concentrated state monopoly capital, facilitates
militarization at an accelerated tempo.

The entire Soviet economy has taken a peculiar form of war
economy. With stress laid on "an economy which can guarantee
the waging of war by either nuclear fragmentation means or
conventional weapons," the new czars all along have given arms
expansion and war preparations top priority and have geared
ever more manpower, material resources, and money to military objectives, steadily intensifying the militarization of the
national economy. Military spending has spiraled year after
year. The proportion of military outlay in the national income
also has registered a yearly increase. It was about 13 percent
in 1960 and 19.6 percent in 1974. As far as the proportion is
concerned, the Soviet Union has not only surpassed prewar Hitlerite Germany (19 percent), but also greatly outstripped U.S.
imperialism at the time of its wars of aggression in Korea
(15 percent) and in Vietnam (10 percent). According to obviously doctored official Soviet statistics, national income is said
to be about 66 percent that of the United States, but actual mili-

tary spending tops the United States by 20 percent. In 1974, it
accounted for about 35 percent of overall Soviet expenditure.
With 60 percent of the industrial enterprises bound up to military purposes, the Soviet revisionist leading clique for years
has channeled more than 85 percent of industrial investment to
production of capital goods, mainly to sectors connected with
armament production; only less than 15 percent is earmarked
for production of consumer goods. The malignant development
of the armament industry has gone hand in hand with serious
backwardness in other industries and agriculture, short market
supplies, soaring prices, and the impoverishment of the laboring people.

While the Soviet Union rapidly increased its weapons and
military equipment of various kinds, the strength of its armed
forces has grown from about 3 million men in the 1960s to the
present 4.2 million. The Soviet revisionists have also taken a
series of measures including a new enlistment act to enlarge
sources of reserves and has put its mobilization system on a
wartime footing. According to data prepared by the London-
based International Institute for Strategic Studies, Soviet reserves of both men and officers total 25 million, of whom nearly
6 million have served in the armed forces in the last five years.

Certain noticeable changes have taken place in the balance of
forces between the two imperialist superpowers, the Soviet
Union and the United States. As present military strength
stands, both now match each other in nuclear weapons as a result of the much faster pace of the Soviet arms drive. Although
the Soviet Union still remains behind the United States in total
naval craft tonnage, the former has outstripped the latter in the
number of vessels, particularly submarines. Though Moscow
has fewer long-distance bombers, it has more combat aircraft.
Soviet ground forces are now better equipped, with four times
as many tanks as the U.S. forces. The Soviet Union has surpassed the United States by almost 100 percent in the numerical
strength of military forces.

In terms of economic strength, the Soviet Union on the whole
is far behind. However, the growth rate of some Soviet heavy

industrial sectors closely connected with armament production and war and the absolute quantity of their products have caught up with or surpassed those of the United States. The cunning tactics of the new czars, who are making more and more use of Western resources to keep up their arms expansion and war preparations, are especially noteworthy. Since 1965, the Brezhnev clique has obtained from the West tens of thousands of millions of U.S. dollars in credits and has imported considerable advanced industrial know-how and equipment and nearly 100 million tons of grain to cope with the staggering consequences of a militarized economy and to boost military strength further. Some sober-minded people in the West have pointed out the perils of giving such blood transfusions to the Soviet war economy.

Europe Is the Focus of Contention

Goaded on by their frenzied ambitions for aggression and expansion, the Soviet social-imperialists pursue a policy of war adventure, ready for both nuclear and conventional wars. From a strategic point of view, it is very clear where the focus of contention is.

As a latecomer to the feast of world imperialism, Soviet social-imperialism is not happy with what is left for it to devour. It is going all out to redivide the world and taking the offensive in its global contention with U.S. imperialism. Over the last few years, apart from political control, military occupation, and economic plunder of some "fraternal countries" within the "Council for Mutual Economic Assistance," it has tried to make its way into and undermine U.S. imperialism's spheres of influence while carrying on feverish penetration and expansion in both the Second and Third Worlds. Soviet revisionist leaders have clamored repeatedly that the Soviet Union is on the "historic offensive" on the "entire front of global confrontation" and, "backed by its military might," must "start an extensive and real general attack" abroad. At a recent Moscow meeting, Brezhnev arrogantly declared that the Soviet Union will "start an active offensive in the international arena" with its "strengthened economic and defense capabilities."

The Brezhnev clique has stressed the necessity to be "ready to fight a war with any weapons," "with nuclear weapons or otherwise," and "under certain conditions, probably only with conventional weapons." The Soviet revisionists have tended more and more to make a show of force and engage in threats of force. They boast that "in all circumstances, the Soviet army and navy will use or will not use nuclear weapons to carry out combat tasks in great depth and at a high speed and successfully accomplish their tactical and strategic missions on whatever scale" and that "the role of a surprise attack has become ever greater and, therefore, surprise attacks have become a factor of strategic importance." They tell the Soviet armed forces to be prepared at all times to "fulfill offensive tasks."

Europe has always been an area of contention among imperialist powers and was the main battlefield in the last two world wars. Today, it is also the focus of Soviet-U.S. rivalry. Placing Europe in the "central position" of its global strategy, the Soviet Union has declared its own "fate depends on how developments evolve in Europe." Having kept Eastern Europe in a firm grip, it tries hard to swallow up Western Europe, a piece of juicy meat. Three-fourths of its troops are deployed in Europe (including the European part of the Soviet Union proper), with their weapons and equipment constantly renewed and the number of soldiers increased. Soviet ground and other forces totaling more than half a million are stationed in the German Democratic Republic, Hungary, Czechoslovakia, and Poland. The Soviet Union is stepping up military deployment on the southern and northern flanks of Europe in an effort to outflank Western Europe. It is very aggressive. Meanwhile, the Brezhnev clique is resorting to "détente" tactics in the European arena to cover up its arms expansion and war preparations and is intensifying its political expansion and economic infiltration in Western Europe, doing everything it can to split and disintegrate Western Europe and squeeze the United States out. Numerous events since the conclusion of the European security

conference masterminded by the Brezhnev clique with pain-
staking effort indicate that far from being a "milestone" of
European security, the conference was a new starting point toward war for the Soviet social-imperialists. Historical experience merits attention. It was precisely amidst the lullaby of
"peace," "security," and "disarmament" that Hitler abruptly
unleashed a "blitzkrieg" and the Nazi iron heel trampled over
nearly the whole West European mainland. Several years ago,
Brezhnev and company suddenly sent troops to occupy Czechoslovakia while holding talks with Czechoslovak leaders and issuing joint statements of "friendship" with them. These facts
are most useful for the people to see clearly the current European situation and the Soviet social-imperialist policy.

Sure Destruction

Soviet social-imperialism is the most dangerous source of
war. This is stark reality. Against this, the revolutionary people and many nations the world over are heightening their vigilance and making preparations. In history, past and present,
those who start an aggressive war all come to no good end. At
present, the world situation has undergone profound changes.
Countries want independence, nations want liberation, and the
people want revolution — this has become an irresistible trend
of our time. Despite their truculence and ferocity, the Soviet
social-imperialists are strong only in appearance but brittle inside; they are beset with difficulties at home and abroad and
plagued by crises. Class antagonism and national contradictions
at home are sharpening day by day with political and economic
crises deepening. The resistance of the people of all nationalities is growing in depth, and the new czars are, so to speak,
sitting on a volcano. Internationally, the Third World nations
and people have seen more and more clearly the true features
of Soviet social-imperialism in their struggle against the two
superpowers. The struggle of the Second World against the
superpowers, the Soviet social-imperialists in particular, continues to surge forward. The tendency of the West European

nations to combat hegemony in unity is gathering momentum.
Chairman Mao pointed out that "imperialism and all reactionaries, looked at in essence, from a long-term point of view,
from a strategic point of view, must be seen for what they
are — paper tigers" (quoted in the explanatory note to "Talk
with the American Correspondent Anna Louise Strong"), and
that the "revisionist Soviet Union is a paper tiger too." The
Soviet social-imperialists are doomed to sure destruction if
they dare unleash a new world war. It is the people who will
win the war, the peace, and progress.

IV

Problems with socialist countries

Documentary Introduction

Three selections are included in this chapter. They deal with the problems that have arisen in several socialist countries owing to their disagreements in policy and theory.

The first document is part of the secret speech of Foreign Minister Huang Hua in July 1977. It uncovered the roots of the present Vietnamese-Cambodian border war, revealed Peking-Hanoi disputes on the ownership of the South Sea islands, made known the basic differences between Albania and China, and defended China's cooperation with Yugoslavia. Peking implied, however, that all the problems came from the "social-imperialist" Soviet Union.

In the second selection, Peking not only rebuffed Moscow's charge that the worsening Vietnamese-Cambodian relations were "provoked" by China, but also accused Moscow of refusing "to be reconciled with" the Cambodian Communists and attempting to capitalize on the armed conflict between these two Indochinese countries.

The third is a very serious and important statement by the Chinese government on the complex issue of Vietnam's expulsion of Chinese residents. This document may well be the first official signal of an escalating Sino-Vietnamese dispute.

PROBLEMS WITH INDOCHINA, ALBANIA,
AND YUGOSLAVIA (Excerpts)*

1

(July 30, 1977)

Huang Hua

The Three Indochina States

There have been border conflicts between Vietnam and Cambodia, and between Laos and Cambodia recently. Cambodia
has issued an order for national mobilization, while Vietnam
and Laos have also taken emergency measures to prepare for
war. At the same time, Cambodia has clashed with Thailand.
Why is it that the three Indochina states, instead of being united
themselves, have clashed on their borders? This is due to historical factors, and also to instigations by social-imperialism.
Historically speaking, there has been a considerable period
of dispute between the Vietnamese and the Cambodians on certain territorial and sovereignty problems. The root of the
trouble can be traced to the demarcation of borders when
France occupied Indochina. When the three Indochinese states
were making concerted efforts against U.S. imperialism, they
did not have the time to consider this problem. Now that the
war has ended, they have become seriously concerned about
this problem again.
As brethren on the same front, they could have emulated the
example of China in solving her border problems with Burma

---

*From Background on China (New York, December 26, 1977).
This title is the Editor's. The original title is "Huang Hua's
42,000-word Foreign Policy Address."

and Afghanistan through mutual respect and mutual concessions.
However, they failed to do so. It became impossible to end the
disputes, and the only solution was war. Why is it that a negotiated settlement has become impossible? This is entirely due
to the sabotage and instigation of social-imperialism.

. . .

After Sihanouk was overthrown, Khieu Sam Phan led the
Cambodian Liberation Army to join the anti-U.S., national-
salvation struggle. At that time, however, they were still very
weak. Vietnam was the strongest in military strength, followed
by the Pathet Lao forces. Vietnam then supported Cambodia
with weapons and equipment she had obtained from the socialist countries, as well as those captured from the U.S. forces.
Meanwhile, like China, she also sent military instructors to
train the Cambodian troops, and a military advisory group to
help direct operations.

In several important campaigns in Cambodia, Vietnam sent
its own crack troops to attack the Lon Nol forces. Finally, in
the battle of liberation for Phnom Penh, Vietnam sent more
than two army divisions into the war. As a result, Phnom
Penh was liberated even before Saigon. Finally, with Saigon's
liberation, political power was transferred smoothly, and the
armed struggle of the three Indochina states ended in victory.

However, this process also produced the following two
problems:

1) Self-conceited, Vietnam deemed that without its help
Cambodia could not have been liberated. Consequently, it assumed the airs of a Big Brother, demanding obeisance from
Cambodia in everything. After the liberation, Cambodia had to
ask repeatedly for Vietnam to withdraw its troops. Although
Vietnam eventually acceded to the request, its troops remained
deployed along the Cambodian-Vietnamese border, seriously
threatening the security of Cambodia. Naturally, it was difficult for Cambodia to swallow this situation, and herein lies
the contradiction.

2) When the war of national liberation was being waged in
Cambodia, the slogan then was whoever opposed U.S. imperial-

ism and its lackey, the Lon Nol-Sirik Matak puppet regimes, whether they were social organizations, groups or armed bands, would all be regarded as brothers in solidarity. Consequently, the components of the Cambodian Liberation Army were extremely complex — some were the original royal troops who had come over, some were the Communist underground, others were organized by patriotic elements, and still more were organized by the oppressed peasants. Some of these troops were trained by us, others by Vietnam which was backed by Soviet revisionism. Thus, Soviet revisionism took advantage of this opportunity and infiltrated into certain units of the Cambodian forces.

After the liberation of Cambodia, simultaneous with the revamping of state organs, the Cambodians also revamped their army. They resolutely disbanded those military organs and units that had been infiltrated by Soviet revisionism, and arrested some impure elements, sending them to the military tribunals for trial, or ousting them permanently from the army, thereby purifying their ranks and strengthening their fighting strength. What they did was strictly their domestic affair and no one could criticize them for it. Still it caused dissatisfaction on the part of Soviet revisionism, which used it as an excuse to sow dissension between Vietnam and Cambodia, thereby further aggravating the contradiction between the two parties.

We have discussed the problems that have arisen in these two countries since the end of the Indochina War. There is another difference concerning anti-imperialism and antirevisionism. It has been our conviction that in order to oppose imperialism, we must also oppose revisionism, and only by opposing revisionism can we gain thorough victory in the anti-imperialist struggle. The Vietnamese view is that they oppose imperialism, but not revisionism. When Vo Nguyen Giap came to China, he even said that they have routed U.S. imperialism without the need to oppose revisionism.

What we told him was that "There is a proverb in China: 'Don't chase away the wolves from the front door, only to ad-

mit tigers and leopards through the back door.'" Within a certain period of time, it will not matter if they do not realize the
situation. There is no need to argue with them. They will realize it when they come to suffer later. Because the Cambodians had suffered from the Soviets before, they understood
that in order to oppose imperialism, it is necessary to oppose
revisionism at the same time. Didn't Sihanouk also cherish
illusions about Soviet revisionism? What has happened to
him? We must have patience in dealing with certain problems.

. . .

There is a great ideological difference between Cambodia
and Vietnam, one being antirevisionist and the other not antirevisionist. As a result of this situation, coupled with the two
factors mentioned above and their historical origins, eventually the two sides came to fight against each other. Once the
war started, troubles came naturally. Sometimes, problems
can be solved by a decisive battle in which one combatant
proves to be definitely superior to the other. Although losses
may be greater, the problems can be settled in a thorough manner. However, where the imbroglio between Vietnam and Cambodia is concerned, no one knows how long this will drag on.
Soviet revisionist social-imperialism has repeatedly invited
Vietnam to send many delegations to the Soviet Union, continuously sowing the seed for war, instigating these two close
neighboring fraternal states to be at each other's throat, with
the attempt of eventually intruding into Cambodia, making it
into an advanced base for Soviet expansion in Southeast Asia....

On the issue between Vietnam and Cambodia, we have made
clear our four-point stand to the three Indochina states:

1) The three states of Indochina should stop all armed conflicts and return to the negotiating table. They should, in accordance with the spirit of the Summit Conference of the Three
Indochina States, based on the common goal of building a prosperous, peaceful and democratic postwar Indochina, seek to
resolve their differences through mutual respect and mutual
concession.

2) All people of the three Indochina states cherish the same

wish for solidarity. Having been neighbors for generations, they have no basic conflicts of interest and they should be united as one. If the three states deem it necessary, China is willing to serve as a mediator in order to enable the three states to return to the negotiating table to resolve their problems and promote their solidarity, friendship, and cooperation. China also hopes that the three states will continue to make their contributions in supporting other Southeast Asian countries in their movement of national liberation, people's revolution and armed struggle.

3) Although China has been and is willing to do whatever she can in giving unselfish aid and in assuming her internationalist duty to these three states in their anti-U.S., national-salvation struggle and in their postwar tasks of building democracy and socialism, China will not take the side of any state to aggravate tension among the three states; nor will she provide any side with military aid that will aggravate tension, or give any other kind of aid.

4) We support the stand of Cambodia and her people against Soviet revisionist social-imperialism and will not watch indifferently any intervention in Cambodian sovereignty or coveting of Cambodian territory by social-imperialism. We will support Cambodia and her people in their struggle and in their actions to protect Cambodia's territorial integrity and national sovereignty by giving all possible assistance.

. . .

There is another important issue which should be mentioned here, that is, the question of the ownership of the South Sea islands. The territory of China reaches as far southward as the James Shoals, near Borneo of Malaysia. These South Sea islands include Tung-sha [The Pratas], Hsi-sha [The Paracels], and Nan-sha [The Spratleys] islands. On the Hsi-sha islands, there is a procurement station of our foreign trade organization. I don't know whether they have representatives attending our meeting here today. The Ministry of Foreign Trade recently held a conference to exchange experience in learning from Taching and Tachai, and it might have repre-

sentatives attending the specialized conference of the Armed
Forces. To go back to these islands, most of them, formed by
coral reefs, are rich in marine products and also in guano,
which is a natural fertilizer. There are also considerable un-
tapped underground resources. We have our troops, fisher-
men and administrative organs on the Hsi-sha and Chung-sha
islands, which have been Chinese territory from time imme-
morial. I remember that while I was still a schoolboy, I read
about the islands in the geography books. At that time, I never
heard anyone say that those islands were not China's.

With the fourth Middle Eastern war, a petroleum war was
unleashed by OPEC, and the capitalist world had to face its
energy crisis. Since then, there have been disputes over the
question of ownership of the Hsi-sha and Nan-sha islands. The
navy of the Nguyen Van Thieu Regime even fought with us at
Hsi-sha, ending in a disastrous defeat for them. The Chiang
Kai-shek clique now occupies some of the Nan-sha islands.
Since Chiang Kai-shek is no more, let us say that Chiang Ching-
kuo's troops are occupying some islands there. The Phili-
pines also occupies some islands, and so does Vietnam.

The Hsi-sha islands are presently under our control. The
Vietnamese claim that the islands belong to them. Let them
talk that way. They have repeatedly asked us to negotiate with
them on the Hsi-sha issue; we have always declined to do so.
Several Vietnamese delegations that came to China recently
also brought up this matter. When Pham Van Dong was here
around April 20, he again asked us to discuss the matter, and
we declined as before. If Vietnam should disregard the historical facts and invade Hsi-sha, the central government has
already instructed our garrison troops there that any invasion
of Hsi-sha by the troops of any country, or any harassment of
the islands, would be a challenge to China's sovereignty and
will be resolutely dealt with, and any invaders thoroughly and
completely annihilated.

The main question now is Nan-sha, on which we will not take
any measures for the time being, although its sovereignty un-
questionably belongs to China. Any exploration of the resources

on the Nan-sha islands and their peripheral waters must have
China's consent if it is to be valid. You may explore them if
you wish, but when the time comes, we will confiscate them
completely. As to the ownership of those islands, there are
historical records that can be verified. There is no need for
negotiation since they originally belong to China. In this respect, Taiwan's attitude is all right, at least they have some
patriotism and would not sell out the islands. As to when we
will recover the islands, this will have to wait until the time
is ripe.

The Albania Question

Recently, Zeri I Populit, organ of the Albanian Party of
Labor, published an article attacking our policy of actively
rallying the Third World nations. The Albanian Embassy in
China distributed copies of that article to all other foreign embassies, further publicizing the differences between the Chinese and Albanian states and between the Parties. The People's Daily did not carry that article, but the "Reference News"
excerpted and published it. At an appropriate time, we will
reproduce articles of other foreign newspapers either in the
People's Daily or the Kuangming Daily in order to clarify certain issues unofficially.

On the basis of instructions of Chairman Hua and Vice Premier Teng, we will not publish any articles openly to refute
the Albanian Labor Party's erroneous views. Instead, we will,
by some other means, publicize Chairman Mao's correct line
and thought concerning the establishment of an international
united front against imperialism and social-imperialism. On
the one hand, this will prevent the further escalation and
publicizing of the differences between the two parties. On the
other hand, this restraint is also for the sake of maintaining
the friendly relations between the two parties and the peoples
of China and Albania, as well as preventing chaos and confusion in the thought and line of the international Communist
movement.

. . .

People have asked: "Why did Albania turn around and is now opposing us ?"

. . .

In the summer of 1966, under the personal leadership of Chairman Mao, our country launched the unprecedented Great Proletarian Cultural Revolution. The purpose of the revolution was to prevent the restoration of capitalism within the Party, which would change our nation into revisionism. In the meantime, ever since the Twenty-second Congress of the Communist Party of the Soviet Union, Albania has stood more and more resolutely with us in opposing revisionism from the standpoint of Marxism-Leninism.

Later on, Albania emulated China's experience in launching the Great Proletarian Cultural Revolution. Albania launched a series of campaigns to oppose and prevent revisionism internally, such as, opposition to bureaucracy, having cadres participate in physical labor, abolition of military ranks, launching of educational reform, and launching of a cultural revolution. The purpose of these measures was also to prevent capitalist restoration, to heighten the awareness and revolutionary alertness of the broad masses, and to prevent subversion and aggression from without.

However, while adopting this series of measures, Albania has neglected theoretical construction in Marxism-Leninism. In dealing with the ideological differences existing within their Party, the Albanians failed to use the method of actively waging ideological struggle to solve the problem. That would, on the one hand, have clearly defined the problem, and on the other hand, united the comrades, so that a new solidarity would have been achieved under the principle of Marxism-Leninism. On the contrary, they either evaded struggle by negative improvisation, or expanded some of the nonantagonistic contradictions into antagonistic contradictions. This has caused discrimination and attack against some of the excellent members of the Party of Labor and brought losses to the Party itself.

For instance, we have recently distributed to certain units Enver Hoxha's speech at the Central Politburo of the Albanian

Party of Labor and also some materials on the Albania problem. It will be seen that in dealing with the problems of Bequir Balluku and Abdyl Kellezi that what the Albanians have done is to emphasize contradictions, thereby enlarging ideological differences into a question of friend and foe. We have also studied carefully the data about Petrit Dume and Xhafer Spahiu and also about Haxhi Lleshi.* Geared to these problems, we have adopted the following principles:

1) We respect the sovereignty of the Albanian Party of Labor and will not interfere in its internal affairs.

2) From the standpoint of the international Communist enterprise, we have the right to submit to them some of our views and opinions, which are different from theirs, with the purpose of upholding the interests of the entire international Communist enterprise and the fraternal friendship between the Chinese and Albanian Parties. We have offered our opinions; whether they will accept them or not is a different matter. For example, if we consider Haxhi Lleshi's speech detrimental to Sino-Albanian friendship, we will state our views whether they accept them or not.

. . .

Albania's present difference with us centers primarily on whether or not we need to unite with the Third World and whether or not the world should be divided into three parts. Should we place our main attention on the Third World and regard the Third World as the principal revolutionary force against imperialism and social-imperialism? What is most important is that we tackle first the question of whether the world should be divided into three parts, and then discuss whether it is necessary to focus our attention on the Third World.

. . .

---

*Balluku was minister of people's defense; Kellezi, president of the Albanian-Chinese Friendship Society; and Dume, chief of general staff. All three have been purged. Spahiu is vice chairman of the Council of Ministers, and Lleshi is president of the Presidium of the People's Assembly of Albania.

A true Marxist must not only understand the ultimate goal
of his own struggle, but also be able to evolve in a timely way
the correct policy and tactic that should be adopted toward
this ultimate goal. This is a question of selecting the means.
To adopt what policy and tactic at what time must be geared
to the needs of a certain stage of the revolution. Hence, a
revolutionary Marxist-Leninist must also recognize that revolution not only should be continuous, but also must be divided
into stages. A continuous revolutionary who nevertheless does
not correctly recognize that revolution has its stages is bound
to make untimely slogans and action programs, thereby causing the whole proletarian revolutionary enterprise to be bogged
down, or fall into the abyss of defeat. Wang Ming and Li Li-
san were totally ignorant of the particular character, tasks,
and objects of the various stages of the Chinese revolution.
Hence, they were not qualified to lead, and were incapable of
leading, the Chinese revolution.

While revolution has its stages, there is also a link between
one stage and the next, instead of each stage being isolated by
itself. The preceding stage serves as the basis for the following stage, while the latter is the continuation of the former.
After completion of the preceding stage of revolution, its foundation must be guided to the following stage which, comparatively speaking, is superior. However, without a lower stage,
there will not develop a higher stage.

Merely to stress continuous revolution, without understanding that revolution has its various stages, will lead only to
revolutionary blindness or leftist adventurism. However,
without the spirit of believing in continuous revolution, and re-
membering only that there are stages in any revolution, will
make it impossible to guide the revolution to advance in a
timely way from a lower stage to a higher stage. Consequently,
the revolution will lose a precious opportunity, retreat and
suffer a setback. Once a revolution stagnates, it will inevitably turn to the Right. We call the "gang of four" extreme
rightists because they not only failed to push our revolution
ahead, but also pulled it back, thereby causing us to lose

more than ten years of our time.

                        . . .

The struggle in the world today is not centered on how to advance to the stage in which the proletariat of the various countries will seize political power through political parties. Instead, this should be the stage in which the people and the government of the various countries in the world unite to eliminate the remnants of colonialism, to demand genuine national independence and sovereignty, to prevent political interference from without, and to seek economic independence, thereby bringing the struggle against hegemony of the two superpowers, especially the struggle against Soviet revisionist social-imperialism, to a high tide.

The extension of territorial waters to 200 miles is a struggle waged by Third World nations to protect their marine resources. The Indian Ocean countries have suggested that the two superpowers stay away from their ocean and that a nonnuclear region be established there. The five ASEAN nations have proposed the idea of establishing a peaceful and neutral zone, guaranteed by the big powers, in Southeast Asia. The aspirations of the OPEC members, whether in relation to the hiking of petroleum prices or to the demands for peace in the Middle East, are all struggles that evolve around the premise of antihegemonism. Antihegemony is the main stream in the global struggle, the demand of the times and the aspiration of the great majority of peoples everywhere. If we Marxist-Leninists do not proceed from the revolutionary aspirations of the majority of nations and peoples in the world, how then can we deserve the name of Marxism-Leninism?

There are certain leading comrades of the Albanian Party of Labor who, like other fervent opportunists, are frantically advocating the advent of a revolutionary high tide but fail to see what is the tide of the times. They want to lead, blindly and adventurously, the present stage of revolution to the realm of socialist revolution. They want to lead the proletarian revolutionary rank and file, a powerful force now in the formative stage, to an adventurous offensive which would only cause the

revolution to suffer another setback and retreat. They oppose
the theory of the Third World, which is tantamount to opposing
the struggle of the proletariat to rally and unite the majority
of the masses.

To ask the proletariat to seize political power alone and
single-handedly is to court defeat. What happened to the leftist adventures and urban riots launched by Ch'ü Ch'iu-pai,
Li Li-san, and Wang Ming? We don't have to mention these
historical evidences. However, history must not repeat itself.
Consequently, we must clearly and firmly establish the theory
of the Third World and do a good job in relation to the Third
World. In presenting the issue this way, does it mean that we
would not support a proletarian party in its armed struggle to
overthrow the ruling class? No, absolutely not....

It is regrettable that the Albanian Party has this time fallen
into the trap of opportunism....

As is well known, the Albanian Party has accused China of
practicing capitulationism and betraying principles....

The problems we had [with Albania] in the past were not
made public. However, we can only face them squarely if they
have become public knowledge. I cannot go into more details
today. We would like to cite an old Chinese proverb: "It takes
more than one cold day to accumulate three feet of ice." The
split between Albania and China at present is limited to ideological differences. Although there are some problems in the
relationships between the two Parties and the two states, they
are not serious....

The Problem of Yugoslavia

Many comrades have raised these questions:

1) Is Yugoslavia a revisionist country? We have advocated that in order to oppose imperialism, we must also oppose revisionism. Then why should we not oppose Yugoslavia?

2) If we denounced Yugoslavia in the past but are now trying to bring her into the ranks of solidarity, does this mean
that our condemnation in the past was wrong? Or does this

mean we have changed our line? Wouldn't that mean that we ourselves are changing to revisionism?

. . .

First, we must confirm the fact that Yugoslavia is a revisionist country. The Central Committee of the Chinese Communist Party, led by our great leader Chairman Mao and such older generation proletarian revolutionaries as Premier Chou, Comrade K'ang Sheng and Comrade Teng Hsiao-p'ing, in its letter replying to the letter of March 30, 1963, from the Central Committee of the Communist Party of the Soviet Union, which was the third commentary of the nine open letters, entitled "Is Yugoslavia a Socialist Country?", has made detailed exposures and analyses on the basic characters of Yugoslav revisionism on the basis of Yugoslavia's state characteristics, ownership of the means of production, domestic and foreign policies, Tito's attitude toward the three peacefuls,* his attitude toward the solidarity of the socialist bloc and toward national liberation movements, his attitude toward the basic principles of Marxism-Leninism, and the policies and systems as carried out in the rural villages and in the country as a whole.

Today, we have not changed our point of view; nor have the ideological and factual bases which supported our point of view been changed. Yugoslavia was, of course, revisionist then, and it still is revisionist now. If you say that Tito is the head of the oldest revisionism, that is all right. . . .

Comrades! Guess who proposed that we invite Tito to visit China? . . . It was Chairman Mao who so instructed us when he was alive. He said: "We should also welcome Tito to visit us. Tito has experience in opposing the Soviet Union and we can learn from him."

. . .

We have only two fists, with which we must cope with Soviet revisionism and its Eastern European lackeys, with the United States and the Western countries, and with young Chiang's dy-

---

*Referring to peaceful transition, peaceful competition and peaceful coexistence.

nasty. You say we must also cope with Yugoslavia. Are there
any more? [Audience mentioned Vietnam and Korea.] Any
more? What about Japan, India, Burma, and Thailand? [Audi-
ence: Yes.] The whole world is our enemy, and no friend any-
where. Nobody else is making revolution, and only we are on
the Left. . . .

Our main task at present is to unite all the oppressed peoples and enslaved nations in the world, to unite all the peace-
loving and progressive countries and peoples in the world, in
order to form the broadest possible international united front
and bring the revolutionary struggle against the two hegemonic
powers, especially Soviet revisionist social-imperialism,
to its high tide. Any country which is opposed to the two hegemonic powers, supports national independence, national liberation and people's revolution, no matter what its social and political system might be, and no matter whether it has had friendly
relations with us or not in the past, can stand together with us
on the same united front. Although the League of Communists
of Yugoslavia is fundamentally antagonistic toward our Party,
nonetheless it is entirely feasible for the Yugoslav state and
people to have friendly contacts with our state and people.

. . .

What shall we do if Tito, when he visits China, should raise
the question of the relationship between our two Parties?
There is nothing to be afraid of. We can frankly state our
point of view. For the sake of opposing our common enemy,
we can, if the views of both sides become closer, tactically
speaking, try to accommodate the other side as a historic task
of this particular stage. To achieve a specific goal of solidarity under certain principles cannot be described as mixing
loose mud together. It is to achieve flexibility in tactics, to
"stress our common agreements while allowing minor differences to remain." This is not bargaining in political transac-
tions; this is merely the means to an end.

President Tito has earned these credits in the following
three areas:

(1) He has achieved people's liberation and national inde-

pendence in the antifascist struggle; (2) he has opposed foreign intervention and followed the road of independence and sovereignty; and (3) he has promoted solidarity among the Third World and the developing nations, supported democratic national movements in recent years, supported China's admission to the United Nations, and opposed the fallacy of "two Chinas" or "one China, one Taiwan." Of course, he has also made contributions in other respects. Now you tell me, should we or should we not unite with this kind of man? [No response from audience.] . . .

WHY DOES MOSCOW RESORT TO LIES
AND SLANDERS OVER KAMPUCHEA-
VIETNAM ARMED CONFLICT?*

2

Hsinhua Correspondent

The Soviet propaganda machine has recently churned out a
string of lies to slander China over the Kampuchea-Vietnam
armed conflict. A Soviet radio commentary on January 3 alleged that "the worsening relations between the Socialist Republic of Vietnam and Kampuchea have obviously been provoked by Peking." The Soviet newspaper, Izvestia, and TASS
time and again spread such rumors as "many Chinese military
advisers have taken part in the military actions of the Kampuchean side."

No one is going to believe these groundless fabrications
which are therefore not worth refuting. But what deserves attention is that, apart from deliberate animosity toward China,
the Soviet Union has an ulterior motive in choosing this very
moment to tell and spread such lies with unusual haste.

A law governing the Kremlin's actions is that, whenever it
wants to provoke an international dispute and interfere in it,
Moscow invariably tries to create a pretext and often plays
the role of a villain bringing suit before his victims in order
to divert people's attention away from its own machinations.

History has repeatedly proven that there is indeed some
villain who makes it a practice to fish in troubled waters by
provoking international incidents, and it is none other than the
Sovict Union itself. In 1971, taking advantage of the dispute

*From Peking Review, No. 4 (January 27, 1978), 24-25.

between India and Pakistan, it supported one party and attacked the other. Trading on the Cyprus situation in 1974, it again stepped in, exacerbating contradictions between the two communities on the island and differences between the countries concerned, in an attempt to infiltrate the area and expand and strengthen its position to contend with the United States for hegemony in the Mediterranean. From 1975 to 1976, it exploited the differences among the three Angolan national-liberation organizations to provoke a civil war by backing one and attacking the other two. Moreover, it sent vast numbers of mercenaries to carry out armed intervention against this newly independent country and turned it into a forward base for Soviet expansion into southern Africa.

In 1977, utilizing the differences between Angola and Zaire, it again instigated mercenaries to invade Zaire. Then, it stretched its hands into the Horn of Africa and the Middle and Near East, cashed in on the disputes among the countries concerned to aggravate contradictions there so as to expand its sphere of influence.

Not long ago, the Soviet Union held an airlift exercise on an amazing scale with the Horn of Africa as the focus. This makes it abundantly clear how it uses disputes among Third World countries for its own strategic ends. It is common knowledge that Moscow has been trying for a long time to establish its hegemony over Southeast Asia and bring the region into its "system of collective security in Asia." Now it is repeating its stock tricks on the question of the Kampuchea-Vietnam conflict. It is Moscow itself that is stirring up trouble for the sole purpose of bringing unrest to the region, yet it mounts a barrage of rumors in order to vilify China. Its purpose, of course, is to divert people's attention and conceal its strategic aim of establishing domination over Southeast Asia.

The other aim of this deluge of Soviet slanders is to sow discord. It has alleged that "the Peking authorities refuse to be reconciled to the presence of a unified, socialist Vietnam...." This cock-and-bull story is the height of absurdity. As is well known, the Chinese people have always given powerful backing to the Vietnamese people in their war against U.S. aggression and for national salvation and in their struggle for the reunification of their fatherland. The Vietnamese people who have been through those difficult war years can testify to this historical fact. On the other hand, it is an irrefutable fact that throughout the five decisive years of war waged by the Kampuchean people against the traitorous Lon Nol clique, the Soviet Union all along sided with the clique and antagonized the Kampuchean people. It smeared their war of national liberation as a "fratricidal war" and, working hand in glove with the Lon Nol clique, it clandestinely tried to rig up a "third force" in that country to sabotage the revolution of the Kampuchean people. The Soviet government maintained diplomatic relations with the puppet Lon Nol regime right up to the last day of the traitorous clique.

Consequently, it is the Soviet authorities who "refuse to be reconciled with" the presence of a revolutionary and socialist democratic Kampuchea in Southeast Asia and will not be satisfied until they get rid of it. It is for this reason that Moscow is zealously telling lies in trying to confuse the picture to mask its wild ambitions.

Soviet lies and slanders, however, have a positive use: they help heighten the vigilance of the people of Indochina and elsewhere in Southeast Asia against the Soviet Union. The people are waiting to see what further acts the Soviet hegemonists are going to commit in an attempt to capitalize on the armed conflict between Kampuchea and Vietnam.

STATEMENT OF CHINESE FOREIGN MINISTRY ON
EXPULSION OF CHINESE RESIDENTS BY VIETNAM*
(Excerpts)

3

(June 9, 1978)

Peking Review

In his statement on the question of the so-called "Hoa people
in Vietnam" of May 27, 1978, the spokesman of the Ministry of
Foreign Affairs of the Socialist Republic of Vietnam distorted
the facts and made unfounded countercharges in an attempt to
put the blame for the expulsion of Chinese nationals on the
Chinese side. With regard to this the Chinese Government
cannot remain silent.

1. In his statement the spokesman of the Ministry of Foreign Affairs of Vietnam tried, in effect, to deny the objective
fact that there are large numbers of Chinese nationals residing in Vietnam and willfully distorted the agreement between
the Chinese Communist Party and the Vietnamese Workers'
Party on the question of Chinese residing in Vietnam, attempting thereby to deceive public opinion and justify the Vietnamese
policy of discrimination against, and ostracism, persecution
and expulsion of, Chinese residents. This is obviously a futile
attempt.

It is well known that there are one million and several hundred thousand Chinese residents in Vietnam, the overwhelming
majority of whom are working people and about 90 percent of
whom reside in south Vietnam. In 1955 the Chinese and Vietnamese Parties exchanged views on the question of their nationality and their rights and duties. Subsequently, after repeated consultations the two sides acknowledged that the Chi-

*From Peking Review, No. 24 (June 16, 1978), 13-16.

nese residing in north Vietnam, on condition of their enjoying equal rights as the Vietnamese and after being given sustained and patient persuasion and ideological education, may by steps adopt Vietnamese nationality on a voluntary basis. As to the question of the Chinese residing in south Vietnam, that was to be resolved through consultations between the two countries after the liberation of south Vietnam. These principles were put forward by the Chinese side out of the desire to deepen the fraternal friendship between the Chinese and Vietnamese peoples, and they are in accordance with China's consistent policy of encouraging overseas Chinese to choose, on a voluntary basis, the nationality of their country of residence, as well as with the general international rule against forcibly naturalizing foreign residents. At that time the Vietnamese Party and Government expressed approval and support for these principles and repeatedly stressed in their documents that "the adoption of Vietnamese nationality by Chinese should be a purely voluntary decision and there should be no coercion whatsoever," and that "those who are not yet willing to adopt Vietnamese nationality are still allowed all rights and may not be discriminated against. It is absolutely impermissible to use rash orders to compel them or to slight them." They also affirmed that politically the Chinese residing in Vietnam would enjoy the same rights and have the same duties as the Vietnamese, that economically they would enjoy the freedom to engage in lawful industrial and commercial undertakings, that culturally they would enjoy the freedom to run schools and papers and that their ways and customs would be respected. In recent years, however, the Vietnamese Government, running counter to the agreement between the two Parties, has compelled Chinese residents to adopt Vietnamese nationality, zealously pursued a policy of discrimination against, and ostracism and persecution of Chinese residents and seriously infringed on their legitimate rights and interests, making it difficult for the mass of Chinese residents to make a living, and has even expelled large numbers of them back to China.

. . .

Facts show that the Vietnamese side long ago thoroughly
violated the agreement between the Chinese and Vietnamese
Parties. Yet the spokesman of the Vietnamese Foreign Ministry now claims that the Vietnamese side "has constantly respected and strictly applied this agreement." This assertion
is not convincing at all.

2. Resorting to sophistry and futile denials, the spokesman
of the Vietnamese Foreign Ministry attributed the massive expulsion of Chinese residents to "information" spread by "certain bad elements among the Hoa people" and said that this was
"a deliberate act." The way things developed fully shows that
it is no other than Vietnam itself that, out of its needs in domestic affairs and international relations, has adopted and
systematically pursued a policy of discrimination, ostracism,
persecution and expulsion of Chinese residents. This is a
grave anti-China step taken by the Vietnamese side in a deliberate attempt to undermine Sino-Vietnamese relations.

Indeed, there have been circulating for some time in Vietnam a number of calculated anti-China rumors to the effect
that "China supports Kampuchea in opposing Vietnam, war
will break out between China and Vietnam," etc. Not a few
Vietnamese officials and public security personnel have used
these rumors as a means to deceive and frighten Chinese residents into returning to China. In their unwarranted complaints
and charges against China early this year, certain Vietnamese
diplomats asserted that an "abnormal situation" had arisen
along China's border, and that China was "calling for an attack on Vietnam." The similarity between these allegations
and the rumors floating around in Vietnam could not possibly
be a mere coincidence, but precisely shows that these rumors
were deliberately fabricated and spread by the Vietnamese side.

The Vietnamese side started early in 1977 to push a policy
of "purifying the border areas" in the provinces adjacent to
China and expel back to China groups of border inhabitants
who had moved from China to settle down in Vietnam a long
time ago. In October 1977 it began to expel Chinese residents
in Hoang Lien Son, Lai Chau, Son La and other provinces in

northwest Vietnam. Then the measure gradually expanded into
the massive expulsion of Chinese residents from various parts
of north Vietnam. The Chinese Government repeatedly tried
to persuade the Vietnamese Government to uphold Sino-
Vietnamese friendship by taking steps to halt the expulsion of
Chinese residents. The Vietnamese side, however, turned a
deaf ear and created on a nationwide scale even more serious
incidents of ostracizing Chinese residents. Tens of thousands
of Chinese were transported overland by the Vietnamese side
to such places as Lao Cai, Dong Dang and Mong Cai along the
Sino-Vietnamese border and then driven back to China, while
a large number of others were forced to return in small boats
across the sea. The numbers of expelled Chinese have increased daily over the past two months, from several hundred
a day in early April to several thousand a day in late May,
with their total exceeding 100,000 by the end of May.

. . .

As for the thousands of Vietnamese residents in China, the
Chinese Government has never subjected them to any discrimination, but has always respected and protected their proper
rights and interests. They enjoy the same rights as Chinese
citizens in respect to work, education and medical care. They
are given more favored treatment than Chinese citizens in respect to the supply of necessities. This is a universally known
fact which brooks no distortion.

3. The sharp increase in the number of Chinese expelled
home due to aggravated discrimination against the Chinese
residents by the Vietnamese side has suddenly created for
China great financial and material difficulties and burdens.
In line with its consistent policy of "protecting the interests
of overseas Chinese and aiding returned Chinese," the Chinese
Government needs to make prompt, adequate arrangements for
the resettlement of the numerous Chinese expelled by Vietnam.
Therefore, it cannot but decide to cancel part of its complete-
factory aid projects to Vietnam so as to divert the funds and
materials to making arrangements for the life and productive
work of the returned Chinese. It is clear that the cancellation

of a part of China's aid projects to Vietnam is a necessary and involuntary emergency measure, it is purely a consequence of the Vietnamese policy of ostracizing the Chinese nationals.

. . .

A great change took place in the situation of Vietnam with the ending of the Vietnam war in 1975. On the other hand, China has encountered tremendous difficulties because of the sabotage of the "gang of four" and as a result of repeated strong earthquakes and other serious natural disasters. Even in these circumstances China has continued to give many-sided aid to Vietnam and undertake many aid projects to the best of its ability. Naturally, the annual sum of China's aid to Vietnam in peacetime showed a reduction as compared with the exceptional case in the war years, but the reason is not difficult to understand. The Chinese side repeatedly explained its own difficulties to the Vietnamese side in the hope that the latter would give a respite to the Chinese people. The late Premier Chou En-lai, during his serious illness, personally said to a Vietnamese leader: "During the war, when you were in the worst need, we took many things from our own army to give to you. We made very great efforts to help you. The sum of our aid to Vietnam still ranks first among our aids to foreign countries. You should let us have a respite and regain strength." At that time Vietnamese leaders expressed understanding on many occasions. But now the Vietnamese side has seen fit to hurl vicious slanders and attacks at Chinese aid. The Chinese people are greatly pained and angered by such an action of returning evil for good.

4. In his statement, the spokesman of the Vietnamese Foreign Ministry proposed that the Vietnamese and Chinese sides "meet" to resolve their so-called "differences on the question of the Hoa people." We consider that in the present circumstances such a proposal was made purely out of propaganda needs.

. . .

5. China and Vietnam are linked by common mountains and rivers and the two peoples share weal and woe. In the long

revolutionary struggles, the two peoples sympathized with and
supported each other and formed a profound brotherhood and
militant solidarity. It is in the fundamental interests of both
the Chinese and Vietnamese peoples and it is the common desire of the two peoples to strengthen and develop steadily this
revolutionary friendship and solidarity. The Chinese Communist Party and the Chinese Government and people have always
valued highly this friendship and solidarity and made unremitting efforts in this connection. Though in recent years the
Vietnamese side has taken a series of actions vitiating the relations between the two countries and a variety of anti-China
steps, the Chinese side, mindful of the overall interest, has
all along exercised self-restraint and tolerance and repeatedly
expressed to Vietnamese leaders its sincere hope that the two
sides would make joint efforts and take effective measures to
uphold the traditional friendship between the two peoples....

V

Energy, economic, and maritime issues

Documentary Introduction

Five issue-oriented selections are included in this chapter. They differ from the geographically oriented documents in the previous three chapters.

The first selection, "Behind the So-Called 'Energy Crisis'" (1974), argues strongly that the crisis was merely a crisis of the capitalist system and a result of the exploitation of the Middle East's energy resources by the superpowers. The "oil weapon" was used by the Arab people simply for their national independence and sovereignty; consequently, it was justified.

The second selection, "Third World Struggle against Hegemony in the Economic Sphere" (1975), again praises the "oil struggle" as an example of the Third World's opposition to the two hegemonic powers and urges Third World countries to strive for food grain self-sufficiency in order to rid themselves of the superpowers' economic domination.

The third selection, "What Motivates 'Economic Cooperation'" (1977), points out that Soviet "economic cooperation" with the West was actually Moscow's scheme to obtain sophisticated technology and equipment from the West.

The fourth selection, "Soviet Social-Imperialism: Maritime Hegemonic Features Fully Exposed" (1976), charges that the Soviet Union has deployed its submarines and surface vessels (including warships) throughout the world, running from the

Barents Sea, to the Atlantic Ocean, to the Pacific Ocean, to the Caribbean Sea. Its expansion in sea power has been growing rapidly.

In the fifth selection, "Another Struggle against Hegemonism" (1977), Peking interprets the Third United Nations Conference on the Law of the Sea as a "struggle" by the developing countries (including a 200-mile coastal limit) against the old maritime privileges of the superpowers.

BEHIND THE SO-CALLED "ENERGY CRISIS"*

1

Ch'ang Ch'ien

The major capitalist countries are now undergoing a serious "energy crisis." Shortages in petroleum supplies have caused a "petroleum upheaval" in their production and life. Factories are closed because of the shortage of electric power. Automobiles are not driven because of the lack of fuel. Room temperatures are down, and the lights have gone out. Prices have soared following the rising price of oil. The stock market value has dropped because of gloomy economic prospects. International political and economic relations are also affected by the "energy crisis." This crisis has caused the major capitalist countries to go through the "coldest winter." There is a phrase in the novel "The Dream of the Red Chamber" that reads: "Gloomy like a dying lamp," which suitably depicts the capitalist world's confusion and darkness and the gloomy outlook of a number of bourgeois representatives.

This situation has led to general discussion. Foreign bourgeois newspapers have said that the cause of the energy crisis is the "exhaustion of energy resources." Some have absurdly blamed the Arabs for using oil as a weapon. These arguments have either evaded the key problem or shifted the blame for

*From Hung-ch'i [Red Flag], No. 2, February 1, 1974. This translation is taken from Selections from People's Republic of China Magazines (Hong Kong: American Consulate General), Nos. 769-770 (February 25-March 4, 1974), 96-100.

the crisis onto others, turning facts upside down.

What is the truth behind the situation?

It has been said that the present "energy crisis" is due mainly to a shortage of petroleum supplies. Superficially, this seems to be a question of natural resources. Actually this is not the case. The energy resources of this world, including a number of major capitalist countries, are abundant. According to the most conservative estimates, they can last up to one thousand years. Moreover, following developments in production and the constant increase of man's knowledge, man is discovering and will continue to discover new energy resources. The "energy crisis" in the capitalist world, in essence, reflects the crisis of the capitalist system; it is an outcome of aggravated contradictions in the capitalist-imperialist system. It is caused by the brutal exploitation and wild plunder of the people at home and abroad by monopoly capital. So far as the present is concerned, it is also a direct result of the frantic external expansion and struggle for world hegemony carried out by the two superpowers, U.S. imperialism and Soviet revisionism.

Under the capitalist system, "the production of surplus value or profit is the absolute law of this mode of production" (Marx, Capital). The aim of the monopoly bourgeoisie is to seek maximum profits. In exploiting energy resources, the capitalists are not concerned with using natural resources rationally, but only with gaining ever greater profits. More often than not, exploitation of various energy resources depends on the profits they produce. In the past, coal was the main source of power and the "food of industry." Today, there are still abundant coal reserves. But the coal industry has generally declined in all major capitalist countries. Even in the United States, which has the largest coal reserves, coal accounts for only one-fifth of the present energy production. The reason for this is that from the angle of profit, coal mining is far less profitable than oil extraction, thus attracting slight attention from the capitalists. Oil can also be extracted from oil shale and oil sand, whose known reserves are several times higher than petroleum reserves. But, these are left in the cold by the greedy capitalists and not developed because they do not produce as much profit as direct petroleum extraction.

Capitalism means waste. In the capitalist world, the anarchic state of production and the extreme extravagancy in living cause serious waste of petroleum. Pockets of oil are destroyed due to wanton drilling, and oil wells are unproductive because of the excessive extraction which has lowered oil pressure, thus leaving a large amount of valuable oil underground. According to estimates, the recovery rate of petroleum is only 35 percent in the United States, meaning that two tons of petroleum are wasted for every ton extracted. Waste in utilizing oil is even more shocking. At present, electric power used for nonproduction purposes is one-third to one-half the total power output in principal capitalist countries. The U.S. press has also admitted that half of the energy consumed in the United States is wasted. Moreover, imperialism and social-imperialism are engaged in arms expansion and war preparations, launching wars of aggression everywhere, thus causing unlimited oil consumption and waste. Such is the basic reason for the existing "energy crisis" in the so-called developed capitalist countries, at a time when the world's energy resources have never been so rich and varied as now. As some Americans have said: "We cannot blame mother nature but Uncle Sam."

Imperialism means aggression and plunder. In view of the economic and strategic value of petroleum and the greater profits gained by seizing the petroleum of foreign countries, the monopoly capitalists have competed in seizing the land and the oil of the Third World countries rather than extracting the petroleum in their own countries. Particularly, they covet the Middle East, which has rich petroleum reserves and holds an important strategic position politically and geographically. The Middle East, which contains two-thirds of the known petroleum reserves in the world, has shallow oil layers which make for a high rate of successful drilling and low production costs. For example, the cost for extracting one ton of petroleum in Kuwait is only one-twentieth of that in the United States. Thus, Middle East petroleum has become a money-producing tree for

foreign monopoly capital in seizing huge profits, and the region
has been the focal point of protracted struggle among imperialist powers. After World War II, replacing Britain, the United
States became the largest plunderer of Middle East petroleum
resources, with U.S. monopoly capital now controlling over
one-half the petroleum production there. At the end of 1972,
direct U.S. private investment in Middle East petroleum totaled
1.8 billion U.S. dollars, with profits of 2.4 billion in that year
alone. The profit rate was as high as 130 percent, or 10 times
the average rate of profits of all U.S. overseas investments.
The false prosperity of imperialism after the war was founded
precisely on the plunder of natural resources and on the blood
and sweat of the people of the Third World.

Soviet revisionist social-imperialism is governed by the
same laws that govern imperialism. Highly ambitious, it has
joined the ranks of imperialist powers in dividing the world.
Unable to extract its own petroleum, it invites and begs for investments from Western countries. Yet it has long thirsted
for Middle East petroleum, making every effort to infiltrate
the Middle East to contend with the United States for the monopoly of petroleum there. With its "military assistance" and
"economic aid," it is going all out to hedge its bets. It has engaged vigorously in such plundering activities as "trading arms
for petroleum" and "trading machines for petroleum," and
gained huge profits from its speculation and manipulations. In
reselling the natural gas of a certain country alone, Soviet revisionism has amassed profits as high as 300 percent. Tricks
used by Soviet revisionism in plundering the Middle East of its
oil even surpass those of the Western imperialist countries!

For a long time now, the true victims on the question of
petroleum have been the Arab countries and other oil-producing
countries of the Third World. The medium and small countries
which have large petroleum resources are poor and undeveloped,
whereas the consumer countries are rich and developed. Where
there is oppression, there is resistance. It is precisely this
irrational situation that has forced the oil-producing countries
of the Third World to rise and fight for their sovereignty and

national resources. Sharing the same hatred against the enemy
this time, the Arab countries are using petroleum as a weapon
to oppose Israeli Zionism and its supporters by reducing their
oil production and raising its price. This is a direct result of
the collusion and contention between the two hegemonic powers
— the United States and the Soviet Union — in the Middle East.
Due to its strategic position and petroleum resources, both
hegemonic powers are trying hard to win over the Middle East.
Essentially, the crux of the Middle East issue is petroleum,
which is closely connected with the struggle for world hegemony. As a Western newspaper wrote: "Whoever has petroleum controls the world, particularly Europe which relies on
the East for oil supply." For this reason, completely ignoring
the interests of the Arab people, the two hegemonic powers are
carrying out "no war, no peace" activities in the Middle East
and supporting and instigating Israeli aggression. This state
of affairs has forced the Arab nations to rise in resistance.
The Arab countries' oil struggle is one against imperialism
and hegemonism. The two hegemonic powers can no longer
completely control the Middle East, nor plunder other countries as they please. The oil crisis has merely reflected the
crisis of their hegemony.

The capitalist world's shock over the Arab countries' use of
oil as a weapon answers this question clearly: Who feeds whom
in the world today? In the past, the imperialists all along
claimed that it was they who fed the people of the developing
countries and that these people could not survive for one day
without their "aid." Now, the oil struggle has once more
shown the truth, that without enslaving and exploiting the developing countries, imperialism and social-imperialism could
not live a day longer. They are all parasites sucking the blood
of the developing countries. Their wealth is wealth from plunder, and the poverty of the Third World is caused by their exploitation and plunder. The oil struggle has emancipated people's minds, further heightening their awakening and strengthening their unity. This will have a far-reaching influence on
the struggle of all peoples.

The "energy crisis" is a manifestation of the great disorder in the world today. It will continue to bring about disorderly changes in the world situation. The various contradictions among imperialist powers are being aggravated, and in particular, the contradictions between the two superpowers — the United States and the Soviet Union — and the people of various countries and between the two superpowers are becoming even more acute. The U.S.-Soviet struggle in the Middle East is becoming more and more frantic and vehement. They will never give up their own interests. Energetically playing up the "energy crisis," spokesmen of U.S. monopoly capital are trying to squeeze the American people in order to shift the crisis onto others and reap huge profits, but their main purpose is to exert pressure on the Third World and strengthen their contention with Soviet revisionism in order to safeguard their vested interests in the Middle East. To contend with the United States for hegemony in the Middle East, Soviet revisionism, while pretending to give support to the Arab people and selling them out in fact, has done its utmost to spread the fallacy that Middle East oil should be made an "international property." It declared: "Although Arab oil is Arab property in form, in fact it is international property." Obviously, the spearhead of this fallacy is directed at the Arab world and at promoting the imperialist fallacy that "plunder is justified." At the same time, it is also directed at the petroleum hegemony of the other superpower, saying: You cannot have it all; let us "divide the profit equally." Such imperialist theory shows that it is the ferocious enemy of the Arab people and also exposes its frantic ambition to expand into the Middle East and the Persian Gulf region after inheriting the mantle of the old tsar. But times have changed. The Arab people are no longer lambs at the mercy of others. They have already taken up the oil and other weapons to fight for the defense of their national independence, sovereignty and the right to existence.

As for the Western fallacy that the energy resources of the world will soon be exhausted, this is groundless anxiety of declining classes. They have always thought of their own crises and doom as the end of the world. Matter will never become extinct. Natural energy resources are inexhaustible, and mankind has unlimited capability to understand and conquer nature, a capability which will never remain at the same level. The development from creating a spark by striking pieces of flint or friction to start a fire to today's coal, petroleum, and atomic and solar energy fully proves this point. Not only are the varieties of energy resources increasing in number, but so are their applications. Therefore, there is no basis whatsoever for pessimism over energy. The question is this: since the beginning of the class society, the development and utilization of energy resources have been linked with modes of social production. The advanced social system spurs the development of social productive forces, whereas the decadent and declining social system obstructs them. For example, China is a large country with rich natural resources. It has all kinds of natural energy resources. But, in semicolonial and semifeudal China, the imperialists not only seized large quantities of its valuable energy resources, but also branded it as a "country poor in oil." Since liberation, the situation in China has changed completely. "The socialist system has promoted the development of productive forces by leaps and bounds." Natural energy resources have been discovered and developed continuously. Under the guidance of Chairman Mao's revolutionary line, the Chinese people, implementing the principle "maintain independence and keep the initiative in our own hands and rely on our own efforts," have in a short time removed the label of a "country poor in oil." The days when China used to rely completely on "foreign oil" are gone for good. Today, China is not only self-sufficient in oil but also exports it. The Chinese people are writing a completely new chapter in the development and utilization of energy resources.

The "energy crisis" is a crisis of the capitalist system. In the world, there will never be such a thing as "energy exhaustion." Only capitalism, "this counterrevolutionary system, has exhausted itself and its social forces" (Lenin, "Today's Russia and Workers Movement"). This crisis shows clearly that imperialism is going further down the road of decline. No matter what kind of situation arises regarding the supply and demand for energy resources in the capitalist world, this general trend in the development of history will never change.

"Were nature sentient, she too would pass from youth to age, but in man's world seas change into mulberry fields." The world is advancing in the midst of disorder. The people are the greatest motive force in changing society and transforming nature. The proletariat and the revolutionary people will ultimately bury the evil system of exploitation which creates all kinds of crises. They will realize the great ideal of communism. Mankind will definitely advance valiantly along the broad avenue of transforming society and nature, "attain freedom from nature," and create miracles which are inconceivable today.

THIRD WORLD STRUGGLE AGAINST HEGEMONY IN THE ECONOMIC SPHERE*

2

Peking Review

Biggest Exploiters in International Trade

The two superpowers have become more and more relentless in exploiting and plundering the Third World. They have intensified their rivalry for sources of raw materials, overseas markets, and spheres of influence and their moves to shift the burden of their crisis onto others at a time when the capitalist world is in the throes of its most severe postwar economic crisis.

Price Differentials between Raw Materials and Manufactured Goods

One of the usual practices of imperialism, especially the superpowers, in trade is to mercilessly exploit the Third World countries by exchange of unequal values through buying cheap and selling dear. This practice has become increasingly sharp in recent years. According to statistics of the United Nations Conference on Trade and Development, prices (in terms of U.S. dollars) of primary products exported by developing countries (not including fuel) went down 56 percent in April this year as compared with the same period last year. The copper price on

*From Peking Review, No. 39 (September 26, 1975), 21-25, 29.

303

the London international market dropped from 1,268 pounds to 561 pounds per metric ton. The price of Philippine copra was down to 287 U.S. dollars per metric ton from 700 dollars. West Africa's palm oil fell from 1,455 U.S. dollars to 444 dollars per metric ton. Prices of other major commodities, such as palm core, natural rubber, cotton, wool, cocoa, coffee, sugar, and coconut oil, all dropped drastically.

On the other hand, prices of manufactured goods, though very high already, keep rising. The U.N. Monthly Bulletin of Statistics shows that the price index (taking 1950 as 100) of industrial goods exported by developed countries to developing countries shot up to 193 in 1973 and to 230 in 1974. Such a big margin of increase topped that of the previous few years. It is noteworthy that prices of goods, large quantities of which are needed by the Third World countries, went up even more sharply. According to newspapers in Southeast Asian countries, prices of chemical fertilizers that they imported from developed countries rose over 100 percent in June 1974 against the same period of the previous year; steel, 65 percent; metal ware, 51 percent, and machinery, 33 percent. International Financial Statistics of the International Monetary Fund shows that in 1974 the developing countries paid 23,000 million U.S. dollars more for imports from developed countries as a result of price hikes.

The two superpowers are the biggest exploiters in this regard. Statistics indicate that in the last few years the United States, through exchange of unequal values, has grabbed an average of 2,000 million U.S. dollars in profits from developing countries annually. By taking advantage of the economic crisis in the capitalist world, the Soviet Union has been wildly robbing the developing countries....

Apart from this, the profit it reaped by reselling at higher prices the Arab oil obtained in exchange for arms reached the rate of 300 percent.

Dumping Commodities

Dumping commodities by boosting exports and restricting imports is another way the superpowers exploit the Third World countries. According to International Financial Statistics, U.S. exports to these countries came to 31,700 million dollars in 1974, or 57 percent more than in 1973. Statistics released recently by the U.S. Department of Commerce show that the favorable balance of trade with developing countries in Asia and Latin America reached 3,200 million U.S. dollars in the first half of 1975, five times the 600 million dollars in the same period of 1974. As a result of the 1974 Trade Act, the United States withholds preferential tariff treatment from the OPEC member states, members of the associations of raw material producers, and countries that have nationalized properties of U.S. enterprises which had a grip on their national economies. On its part, the Soviet Union has taken every opportunity to dump manufactured goods on Third World markets. According to the Soviet Economic Gazette, Soviet exports to developing countries in 1974 were valued at 4,620 million U.S. dollars, some 630 million more than in 1973. As a result, the Soviet Union had a 1974 favorable balance of 1,360 million dollars.

Exports from the developing countries, however, present an entirely different picture. According to International Financial Statistics, Third World countries' exports in the world's total for 1974 did not reach the 1950 level, even with the greatly increased exports of the OPEC members included. If the few petroleum-exporting countries were excluded, Third World countries' exports would account for a mere 12.4 percent of the world's total. At the same time, these countries' imports in 1974 increased by 79 percent over 1973.

To obtain cheap labor and plunder natural resources, the superpowers have stepped up the pace of their capital exports to the Third World in recent years. This in turn has stimulated their commodity exports. Transnational companies set up by the United States in Third World countries control production and sales of many raw materials to ensure markets and superprofits for the holding companies. These companies control nearly 30 percent of the exports of developing countries the world over.

The Soviet Union does not allow itself to be outdone in this aspect. While greatly increasing capital exports to Asia, Africa, and Latin America by means of loans, "assistance," and "cooperation," it treads in the steps of Western transnationals by setting up "joint enterprises" or "companies" and extending their tentacles into mining, processing, transport, trade, and other important sectors of the developing countries. It is also plundering these countries by selling outmoded machinery and equipment and other manufactured goods at high prices and buying agricultural and mineral products cheaply.

Arms Dealers

What merits special attention is that since the outbreak of the current economic crisis in the capitalist world, the superpowers have been going in for arms deals in a big way, turning the Third World into their principal munitions market. According to a UPI report, the United States exported 8,300 million dollars worth of munitions in fiscal 1974, more than doubling the 3,900 million dollars of 1973. Of this, some 7,000 million dollars worth of munitions went to the Middle East.

The Soviet Union is not reconciled to falling behind. According to the Japanese weekly Toyo Keizai, Soviet munitions exports totaled 5,500 million U.S. dollars in 1974, more than double the figure of 2,500 million dollars in 1973. The U.S. magazine Time reported that 45 percent of the 1974 Soviet munitions exports were sold to Middle East countries.

The two superpowers have made enormous profits from munitions sales. The Toyo Keizai reported that the export price of the U.S. F-14 plane more than doubled in 1974, the year which saw a drastic drop in prices of primary products on the world market. The Soviet Union, on its part, is selling out-of-date weapons to developing countries at high prices. According to an August 16 report in Oman, a paper in the Sultanate of Oman, Ahmed al Ghasmi, vice commander-in-chief and concurrently chief of staff of the armed forces of the Yemen Arab Republic, said the arms his country obtained from the Soviet Union "are outmoded leftovers from World War II, some are mere trash from World War I. They should be sent to the military museum."

The Significant Oil Struggle

The Third World oil-producing countries have persevered in united struggle since the Sixth Special Session of the U.N. General Assembly last year. They have made common cause with other raw material-producing countries. This has resulted in new victories in the struggle against hegemonism.

The oil struggle in the last year or so has been revolving mainly around the price question. With the aggravation of the capitalist world's economic crisis and the decline in oil sales on the world market, the United States seized the opportunity to make a big noise about "overproduction of oil" in an attempt to force the producing countries to lower prices. The Soviet Union time and again has advocated that prices should be "beneficial to all countries" and accused the producing countries of "unilaterally raising the oil price." Maintaining equitable oil prices thus has become the focus of the Third World oil-producing countries' struggle against hegemonism.

Because of the grave economic crisis in the major capitalist countries, oil consumption last year in the United States, Western Europe, and Japan dropped 5 percent, by a total of 80 million to 100 million tons. The United States thus put economic, and even military, pressure on the producing countries to cut the price. The latter, however, refused to be cowed. Instead, they cut production to maintain the price. Since the beginning of this year, the U.S.-controlled "International Energy Agency" has threatened to cut oil imports by 100 million tons this year, that is, 2 million barrels a day. OPEC member states responded by reducing production — by over 10 percent in the first quarter of the year, or about 4 million barrels a day — thereby thwarting the superpower's schemes. Owing to the struggle of the producing countries, the posted price of crude oil has been frozen at 11.651 U.S. dollars (nearly four times that before the 1973 October War in the Middle East) per barrel since January last year. Meanwhile, they have raised the rate of taxation. Rent for oil fields of foreign companies has increased to 20 percent from 12.5 percent in a year, and the oil tax to 85 percent from 55 percent so as to limit the profits of foreign capital and

guarantee an increased real revenue for the oil-producing
countries.

Inflation and the dollar devaluation in the capitalist world,
however, have caused prices of manufactured goods imported
by the Third World oil-producing countries to skyrocket (the
average increase was 26 percent in 1974 alone), while the real
purchasing power of oil earnings has declined by a big margin.
To safeguard the purchasing power, it was decided at the OPEC
ministerial conference in Gabon last June that oil prices would
be readjusted from October 1 and the oil trade would be carried
on in terms of the International Monetary Fund's Special Drawing Rights instead of the devaluated U.S. dollar.

Stepping Up Nationalization

Meanwhile, to safeguard state sovereignty, the Third World
producing countries over the last year and more have stepped
up nationalization and tightened their control of foreign oil companies' shares. In 1974, Saudi Arabia, Kuwait, Qatar, and the
United Arab Emirates controlled 60 percent of these companies'
shares, eight years in advance of the agreements signed with
Western oil companies at the end of 1972. Furthermore, Kuwait
and Dubai in the United Arab Emirates took over 100 percent of
the shares of foreign companies last January. On the basis of
the nationalization of a major part of their oil industry, Iraq
and Libya and other countries nationalized some more foreign-
owned companies or took over more foreign shares. Nigeria
holds 55 percent of the shares in foreign oil companies. Venezuela will nationalize the entire oil industry starting January 1
next year.

The producing countries now own a major part of the crude
oil turned out in their countries. One-fifth (approximately 300
million tons) of their total output can be sold freely on the international market without having to resell it to foreign companies.
Moreover, step by step, they have taken control of prospecting,
exploiting, processing, storage, transport, sales, and use of oil.
These tremendous changes marked the collapse of the oil con-

cessions imposed on the producing countries by the imperialists in past decades and the important move to deepen the oil struggle.

As a result of the price rises, the Third World oil-producing countries have greatly increased their income. In 1974, the oil revenue of the thirteen OPEC members totaled more than 100,000 million dollars, more than four times the figure for 1973. "Petrodollars" have strengthened the Third World's economic power against hegemonism. They not only help the oil-producing countries develop their national economies and strengthen their national defense, but facilitate their efforts to support other developing countries and promote economic cooperation. The OPEC in 1974 granted to other developing countries 17,000 million dollars in aid. Of this, 3,870 million dollars have been allocated. This has dealt a heavy blow to the two hegemonic powers in their schemes to sow discord in the Third World.

The Oil Struggle Sets the Example

The oil struggle gives a new impetus to the Third World's struggle in the economic sphere. From the victories in this struggle, the Third World countries see the light of their hopes. At the conference of developing countries on raw materials in Dakar last February attended by delegates of more than eighty countries, a resolution was adopted in support of the oil struggle, and it was declared that the oil struggle would be integrated with the struggle in connection with other raw materials. In the past year or so, a number of new organizations of raw material-producing countries has been set up by the Third World. Organizations for regional cooperation are also growing. These struggles have merged into a powerful current changing the old international economic order and battering at the biggest raw material plunderers in the world, the United States and the Soviet Union.

The Third World oil-producing countries are in favor of the policy of "dialogue" adopted by certain major oil-consuming countries in the Second World. Brushing aside the superpowers, some West European countries are developing their economic and trade relations with oil-producing countries. They have advanced from concluding barter agreements to exchange arms, machinery, and other equipment for oil to establishing long-term cooperation with the oil-producing countries in the economic, trade, and technical fields. A number of East European countries which have depended on the Soviet Union for oil supplies have, one after another, made direct deals with the producing countries, a trend that is worrying the Soviet Union.

Striving for Food Grain Self-Sufficiency

In order to get rid of superpower domination, an increasing number of Third World countries is developing agriculture based on grain production and doing away with the need to consume imported food. This is an important part of the Third World's struggle against hegemonism.

Despite vast land areas and abundant natural resources, many of these countries had to live on imported food as a result of the single-product economy arising from long-time domination and plunder by colonialists, imperialists, and superpowers. Statistics show that the Third World, with a population of more than 70 percent of humanity, produces only 45 percent of the world's grain output. In 1973, the developing countries and regions as a whole imported a net quantity of 38.2 million tons of cereals, the estimated volume for 1974 being well over 40 million tons.

Victims of Two Hegemonic Powers

Such a situation gives the two hegemonic powers, the Soviet Union and the United States, an opening for utilizing the question of food grain to intensify their efforts to control and plunder the Third World countries. The Soviet Union this year again is making heavy purchases of grain and sending grain prices soaring on the world market. Its 1972-73 purchases of approximately

30 million tons shoved wheat and rice prices up more than two-fold. It then used that grain for speculation. In 1972, the Soviet Union bought 440 million bushels of U.S. wheat at 1.63 dollars a bushel. In August 1973, it sold a good part of that for 4.7 dollars per bushel, thereby gathering in a fabulous profit. The other superpower, the United States, uses food as a weapon for political blackmail against, and economic control of, the Third World countries. Taking advantage of world food shortages, it sells grain at huge profits. For instance, in fiscal 1972-73 alone, it raked in 11,800 million dollars through trade in farm products.

More and more government leaders and people have come to realize the extreme importance of developing agricultural production and especially of becoming self-sufficient in grain for smashing the imperialist shackles and safeguarding their political and economic independence. Guinean President Sekou Touré has pointed out: "Agriculture is the foundation of economic development." Prime Minister Madame Sirimavo Bandaranaike of Sri Lanka has stressed developing food production as a means of solving the country's economic problem and saving it from economic exploitation by foreign powers. Tunisian Prime Minister Hedi Nouira has declared: "We should mobilize all our force and capability to give priority to agricultural production so as to ensure self-sufficiency in our food requirements and cease to suffer from dependence on foreigners." King Hassan II of Morocco has pointed out that vigorous agricultural development is necessary not only "for the consolidation of independence, but also for the opening up of a new prospect for this independence" and that without it, freedom, sovereignty, and dignity would be lost. The Government of the Congo declared that "self-support in food is one of the attributes of the independence of a country." In its Arusha Declaration of 1967, Tanzania made it clear that "agriculture is the base for development."

Many Third World countries in fact have already taken steps to promote agriculture. In Zaire, all privately owned foreign and Zairian plantations, farms, and ranches have been taken over by the state. Morocco has recovered 170,000 hectares of land from foreign ownership. The Zambian government has confiscated abandoned and idle land, which is mostly owned by foreigners. A U.S. military base in Trinidad and Tobago has been converted into a state farm. Many countries have increased their allocations for agricultural projects. In Trinidad and Tobago, government funds for food production this year are four times last year's. In Togo, 67 percent of the capital expenditure for its second five-year plan is assigned to agriculture. In addition, many countries are building water conservancy works to expand irrigated areas and prevent flood and drought. In Iran since 1967 when water resources were nationalized, twelve large dams and a number of smaller ones have been built with a capacity of holding a total of 13,000 million cubic meters of water. Thanks to impressive water conservancy projects, Mexico extended the area of irrigated land by nearly 60,000 hectares in 1973 and by over 107,000 hectares last year. The Mahaweli River Diversion Program is in full swing in Sri Lanka. Completion is expected at the end of this year, and the project will substantially increase the acreage of arable land and enable certain areas to yield two crops a year instead of one as at present. In some countries, attention is being paid to reclamation of wasteland, desert transformation, improvement of cultivation methods, training of their own agrotechnicians, and so forth.

Encouraging Results

Through their endeavors, quite a number of countries have achieved encouraging results in grain production. Statistics show that more than thirty Third World countries have already become self-sufficient or basically self-sufficient (95 percent or more) in grain, and more than twenty others are 90 percent self-sufficient. Ignatius Kutu Acheampong, head of state of Ghana, declared in July: "Gone are the days when we relied on foreign imports of food." Nepal is more than self-sufficient in grain and is exporting its surplus. The Sudan is self-sufficient in sorghum, its people's staple food. Annual production of wheat

in Mexico over the last several years has risen. Its output hit
an all-time high of 2.7 million tons in 1974-75. Besides meeting its own needs, Guyana has been able to export rice in recent
years.

Furthermore, some countries have brought about increases
in cotton, hemp, beet, and other industrial crop production. As
a result of the growth of cotton production, the textile industries of Tanzania, Sri Lanka, Cameroon, Ghana, and Ecuador
have registered corresponding development. In the main, these
countries have become self-sufficient in cotton cloth. Tanzania
also has built mills to produce hemp sacks and hemp cord, thus
bringing about a change in the abnormal situation of exporting
large quantities of sisal hemp and importing all the hemp sacks
and cord it needed. Sri Lanka has, since 1974, used domestic
kenaf to make paper pulp as a substitute for imported long fiber
pulp. Iran's 1973 bumper beet harvest greatly reduced its sugar
imports. Pakistan produced last year some 600,000 tons of
sugar which can meet the basic domestic requirements.

Facts prove that the countries of the Third World possess a
vast potential for developing agricultural production, particularly in grain, and that the superpowers' policy of using grain
to enslave and exploit them can be defeated.

[Appendix]

Raw Material Producing and Exporting
Countries' Organizations

Raw material production makes up a major portion of the national economy of many developing countries whose exports are
mainly primary products. To counter the superpowers' practice of forcing down prices of raw materials and shifting the
burden of economic crises onto them, these countries have set
up a number of raw material-producing and exporting organizations [outlined in the following chart].

Name	Date of Founding	Members
Organization of the Petroleum-Exporting Countries (OPEC)	September 1960	Iraq, Iran, Saudi Arabia, Kuwait, Venezuela, Qatar, Indonesia, Libya, United Arab Emirates, Algeria, Nigeria, Gabon, Ecuador.
Inter-African Coffee Organization (IACO)	December 1960	Burundi, Cameroon, Central African Republic, Congo, Dahomey, Ethiopia, Gabon, Ivory Coast, Madagascar, Nigeria, Rwanda, Sierra Leone, Tanzania, Togo, Uganda, Zaire, etc.
Association of Natural Rubber-Producing Countries (ANRPC)	1970	Malaysia, Singapore, Indonesia, Thailand, Sri Lanka, etc.
Intergovernmental Council of Copper-Exporting Countries (CIPEC)	June 1967	Chile, Peru, Zambia, Zaire.
International Bauxite Association (IBA)	March 1974	Jamaica, Guyana, Surinam, Guinea, Sierra Leone, Yugoslavia, Ghana, Haiti, Dominican Republic, etc.
Cocoa Producers' Alliance (COPAL)	May 1962	Ghana, Nigeria, Ivory Coast, Cameroon, Brazil, Togo.
Organization of Mercury-Producing Countries	May 1974	Algeria, Turkey, Mexico, Yugoslavia, etc.

Association of Iron Ore-Exporting Countries	April 1975	Algeria, Brazil, Chile, India, Mauritania, Peru, Sierra Leone, Tunisia, Venezuela, etc.
Association of Tungsten-Producing Countries	April 1975	Bolivia, Peru, Thailand, etc.
International Phosphate Association	1975	Morocco, Algeria, Tunisia, Senegal, Togo.
Organization of African Oilseeds Producers	August 1974	Algeria, Burundi, Dahomey, Ivory Coast, Mali, Nigeria, Senegal, Sudan, Gambia, Chad, Upper Volta, Zaire.
Inter-African Organization of Forestry and Timber Trade	May 1975	Cameroon, Central African Republic, Congo, Gabon, Ghana, Equatorial Guinea, Ivory Coast, Liberia, Madagascar, Tanzania, Zaire.
Southeast Asia Lumber Producers' Association	December 1974	Malaysia, Indonesia, Philippines.
Union of Banana-Exporting Countries (UPEB)	September 1974	Panama, Costa Rica, Honduras, Guatemala, Colombia, etc.
Group of Latin American and Caribbean Sugar-Exporting Countries	November 1974	Argentina, Barbados, Brazil, Colombia, Costa Rica, Cuba, Dominican Republic, Ecuador, El Salvador, Guatemala, Guyana, Honduras, Jamaica, Mexico, Nicaragua, Panama, Paraguay, Peru, Trinidad and Tobago, Venezuela.

WHAT MOTIVATES "ECONOMIC COOPERATION"* 3

Hsu Keng-sheng

Inadequacy in the economic strength is the Achilles' heel of Soviet social-imperialism in its cutthroat rivalry with U.S. imperialism for world hegemony. To alleviate its economic difficulties, the Soviet Union has in recent years steeply increased its trade with the West and sought enormous credits to finance the import of sophisticated equipment and technology and grain. All this is done by mouthing "materialization of relaxation" and "economic cooperation" and cashing in on the appeasement trend in the West. The Brezhnev clique thus has managed to boost the Soviet economic potential for the arms drive and war preparations and strengthen its hand in contending for world domination. Numerous facts show that all these enormous material benefits from the West have only served to help the Soviet Union keep up the momentum of its rapid military buildup and encourage its aggressive and expansionist pursuits abroad.

Appeasers in the West preach that placating the Soviet Union economically can soften up and ensnare that country and put a spoke in its expansionist wheel abroad. They even claim that such a course of action can change the antagonism existing between the West and the Soviet Union and bring about a relaxation of strained relations. Such appeasement thinking will get the West nowhere and, instead of curbing Soviet expansionism, can only further aggravate the danger of a new war.

*From Peking Review, No. 52 (December 26, 1977), 26-27, 32.

Storing Up Strategic Grain Reserves

Grain shortage has been a chronic illness of the Soviet Union. Eight out of the thirteen years since Brezhnev's assumption of power have seen agricultural shortfalls. At the meeting marking the sixtieth anniversary of the October Revolution, Brezhnev acknowledged that Soviet grain output this year would be 20 million tons less than the planned quota, that is to say, 13 percent less than the 1976 figure, or 21 to 26 million tons lower than the average annual output of the tenth five-year plan. Livestock breeding was also affected in many places because of inadequate feed. In the circumstances, the Soviet Union had to purchase vast amounts of grain and feed on the world market.

According to official Soviet statistics, Soviet grain imports in the 1965-76 period totaled 107 million tons, with over 83 million tons imported between 1972 and 1976. It is estimated that as a result of crop failures this year the Soviet Union must import 20 to 25 million tons of grain in the agricultural year ending September 1978. Meanwhile, it is increasing strategic grain reserves in a big way. U.S. satellite photos, reports say, reveal many large-sized underground granaries in the Soviet Union. The Soviet authorities have decided on a total granary capacity of 30 to 40 million tons to be built and made ready for use during the period of the tenth five-year plan. With the millions of tons of grain supplied by the West, they not only meet current needs but also fill the granaries of strategic reserves. In the calculations of the new tsars who are preparing for a new war, this grain reserves buildup is indispensable.

Developing War Industry

For years the Kremlin's all-out drive to expand the war industry has left the Soviet economy in a state of lopsided development — the consumer industries are backward, and the growth of production has fallen markedly. According to Western estimates, the technical level in many Soviet enterprises,

as compared with the West, generally lags behind twelve to
twenty years. So with "economic cooperation" as blandish-
ments, Moscow tries as best it can to obtain sophisticated technology and equipment from the West. In 1976, for example,
machinery and transport vehicles accounted for well over one-
third of the total exports by the Western countries to the Soviet
Union. Importation of such equipment is not only conducive to
making up Soviet deficiencies, but much of it can be made to
suit military purposes, or directly put to use for the military
industry in the event of war. Take the Kama River Truck Plant
built with the help of several Western countries for example.
When fully commissioned, it will turn out 150,000 to 200,000
multishaft trucks and 250,000 diesel engines annually. In case
war breaks out, it can easily be converted to produce tanks,
reconnaissance military cars, rocket launchers and military
transport vehicles. Some equipment is urgently needed by the
Soviet Union to develop its military technology. The U.S. Cyber
73 computer system which is widely used in the United States
for military purposes was bought by the Soviet Union last year.
This will make the Soviet computer technique leap forward by
as much as ten years. What is more, it will help the Soviet
Union improve its military research and production. Besides,
Moscow is intent on purchasing more sophisticated U.S. computer systems and "CF-6" jet engines with the biggest horse-
power and parts and accessories essential to producing items
for military purposes. The Soviet Union has also imported
other equipment from the West, including an array of items of
strategic significance such as rolling equipment for ferrous
and nonferrous metals with an annual capacity of over 6 million
tons, complete sets of equipment for chemical industry, large-
diameter natural gas pipes with a total length of 5,000 kilometers and large quantities of equipment for the petroleum industry. In 1972-73, the Soviet Union bought from the United
States 164 precision grinding machines capable of making precision miniature ball bearings needed for mass production of
guidance mechanisms for the multiple independently targetable
re-entry vehicles (MIRVs). In short, industrial equipment from

the West provides favorable conditions for the Soviet Union to build up its strength both economically and militarily.

Rearing a Tiger to Devour Oneself

The Soviet Union is low in funds because of militarization of the national economy. Huge military expenditures have consumed much of the country's resources, and this gives one the impression of a beggar dressing up as a "military giant." Time and again, Moscow went hat in hand to Western countries for large loans to import food grain, technology and equipment and ease the economic difficulties at home. Rough estimates put Soviet debts to Western countries at between 15,000 and 20,000 million U.S. dollars by the end of 1976. By giving Soviet social-imperialism shot after shot in the arm, the Western countries have given the Soviet Union a free hand to concentrate on building up its military strength at a faster tempo and to pose a greater threat to the West.

In the past few years, taking advantage of the appeasement trend in some Western circles to mislead the West, the Kremlin's new tsars have done their best to disguise themselves as partners in "economic cooperation" with the Western countries. They are never weary of advertising the benefits Western countries will reap from this cooperation which, they even assert, is "conducive to consolidating universal peace." But the stark reality has laid bare the new tsars' gimmick.

In this connection it is useful to review lessons in history. On the eve of World War II, when Germany embarked upon a course of rearmament and set to plotting a war of aggression, the United States, Britain, France and other countries energetically pushed a policy of appeasement in the economic sphere and gave Germany some bolstering up, in order to gain a breathing space for themselves. In addition to food grain, cotton and crude oil, Berlin was offered huge loans, technology, patent rights and supplies of industrial raw materials, and military equipment ranging from plane engines to spare parts. It was a case of rearing a tiger to devour oneself. The United

States, Britain, France and other countries had to pay for this
heavily. The appeasers of today have provided the superpower,
which is more ferocious and greedy than Hitlerite Germany,
with more food grain, more advanced technology and larger
loans. But they can neither soften the superpower up nor pin
it down. On the contrary, they will only whet its expansionist
ambitions and precipitate its launching of a new world war.

An increasing number of people in the West are now disturbed by the grave consequences of economic appeasement.
Articles in recent issues of the U.S. weekly Human Events
pointed to the fact that "U.S.-Soviet trade fuels the Soviet war
machine" and that "business deals" with the Soviet Union "en-
tail for the United States and the West significant political or
strategic risks" and are "contributions to Soviet military
power."

The U.S. press pointed out that Western countries are helping the Soviet Union and some countries in Eastern Europe to
revive their economies and expand their already bloated war
machines by offering them huge loans with low interest. A
newspaper in the West even figuratively said: "When the Soviet
Union pounces upon the West some day, people in the West will
"find" that "guillotines were built by Western contractors and
financed by Western banks with the low-interest loans."

MARITIME HEGEMONIC FEATURES
FULLY EXPOSED*

4

Soviet Social-Imperialism

Chiang Chien-tung

The seas and oceans have always been an arena of fierce
contention among colonialists, imperialists and hegemonists.
The scramble for maritime hegemony figures high in the
global strategy of Soviet social-imperialism in its bid for
world domination. Since the 1960s, it has made desperate efforts to beef up its naval forces, frequently held military exercises as a show of strength in the oceans, intruded into the
territorial waters of other countries and clamored for expansion. It has indeed become an out-and-out overlord of the seas.

New Tsars More Ambitious Than the Old

In the early years of the eighteenth century, Peter I, tsar
of Russia, declared: "Areas of water — this is what Russia
needs." "A monarch with an army is a person with only one
arm, but with an army and a navy he is a person with two
arms." To realize this ambition, the old tsar frantically
pushed a policy of strength on the seas. It was in those years
that tsarist Russia built its Baltic Fleet, its first naval force
of forty-eight warships. Toward the end of that century, Yeka-
terina II built Russia's second fleet — the Black Sea Fleet. It
was tsarist Russia's fond dream to establish a great "Slav em-
pire" stretching from River Elbe to China and from the Adri-
atic Sea to the Arctic Ocean.

---

*From Peking Review, No. 18 (April 30, 1976), 25-26.

The new tsars' ambitions are even greater. They have not
only taken over their predecessors' blueprint for aggression
and expansion, but have also mapped out a wild plan which the
old tsars dared not even imagine. They have declared that
whoever has a "powerful" navy can "extend his hegemony to
new areas." Their pipe dream is to build a big colonial em-
pire straddling Europe, Asia, Africa and Latin America. They
have opened a sea route from the Black Sea through the Mediterranean, the Indian Ocean, and the Pacific Ocean to the Sea
of Japan. Linking the three continents of Europe, Asia and
Africa, the route is intended to serve their contention for maritime hegemony with U.S. imperialism and their sabotage and
suppression of the revolutionary struggle of the people of the
Third World.

Wild Expansion of Naval Forces

In order to carry out its marine strategy for global expansion, the Soviet Union has changed its naval strategy from "offshore defense" to "attack in the distant seas." It has frantically expanded its naval forces, vigorously developed nuclear
submarines, and built aircraft carriers and other warships for
launching an offensive far from home waters. Soviet appropri-
ations for expanding its navy have reportedly increased from
about 15 percent of its defense budget during the Khrushchev
rule to 30 percent today, and the Soviet Union has outstripped
the United States by more than 33 percent in expenditure on
building warships. In the last decade, it has built 911 warships, and the total tonnage of Soviet warships has doubled.
It has surpassed the United States in both the number of warships and the speed of building. From 1967 to 1973, the Soviet
Union produced about 12 types of important warships of a new
class, including the helicopter carriers Moscow and Leningrad
equipped with missiles. In the past four years, the total tonnage of Soviet nuclear submarines rose 450 percent, and its
submarine-launched ballistic missiles increased more than
40 percent. From 1972 to 1974, it built on an average 39 big

surface warships and 6 guided-missile nuclear submarines
each year. The Soviet Union's first aircraft carrier — the
40,000-ton Kiev — has been launched, and its second — the
Minsk — is under construction. It now has a huge navy con-
sisting of 475,000 men. In addition to its Black Sea, Baltic,
Northern and Pacific Fleets, which are permanent setups, the
Soviet Union now has a permanent flotilla in the Indian Ocean
and a task force in the Mediterranean Sea, a naval air force
with 1,200 aircraft and a 20,000-strong marine corps.

Besides frenziedly expanding its navy, the Soviet Union has
built huge fishing, mercantile and scientific research fleets,
serving as important auxiliary forces for maritime expansion.
Some of these ships are armed with military equipment, others
are spy ships in disguise, and still others can be converted at
any time for military use. It is reported that many of the new-
type Soviet "long-hatch" freighters can carry aircraft, tanks
and other heavy arms and equipment. The passenger ships the
Soviet Union has today constitute an important logistical supporting force in wartime. In its recent criminal armed intervention in Angola, the Soviet mercantile fleet transported most
of the arms.

The Brezhnev clique was highly pleased with its rapidly expanding naval strength. Gorshkov, chief of the Soviet navy,
boasted that the Soviet navy "has all the necessary means for
simultaneous operations in the oceans." The Soviet Union's
rabid expansion of its naval forces fully exposes its wild ambitions to dominate the world.

Behavior of a Sea Overlord

Denouncing the old tsars, Engels said that they "are as
treacherous as they are talented" (The Foreign Policy of Russian Czarism [1890]).

Banking on its growing naval strength, the Brezhnev clique
is trying to lord it over the world's waters. Soviet fleets have
on different occasions intruded into the waters of over sixty countries. Such hegemonic acts are part of Soviet tactics in con-

tention for maritime hegemony with U.S. imperialism and in
its efforts to intimidate the littoral countries.

Making Europe the focus of its contention for hegemony, the
Soviet Union has deployed 70 percent of its submarines and 75
percent of its surface vessels in European waters.

On the northern flank, the Soviet Union has built a big naval
base on the Kola Peninsula bordering on northern Norway. It
has expanded the White Sea-Baltic Sea Canal inside its territory so that this canal, which formerly served civilian navigation only, is now navigable for 5,200-ton-class warships. It
has pushed its forward naval "defense areas" to places between Greenland, Iceland and the Faroe Islands and is continuing to extend them far into the Atlantic Ocean. The Barents
Sea and the Norwegian Sea have virtually become its inland
seas, and the Baltic Sea, a "publicly acknowledged Russian
lake." On the southern flank, it has tried hard to control all
the way from the Black Sea to the Strait of Gilbraltar and open
a passage leading from the Black Sea to the Mediterranean Sea
and then to the Atlantic Ocean so that its Mediterranean Fleet
could act in concert with its Baltic, Black Sea and Northern
fleets in wartime and form a pincers encirclement of Europe.
All this is posing a serious threat to the security of West and
North European countries. Soviet warships permanently stationed in the Mediterranean now number fifty to sixty, sometimes exceeding ninety. Various types of Soviet spy trawlers
and military supply ships frequently shuttle between Italy's
Sardinia and Sicily islands and prowl along Malta's rocky
coasts.

The Soviet Union deploys a fleet of over twenty warships in
the Indian Ocean and has set up floats for anchoring warships
and actually grabbed the right to use a dozen or so ports and
military bases in the area. On the strength of all this, it has
carried out threats, infiltration and aggression against the
coastal countries in a vain attempt to establish its hegemony
in the Indian Ocean.

The Soviet Pacific Fleet consists of 750 warships, including
30 nuclear submarines, with a total capacity reaching about

1.1 million tons. The Soviet Union has refused to return to Japan the four northern islands under its forcible occupation, and the northern waters have become one of the vital strategic points for the Soviet navy, posing an increasing military threat to Japan. To facilitate its Pacific Fleet's unhampered entry into the Indian Ocean, the Soviet Union has been energetically advocating the "internationalization" of the Strait of Malacca and "free" passage through it. This is a plot to turn the strait into its "private strait" through which Soviet warships can pass freely.

Soviet fleets are just as unbridled in other areas. They prowl along the 4,000-mile-long oil line of the West, in the Caribbean Sea which is a "forbidden zone" of the United States, along the east and west coasts of the United States and sometimes in places only 350 miles away from U.S. territory, and even in the south Atlantic Ocean, which is called a "no-man's sea." Wherever they are, they make a great show of strength.

Expansionist Fallacies

To legitimatize its attempt to lord it over the oceans, the Soviet Union has created various fallacies for maritime expansion. It babbled: "The Soviet fleets" will "sail in all places required by the security and interests of the Soviet Union." What interests do the Soviet fleets have to safeguard in places several thousand kilometers away from the Soviet coast? And who is threatening its security? Can it be that the Soviet fleets, which far exceed the defense needs of the Soviet Union, are protecting its security when they cruise around the British Isles, sail in the Indian Ocean day and night and carry out maneuvers in the Tsushima Strait and the Pacific Ocean? This fallacy is obviously a rehash of the old tsars' slogan "in the interests of Russia" when they carried out expansion abroad, and a typical manifestation of the "theory of interests involved" in the service of the imperialist policy of aggression.

The Soviet Union, a sea overlord, undisguisedly resorts to power politics with regard to the question of maritime rights.

It willfully bullies the small and medium-sized countries, attacks those countries which have declared a territorial water limit of over 12 nautical miles as having "violated international laws," assails the Third World countries' just demands for maritime rights within the 200-nautical-mile water limit as "extremist," energetically harps on the imperialist old tune of "freedom on the high seas," "freedom of navigation," "freedom of fishing," "freedom of overflight," "freedom of scientific research" and so on and so forth. In a word, the Soviet Union has the freedom to send its fleets to do what they like on the oceans, to encroach upon the territorial waters and airspace of other countries, to plunder their fishery resources and carry out espionage activities, but the small and medium-sized countries do not have the freedom to defend their own territorial waters and safeguard their maritime rights and marine resources. All this has thoroughly exposed the maritime hegemonic features of the Soviet Union.

ANOTHER STRUGGLE AGAINST HEGEMONISM*

U.N. Conference on the Law of the Sea

5

Hsinhua Correspondent

The Sixth Session of the Third United Nations Conference on
the Law of the Sea held in New York from May 23 to July 15
was attended by representatives from more than 140 countries.
During the eight-week session, a large number of developing
countries again waged an acute struggle against the superpowers over the provisions of a new law of the sea.

After the conclusion of the conference, while commenting on
the session, some representatives of Third and Second World
countries censured the superpowers' stand of maritime hegemonism and expressed the determination of the coastal states
to fight together to defend their sea rights on the basis of the
identity of their fundamental interests. Some representatives
from Third World countries pointed out that the tough stand
of maritime hegemonism adopted by the two superpowers, the
Soviet Union and the United States, was the root cause of the
failure of the session to reach agreements acceptable to the
developing countries on a number of important questions.

Drawing up a new sea law convention in conformity with the
fundamental interests of all peoples in the world constitutes an
important part of the struggle for establishing a new, just and
reasonable international economic system in the present world.

The numerous small and medium-sized countries have won
outstanding achievements in the struggle to protect state sov-

_____

*From Peking Review, No. 31 (July 29, 1977), 25-27.

ereignty and maritime resources from the expansion and plunder of the superpowers since Latin American countries took the lead in striving for a 200-mile maritime right. With their united struggle, they finally broke down some of the superpowers' privileges, such as their long-standing control of the sea in the name of ensuring "freedom of the high seas." They had a resolution adopted by the U.N. General Assembly which explicitly stipulates that the international seabed and its resources are the common heritage of mankind and are not subject to willful exploitation or plunder by any country or private corporation. Establishing 200-mile exclusive economic zones, proposed by several developing countries and supported by more and more states, has become an irresistible trend.

However, the road of struggle is never a straight one. Every step of the way, the developing countries have encountered obstruction and sabotage by the superpowers. In and outside the meeting hall during the sixth session of the conference, the U.S. delegation tried to lure and curry favor with some developing countries. Meanwhile, it openly put pressure on the conference, brazenly threatening that if no agreement were reached at the session, the U.S. Congress would pass an act on the unilateral exploitation of international seabed resources. The United States was trying to subordinate an international conference of more than 140 sovereign states to the timetable of its Congress. Such arrogance can only lay bare its true features as a hegemonic power.

The delegate of that self-styled "natural ally" of the developing countries, the Soviet Union, tried to deceive people by unfurling, with an ulterior motive, the banner of "opposing monopoly" when the system of international seabed exploitation was under discussion. Nominally opposing the monopoly of international seabed exploitation by Western transnational corporations, the Soviet Union in reality was driven by the fear that there may be additional unfavorable factors in its contention for hegemony with the United States if Washington is ahead, technically and financially, in the exploitation of international seabed resources. Delegates from some developing countries put it well: If the Soviet Union is antimonopoly as it claims, why is it that at the conference it was as obstinate as the United States in opposing the proposal of the "Group of 77" for the direct exploitation of international seabed resources by an international seabed authority and for full and effective control of all activities in international seabed areas?

It is well known that the Soviet Union has long been opposed to the 200-mile maritime right. Later on, forced by circumstances to change its tune, it pretended to agree to the establishment of 200-mile economic zones by coastal countries. However, it has all along attempted to kill the substance of the proposal for the exclusive economic zone. Striking a compromise posture at the session, the Soviet delegate, on the one hand, expressed willingness to "accept the concept of exclusive economic zone" and "recognize the rights of the coastal states over their exclusive economic zones" but on the other, acting exactly like the U.S. delegate, obstinately maintained that the economic zone is "part of the high seas." This was nothing but an ill-disguised attempt to distort the basic nature of the exclusive economic zone so that the Soviet Union could continue to do as it likes within exclusive economic zones under the cover of "freedom of the high seas."

Soviet social-imperialism has a guilty conscience and is very much afraid of the unity of the numerous small and medium-sized countries in their struggle against the superpowers.

During a discussion of the rules and procedures of the U.N. sea law conference a few years ago, the Soviet delegate stressed "a package deal" and insisted on a "consensus" vote on questions of substance so that it could exercise a veto on a number of relevant questions. The opposition of numerous small and medium-sized countries compelled the Soviet Union to revise its tactics a little bit, but it alleged that a question of substance should require a 90 percent overwhelming majority vote. This was tantamount to a claim to its right of veto. In discussing the functions and powers of the international seabed authority at the recent session of the sea law conference, the Soviet representatives, while resorting to their old tricks on voting procedures, tried in every way to restrict and weaken the powers of the supreme organ of the administration and expand the real powers of the council, the executive organ of the administration. This was because the superpowers would find it difficult to manipulate the supreme organ, at which the developing countries would account for a majority of the participants, and comparatively easy to control the council, whose membership would be limited. On the question of the council's composition, the Soviet delegate was openly opposed to the principle of equitable geographical representation as proposed by many developing countries. The Soviet delegate suggested that of the thirty-six council seats, only twelve should be allotted according to the principle of geographical representation, and all the rest distributed among the five "special interest groups" as proposed by the Soviet Union (industrialized developed countries, developing countries, landlocked and geographically disadvantaged states, land-based mineral-producing countries and mineral-consuming countries). The delegate also claimed that at least five seats should go to the "Soviet and East European group." According to Soviet logic, more than one hundred developing countries would have no more than eighteen seats while the "Soviet and East European group" comprising a few countries would be entitled to proportionally more seats in the council. All this shows why the Soviet Union, with meager support for its unjust cause at the session, was so afraid of the majority of the countries.

What warrants attention is that at the sixth session the Soviet Union instigated the delegate of Byelorussia, a landlocked union republic, to squeeze the republic into the ranks of landlocked and geographically disadvantaged countries. This was an attempt to sow discord between the landlocked developing countries and coastal ones. It serves to prove that the unity of the developing countries is an important prerequisite for working out a new convention of the law of the sea.

The foul performance of the Soviet delegates at the conference on the law of the sea in the past few years has helped to make an increasing number of small and medium-sized coun-

tries more clear-sighted and awaken them to the fact that the
superpowers will never renounce their maritime hegemony of
their own accord. Delegates of several African countries at
the sixth session in strong terms urged developing countries
to recall the inglorious history of the 1884 Berlin Convention —
a design for a division of colonial interests among imperialist
powers. They expressed their firm resolve under the present
international situation not to allow a few big powers to use the
international conference for pushing neocolonialism. A delegate of a developing country stressed that the establishment of
200-mile exclusive economic zones by the developing countries
is an exercise of their legitimate right, and it is by no means
a favor bestowed on them by the superpowers. His statement
represented a strong call of a vast number of developing countries which have been subjected to prolonged oppression and
exploitation and are pressing for a new international economic order.

VI

Taiwan and normalization

Documentary Introduction

There are four selections in this chapter. The first one, Keng Piao's speech of 1976, is the first document that ever indicated clearly that the Taiwan issue was not the most urgent problem to Peking. For the present, the document states, Peking will "let the United States defend" Taiwan against the Soviet Union, but when "the time is right," the issue will be settled, and Peking will ask the United States to leave the island.

The second document, Huang Hua's speech of 1977 on the occasion of Secretary of State Vance's visit to Peking, reveals the Peking leaders' observation that Taiwan may not be "liberated" by force within one decade, but that China-U.S. trade, sciences, and technology can be discussed and promoted.

The third selection, Teng Hsiao-p'ing's interview of September 1977, about two weeks after Vance's visit, unprecedentedly states Peking's rejection of the reverse-embassy-liaison-office proposal presented by Vance. To Teng, the normalization process was in a dilemma.

The fourth document, Hua Kuo-feng's speech of February 1978 at the Fifth National People's Congress, officially reiterates China's sovereignty over Taiwan and Peking's three conditions for the normalization of China-U.S. relations.

TAIWAN AND PEKING-WASHINGTON RELATIONS

Keng Piao's Talk on "A Turning Point in
China-U.S. Diplomatic Relations" (Excerpts)*

(August 24, 1976)

The Soviet Union is no longer the Soviet Union of twenty
years ago. But the U.S. remains the same as she was twenty
years ago and is one of the two superpowers. The U.S. still
maintains a capitalist system domestically, and, externally,
continues to accelerate the expansion of its military preparedness and the nuclear race. The Seventh Fleet is still haughtily
plying the Pacific Ocean. The U.S. no longer has military bases
in Thailand and not a soldier in Vietnam, but she still has military bases in the Philippines, a large contingent of troops stationed in South Korea, air bases in Okinawa, and troops stationed in Europe. The U.S. has declined in military strength
in comparison with the past and has thus become less flagrant
in her behavior. But she has not changed her aggressive nature.
For this reason, we should not only direct the spearhead of our
struggle at the Soviet revisionists but also should not miss any
opportunity to continue directing it at the U.S. Now we seldom
use the term "U.S. imperialism" and use instead "one of the
two superpowers." Does this mean that we have discarded the
basic principles of Marxism-Leninism and no longer oppose

*Keng Piao chiang "Chung-Mei wai-chiao kuan-hsi shang ti
i-ko chuan-tse-tien." Fei-ch'ing yüeh-pao [Chinese Communist
Monthly], XIX: 7 (Jan. 1977), 105-106. This translation is
adapted with permission from Issues & Studies, XIII: 1 (January 1977), 128-131. The title is the Editor's.

imperialism and colonialism? So far, quite a few comrades still have very nebulous ideas on this question while many fraternal parties do not understand or even misinterpret it. We must carry out educational and propaganda work, talk the matter over, and constantly cite evidence from both sides of the question so as to help everyone understand thoroughly Chairman Mao's revolutionary line in foreign policy. Soviet revisionism and U.S. imperialism have always been the source of war. In the current international situation, this fact remains unchanged.

Since the revisionist Soviet Union has changed from a socialist country into a social-imperialist one, the excellent revolutionary situation has undergone a precipitous change, and a sinister storm and evil clouds have appeared. Faced with such a situation, we cannot help but institute a big shift in our foreign policy. Today we are squeezed between two imperialist blocs. The U.S. and the USSR are contending for hegemony and are unwilling to compromise with each other in some respects, but in others they are colluding with each other, trading behind the scenes and dividing up the winnings. If we put the two superpowers together and deal with them both as one, the outcome will be unthinkable. Therefore, for the sake of survival, we must, in the first place, put one aside and deal with the other. Speaking from the strategic viewpoint as a whole: if we shelve the China-U.S. controversy, we will be able to deal with one side with an all-out effort and even gain time to solve our domestic problems first in order to build up our country in a comparatively peaceful milieu. Therefore, striving to foster good U.S.-China relations to diminish [the threat of] one enemy and uniting with still more friends are concrete expressions of Chairman Mao's revolutionary line in foreign policy which are put forth in accordance with the requirements of the situation.

As to our relations with the U.S., a few revolutionary putschists and adventurists do not see accurately the two-sidedness of the U.S. ruling class. They see mostly its reactionary side only and emphasize struggle. They do not perceive at all that

its weak side is exploitable and they deny the idea of carrying
out necessary struggle against and exploitation of the weaknesses of the U.S. No matter what angle we view it from, we
must have a correct conception in our policy toward the U.S.,
that is: first, the U.S. is still an imperialist country; second,
in accordance with the development of the situation, we have
to foster good relations in a positive way between China and
the U.S. in certain respects. These two points embrace the
philosophy of both unity and struggle and reflect the putting
into practice of a policy based on fundamental principle combined with flexible strategy.

As long as we fully realize the dual nature of U.S. imperialism, it will be easy to comprehend our current policy toward
the U.S. which may appear contradictory but is not contradictory in essence. For example: on the one hand, we denounce
U.S. imperialist troops for refusing to clear out of some countries, while on the other hand we support the stationing of U.S.
troops in such places as Western Europe and the Philippines.
It is not strange at all when we lay things out. Although stationing U.S. troops in Western Europe cannot stifle the aggressive ambitions of the Soviet revisionist new Czars, it can at
least accomplish temporary stability and attain the effect of
deterrence which would delay the outbreak of war. The delay
will do us and the whole world good. As a matter of fact, it is
our consistent foreign policy to oppose the U.S. troops' refusal
to clear out of others' land. But we agree that U.S. troops
should remain stationed in some areas. This amounts to flexible use of strategy under the premise of major principles. If,
on the contrary, we drive the U.S. entirely to the antagonistic
side and treat her as we do the USSR, we will very obviously
be caught between the devil and the deep blue sea and find ourselves in a situation which would be hard to deal with.

Taiwan today no longer exercises great political influence
internationally. But it is still impossible to solve the Taiwan
issue in a short period of time. It might take ten or twenty
years, or even a longer period of time. Even if U.S.-China
relations were normalized, it would still be impossible to

liberate Taiwan immediately. But since it is part of the territory of China, it is absolutely impermissible not to persist [in the matter of Taiwan] on the basis of reason and to allow a big country like the U.S. to create a theory of "two Chinas." So we say that the prerequisite for the U.S. to establish diplomatic relations with China is to acknowledge the government of China as the only legitimate government and to recall the U.S. ambassador in Taiwan. We do not oppose her maintenance of trading and civilian travel with Taiwan after she establishes relations with us. Other countries such as Japan, Malaysia, Canada, and Britain have already established diplomatic relations with us, yet they still maintain relations such as trade and civilian travel with Taiwan. We do not condemn this. To acknowledge one China is the major premise; everything else is of secondary importance. However, the U.S. has not yet acted accordingly.

To liberate Taiwan is our firm policy, but one must consider the development of the international situation as a whole and our own preparations. If the matter cannot be solved by force, peaceful liberation is the best. For the present, it is better to maintain the status quo. If as the existing status of this strategic area remains unchanged for awhile, when the time is right the ripe melon will fall off the vine. For now, let the U.S. defend us against the influence of Soviet revisionism and guard the coast of the East China Sea so that we can have more strength to deal with the power in the north and put more effort into nation-building. When we feel the time is right, we will candidly say: "Please, Uncle Sam, pack your bags and go."

What we are concerned with now is not exclusively the Taiwan issue. Taiwan is the greatest obstacle in the normalization of the U.S.-China relations. However, that is not our most pressing concern. We can still wait. Since we have already waited almost twenty-six years, so we can still wait. In today's world situation, it is Soviet social-imperialism, the No. 1 enemy, that should be dealt with first; all other problems are of secondary importance. Following the general trend, the U.S.

will carefully consider this issue and change her policy. Only
the increasing atmosphere of détente with the USSR within the
U.S. ruling class is a major development with which we must
be concerned. Both Nixon and Ford have visited us. Members
of both the Senate and the House of Representatives, Congres-
sional leaders of both Parties, and former Defense Secretary
James Schlesinger are all on our invitation list. From now on,
we will invite more prominent American guests who are influential in U.S. political and military circles and in society.
There is only one purpose to this: to explain to them repeatedly
our views on the situation and point out that to promote a policy
of détente with the USSR will not do, that it is capitulationist
and retrogressive, and not a positive way of solving world problems. We all stand to lose by it.

VANCE'S VISIT TO PEKING AND NORMALIZATION (Excerpts)*

2

(July 30, 1977)

Huang Hua

Mr. Vance, secretary of state of the Carter administration, will visit China next month. The Vance visit will take place just after our Eleventh Party Congress has been successfully convened.** The timing is significant. In making the arrangement for his visit, we have considered the recent domestic and international situation beforehand. Prior to Vance's visit to China, he has been to Europe, and has also visited Israel and talked with some Middle East countries. However, that journey was not fruitful. At present, on the diplomatic front, the United States is anxious about solving the problems of peace negotiations for the Middle East, arms limitation with Soviet revisionism, the Rhodesian problem together with Britain, and normalization of relations between China and the United States.

After President Carter's inauguration, although his administration professed the desire to push Sino-U.S. relations one step further on the basis of the Shanghai Communiqué and to gradually remove the obstacles to normalization, nonetheless,

---

*From "Huang Hua's 42,000-word Foreign Policy Address." Background on China (New York, December 26, 1977). The title is the Editor's. The original title of this section was "Secretary of State Vance's Forthcoming Visit."

**The Eleventh Congress of the Chinese Communist Party was held August 12-18, almost two weeks after Huang's secret speech.

judging from recent changes in the situation, because the United
States still refuses to accept the three principles for the solution of the problems of Sino-U.S. relations, there will be no
possibility for the establishment of diplomatic relations in the
next one or two years. However, there will be progress in
trade relations and in such exchange areas as science, education, culture, sports and contacts on a people-to-people basis.

. . .

It is necessary to win over the United States in order to focus our strength to cope with the No. 1 enemy — Soviet revisionist social-imperialism. This is why, although we know
that Sino-U.S. relations will remain at the status quo, we must
still bring our relationship with the United States one step
further. This is also why, while stressing the importance of
Sino-U.S. relations, we must, in the meantime, continue to expose the conspiracy of the double-faced strategy of the United
States on the question of war and peace and the perils of its
struggle with Soviet revisionist social-imperialism for world
hegemony, thereby cautioning the people of the world that they
must proceed from the premise of ideological preparation for
war.

Of course, we have no illusions toward the United States. We
have seen its face clearly — the past as well as the present and
the future. Although the Shanghai Communiqué has stated the
key points clearly, what has been agreed upon is not the same
as what has already been realized. . . .

Although the Shanghai Communiqué, signed jointly by President Nixon and Premier Chou on behalf of their governments,
has passed through three different presidents — Nixon, Ford
and Carter — nobody has yet denied that it is necessary to implement it. We hope our comrades will bear in mind that the
communiqué, like other agreements and treaties is merely
something on paper, and so, before its realization, do not cherish naïve illusions about it. When Vance comes this time, the
China-U.S. relationship will remain on its existing foundation,
and it is rather unlikely that there will be any new proposals
in the nature of a breakthrough. How then should we discuss

the problems of bilateral relationships of concern to both
countries?

Taiwan is Chinese territory. This is recognized by the
whole world, and even the Kuomintang regime on Taiwan does
not deny it. Therefore, in regard to the liberation of Taiwan,
what means would be employed, under what circumstances,
and when will this task be completed is the internal affair of
China, which no other nation, including the United States, will
be allowed to interfere with. This is what we are going to tell
the U.S. government; not a sentence more, nor a word less.
Incidentally, on this question, we will convey these two hints
to their government. Whether they can comprehend it or not
is their business:

1) The U.S. does not have the strength to deter the resolution
of the Chinese people to liberate Taiwan. This does not mean
that American atomic bombs cannot be dropped on Peking or
that American airplanes, guns and tanks are all useless scrap.
It is rather that the U.S. government cannot manipulate such a
crisis that might lead to war, and the American people will not
allow it to do so. The United States and Taiwan have signed
many agreements and treaties, one of which, the U.S.-Taiwan
mutual defense treaty, is one of the obstacles to the solution of
China-U.S. relations. It stipulates that if Taiwan should be attacked by some other party, under this treaty, the United States
must come to the aid of Taiwan, by sending troops, by supplying arms, and by joint counterattack.

Nonetheless, we will simply regard this treaty as a scrap of
paper. We dare say that, in fact, to the United States, although
the treaty is an obligation, the United States does not regard it
as a responsibility. Why is it that the U.S. would not assume
the responsibility? When the Chinese people deem the time
to be ripe to liberate Taiwan by force, would the American people really have the resolve to live or perish with the Chiang
dynasty and share the fate of the island of Taiwan? Go read
American history. We have not seen an instance in which the
United States has had such resolve and courage to sacrifice
for others. This has been determined by the intrinsic charac-

ter of the bourgeoisie. That is why we dare to conclude that the
United States is a paper tiger. It can be said that we have the
deepest insight into the United States and, after having dealt
with it for such a long time, we can paint not only its skin, but
also its bones.

. . .

This treaty may be useless, but unless it is scratched, it
will mean that we tacitly recognize the existence of "two Chinas" or "one China and one Taiwan." This is a question of
principle on which we cannot accept any compromise.

2) We need to let the U.S. government know that, even when
China-U.S. relations are normalized, the U.S.-Taiwan mutual
defense treaty is invalidated, and U.S. forces are withdrawn
from Taiwan, we will not, within the next decade, use force to
liberate Taiwan. In diplomatic parlance, even if U.S. troops
should evacuate from Taiwan, we won't at least "for the present" liberate Taiwan by force. Although we are impatient with
the prolonged stalemate in China-U.S. relations, we do have
the patience to temporarily shelve the Taiwan question until
all preparations have been made. This is to ensure that when
the time becomes more ripe in the future and we are more
sure of the prerequisites, we will then liberate Taiwan, completely unify the fatherland, and consummate Chairman Mao's
last behest. Because the main point of my talk today is not the
Taiwan issue, I will not dwell on the present conditions and the
future of Taiwan or on how to undertake the work of liberating
Taiwan.

Let us go back to Vance's visit to China and see during which
time, besides exchanging views on China-U.S. relations, what
other topics should be broached.

. . .

We are resolved to support the revolutionary liberation movements of the peoples of various countries in the world, but we
will not export revolution. Since neither side wants to invade
the other, and since the Taiwan issue cannot be resolved for
the time being, why don't we first leave this matter alone?
While there are wide divergencies between our social and po-

litical systems and since there are many things in the world that are more important and more urgent and that must be dealt with and examined, we should seek what is common between us. This is our attitude toward the Vance visit today.

We are prepared to exchange views more extensively, not just limited to the Taiwan issue. In the meantime, we also would like to understand through this meeting, the directions of movement of the Carter administration's foreign policy and convey to the United States our views on the expansion of the Soviet revisionist influences, the possibility that World War III might start in Europe, and the question of European defense.

. . .

In regard to the wavering policy of the U.S. government, we will convey our views at a proper time during Vance's friendly visit. If both sides are sincere, the visit will bring good results. I believe Vance will bring with him the U.S. views and policies on current international issues. We also hope that following the Vance visit, President Carter may also come to visit us at an appropriate time. We will be happy to welcome him.

We will also discuss trade, with a view to expanding it and to opening the door wider in order to expand our trade with the United States on a fair and mutually beneficial basis. In the next few years, our country will enter a stage of great construction, during which we will need to learn the experiences of advanced science, technology and business management of the United States. We need to buy equipment, precision instruments, and scientific research facilities from her, and through diverse forms of exchanges obtain more data on industrial construction and scientific research for our reference. We hope that more communication will promote more friendly contacts between the peoples of China and the United States. Such kind of exchange is beneficial not only to us, but also to the United States. It would be beneficial to our efforts in opposing Soviet revisionism and to world revolution as a whole.

The United States is a developed capitalist nation, whose industrial workers are very powerful and constitute a vast reservoir of strength for revolution. By means of such exchanges, Marxism-Leninism-Mao Tse-tung Thought will be propagated there and, like seeds, will take hold, grow and flourish. This will accelerate the nurturing of the domestic revolutionary movement in the United States. By opening the door of China-U.S. relations, we are opening wide the door which leads to revolution in the United States. We believe that there will be such a day when more people will see the crystallization of revolution. Chairman Mao said: "There is hope for revolution in America." The people of the world are bound to witness this great prophecy come true earlier than they think.

3

Deputy Prime Minister Teng Hsiao-p'ing said today [September 6, 1977] that efforts to establish normal diplomatic relations between the United States and China had suffered a setback during the visit last month of Secretary of State Cyrus R. Vance.

In an interview with executives and directors of the Associated Press, who are on a sixteen-day visit to China, Mr. Teng said that the discussions with Mr. Vance represented a retreat from proposals advanced by former President Gerald R. Ford and former Secretary of State Henry A. Kissinger.

In the interview, his first since he returned to office in July, Mr. Teng made these points:

1) President Ford promised in December 1975 that if he was reelected he would break diplomatic relations with the Chinese Nationalist Government on Taiwan and establish relations with Peking.

2) Secretary Vance discussed setting up a United States liaison mission in Taiwan and a full diplomatic mission in Peking, but the Chinese rejected that.

3) Though the Chinese regard Taiwan as an internal problem that permits no foreign interference, they would take into consideration the special conditions prevailing on the island in

---

*From the New York Times, September 7, 1977. © 1977 by The New York Times Company. Reprinted by permission. The title was added by the Editor.

trying to solve the problem with the United States.

4) Reports of progress that have grown out of Mr. Vance's trip are wrong.

The Japanese Formula

No direct quotations were permitted because, Chinese officials said, there was no official translation. Mr. Teng spoke in Chinese through an interpreter.

Mr. Teng said that Mr. Ford had promised during his visit to China twenty-one months ago that if he was reelected he would resolve the Taiwan problem in the same way as the Japanese had done. Japan severed diplomatic relations with the Nationalists on Taiwan but has maintained nongovernmental contacts, including substantial trade, with the island.

In December 1975, after Mr. Ford and Mr. Kissinger visited Peking, Mr. Kissinger told reporters he felt that Mr. Teng and Mao Tse-tung, the Chinese Communist Party chairman, clearly had signaled that they would accept an arrangement for diplomatic relations with the United States similar to the Japanese formula.

Mr. Kissinger said that the United States had no timetable for breaking diplomatic relations with the Taiwan government. . . .

Just before Secretary Vance came to China, Mr. Teng said, Mr. Ford made a speech taking a different view of how to resolve the Taiwan issue, but the deputy prime minister insisted that Mr. Ford had made such a promise in 1975.

Three Conditions Set by Chinese

Mr. Teng said that the United States had promised to take the three actions China has demanded for bringing about normal relations: breaking diplomatic relations with Taiwan, abrogating the United States-Chinese Nationalist defense treaty and withdrawing the 1,200 American troops on the island.

Mr. Teng said that Mr. Vance had come to Peking with a proposal that was a retrogression from that position. He said the secretary had discussed establishing full diplomatic relations with China but at the same time establishing a diplomatic liaison office on Taiwan. In effect, this would reverse the present situation. The United States has full relations with Taiwan and only a liaison mission in Peking.

The reverse liaison proposal was unacceptable, the deputy prime minister said, because it would mean continued diplomatic links between the United States and Taiwan.

Mr. Teng said his discussions with Mr. Kissinger about Taiwan had been based on the idea that eventually it would be the United States that would have to make the moves necessary to normalize relations.

However, he said, Mr. Vance came to Peking saying that both sides would have to make efforts for normalization, and this, Mr. Teng said, was a step back from the position taken by Mr. Ford and Mr. Kissinger.

Exchange of Views Called Useful

Mr. Teng stressed that the meeting with Mr. Vance had been cordial and useful for the exchange of views but that reports of progress were wrong.

The deputy prime minister, who is also deputy chairman of the Chinese Communist Party, under Chairman Hua Kuo-feng, reiterated the Chinese position that the Taiwan problem was an internal matter for the Chinese.

He said the American side had been responsible for creating an impression after Mr. Vance's visit that the Chinese would be flexible about promising not to take Taiwan by force if the United States withdrew. He said there was no such flexibility on the part of the Chinese.

Mr. Teng said he had told Secretary Vance that the Chinese people had patience but that the patience could not last forever. He said there had been no talk of a deadline.

Possible Conflict Foreseen

Asked what would happen if the people of Taiwan resisted a

takeover by the Chinese government. Mr. Teng said that this would lead to a conflict.

He said that in finding a solution to the Taiwan problem the Chinese would take into consideration the special conditions on the island. He also commented that if the United States did not interfere, the Chinese would not rule out the possibility of solving the problem peacefully. He did not elaborate on either of these points.

The question of continued American sale of arms to Taiwan after some change in the diplomatic relationship did not come up while Mr. Vance was in Peking, Mr. Teng said.

He said Mr. Vance had told him that the Chinese view would be considered and that there would be further talks. Mr. Teng said he agreed.

TAIWAN AND NORMALIZATION (Excerpts)* 4

Hua Kuo-feng

. . .

Taiwan is part of the sacred territory of China. The people in and from Taiwan are our kith and kin. The liberation of Taiwan and the unification of the motherland are the common aspirations of the whole Chinese people, our Taiwan compatriots included. We resolutely oppose anyone scheming to create what is called "two Chinas," "one China, one Taiwan," "one China, two governments" or an "independent Taiwan." We place our hopes on the people of Taiwan and resolutely support their patriotic struggle against imperialism and the Chiang clique. As for the military and administrative personnel of the Kuomintang in and from Taiwan, it has been our consistent policy that "all patriots belong to one big family," "whether they come over early or late." It is our hope that they will clearly see the general trend of events and take the road of patriotism and unification of the motherland. The Chinese People's Liberation Army must make all the preparations necessary for the liberation of Taiwan. We are determined to realize the behest of Chairman Mao and Premier Chou and, together with our Taiwan compatriots, accomplish the sacred

*From Hua Kuo-feng, "Report on the Work of the Government Delivered at the First Session of the Fifth National People's Congress on February 26, 1978." Peking Review, No. 10 (March 10, 1978), 35, 39. The title is the Editor's.

349

task of liberating Taiwan and unifying the motherland.

. . .

China and the United States differ in social system and ideology, and there are fundamental differences between them.
Yet the two countries have quite a few points in common on
some issues in the present international situation. The Sino-
U.S. Shanghai Communiqué issued in 1972 has brought a new
turn in the relations between the two countries. These relations will continue to improve provided the principles laid
down in the communiqué are seriously carried out. At present, the attitude of the U.S. government toward the question of
Taiwan is the obstacle to the normalization of Sino-U.S. relations. The Chinese people are determined to liberate Taiwan.
When and how is entirely China's internal affair, an internal
affair which brooks no foreign interference whatsoever. If the
relations between the two countries are to be normalized, the
United States must sever its so-called diplomatic relations
with the Chiang clique, withdraw all its armed forces and military installations from Taiwan and the Taiwan Straits area and
abrogate its so-called "mutual defense treaty" with the Chiang
clique. This is the unswerving stand of the Chinese government.
The people of China and the United States have always been
friendly to each other. We are willing to increase contacts between the people of our two countries and promote mutual understanding and friendship.

. . .

VII

Modernization and foreign relations

Documentary Introduction

"Modernization" is very much in the air in the post-Mao era. The problems of how and what modernization projects should be carried out, how foreign relations in the modernization era should be guided, and in what way the principle of self-reliance and foreign technology should be made to complement each other are only a few key issues concerning modernization and foreign relations that Peking has to cope with during the modernization era.

In this chapter, the first selection, "Speed Up Socialist Economic Construction" by Hua Kuo-feng, outlines ambitious priorities, projects, and measures for economic development. They include agriculture, industry, foreign trade, technical revolution, relationships between central and local authorities, and the improvement of the people's livelihood.

The second selection, "The Relationships between China and Other Countries" by Mao Tse-tung, is from the 1977 text which differs somewhat from its 1956 version. Mao points out that in 1949 and 1950 Stalin's pressure on China "was very great indeed" but that China must make a special effort to learn advanced sciences and technologies from foreign countries, including capitalist nations.

The third selection, "Self-Reliance and Making Foreign Things Serve China," expresses Peking's view that China herself should select and introduce new foreign techniques and useful experience to serve her modernization projects, that is, use foreign science and technology for self-reliant growth and economic development.

The fourth selection, "Speed Up the Modernization of National Defense," should actually be regarded as a policy statement by Peking on military modernization. In fact, such a modernization project is already in progress.

SPEED UP SOCIALIST ECONOMIC
CONSTRUCTION (Excerpts)*

1

Hua Kuo-feng

In order to make China a modern, powerful socialist country
by the end of the century, we must work and fight hard in the
political, economic, cultural, military and diplomatic spheres,
but in the final analysis what is of decisive importance is the
rapid development of our socialist economy.

At the Third National People's Congress and again at the
Fourth, Premier Chou, acting on Chairman Mao's instructions,
put forward a grand concept for the development of our national
economy which calls for the all-round modernization of agriculture, industry, national defense and science and technology
by the end of the century so that our economy can take its place
in the front ranks of the world. . . .

According to the ten-year plan, by 1985, we are to produce
400 billion kilograms of grain and 60 million tons of steel. In
each of the eight years from 1978 to 1985, the value of agricultural output is to increase by 4 to 5 percent and of industrial
output by over 10 percent. The increase in our country's output of major industrial products in the eight years will far exceed that in the past twenty-eight years. In these eight years,
state revenues and investments budgeted for capital construc-

---

*From Hua Kuo-feng, "Report on the Work of the Government
Delivered at the First Session of the Fifth National People's
Congress on February 26, 1978." Peking Review, No. 10
(March 10, 1978), 18-26.

tion will both be equivalent to the total for the past twenty-eight years. As fellow deputies have reviewed the various economic targets in the ten-year plan, there is no need to list them now. The accomplishment of the ten-year plan will bring about tremendous economic and technological changes and provide the country with a much more solid material base, and, given another period of hard work over three more five-year plans, the stage will be set for China to take its place in the front ranks of the world economy.

· · ·

To turn the plan into reality, we must also adopt effective measures and strive to solve a number of problems bearing on our whole economy.

1. Mobilize the Whole Nation and Go in for Agriculture in a Big Way

Agriculture is the foundation of the national economy. If agriculture does not develop faster, there will be no upswing in our industry and economy as a whole, and even if there is a temporary upswing, a decline will follow, and there will be really serious trouble in the event of major natural calamities. We must have a clear understanding of this. Predominantly agricultural provinces must make an effort to develop agriculture, and predominantly industrial provinces must make still greater efforts. All trades and professions must do their best to support and serve agriculture.

In order to effect an upswing in agriculture, we rely mainly on learning conscientiously from Tachai, practicing scientific farming and speeding up mechanization. In line with the principle of "taking grain as the key link and ensuring an all-round development," the state is planning to take the following measures to develop agricultural production:

1) While attaining a countrywide increase in grain production, focus on the two following tasks. One, run the twelve large commodity-grain bases and all our state farms efficiently and enable them to achieve a twofold or threefold in-

crease in marketable grain in a space of eight years. Two, help low-yield, grain-deficient areas to become self-sufficient and achieve a surplus within two or three years.

2) While ensuring a rise in yields per unit, organize planned reclamation of wasteland by the state farms and people's communes so as to obtain a fair increase in cultivated acreage year by year, provided such reclamation does not affect water and soil conservation and the protection of forests, grasslands and aquatic product resources.

3) In accordance with the principles of specialized planting and rational distribution, build a number of bases for the production of cotton, edible oil, sugar and other cash crops where conditions are suitable, and turn them into the state's main sources of supply for these products.

4) Strive to develop forestry, animal husbandry, sideline production and fisheries, do a good job of developing the forest regions, plant trees around every house and every village, by roadsides and watersides, build livestock-breeding areas, set up freshwater and marine fishing grounds, and actively promote rural sideline occupations and commune- and brigade-run enterprises. In this way it will be possible considerably to expand the afforested areas and greatly increase the output of animal and aquatic products and increase the proportion of commune and brigade income derived from sideline occupations and enterprises.

5) Mobilize the masses to forge ahead with farmland capital construction and stress soil improvement and water control. The state must take charge of large-scale water conservancy projects, continue to harness such big rivers as the Yellow River, the Yangtze, the Huai, the Haiho, the Liaoho and the Pearl River, carry out the key projects to relieve drought in northwest, north and southwest China properly, and undertake projects to divert water from the Yangtze to areas north of the Yellow River. In the localities work must be initiated to build medium-sized and small water conservancy works suiting local conditions and to improve low-yield fields on mountain slopes, alkaline land and red soil.

6) From the top organs to the grass-roots units, set up and perfect a system of agroscientific research and agrotechnical popularization; implement the Eight-point Charter for Agriculture in an all-round way, with stress on cultivating and popularizing fine strains of seed, improving farming methods, extensively exploring various sources of fertilizer, making a big effort to develop organic fertilizer and making proper use of chemical fertilizer.

7) In order to hasten the mechanization of agriculture, strive to manufacture more, better and cheaper farm machinery, chemical fertilizer and insecticide that meet specific needs, do a good job of supplying complete sets of farm machinery and of their maintenance, repair and management, and step up the training of farm technicians.

8) Make an extra effort to build up mountain areas and in particular give attention and assistance to construction in the old revolutionary base areas so as to accelerate their economic progress.

9) Strengthen the leadership of the poorer production teams and help them to transform themselves economically and catch up with the richer teams as soon as possible.

. . .

2. Speed Up the Development of the Basic Industries and Give Full Scope to the Leading Role of Industry

As the economy becomes modernized, the leading role of industry, and especially that of the basic industries, becomes more and more prominent. We must take steel as the key link, strengthen the basic industries and exert a special effort to step up the development of the power, fuel and raw and semi-finished materials industries and transport and communications. Only thus can we give strong support to agriculture, rapidly expand light industry and substantially strengthen the national defense industries.

In developing the basic industries, we must endeavor to

strengthen our work in geology and in the opening up of new
mines so that geological surveying and the mining industry will
meet the needs of high-speed economic construction.

In developing the basic industries, we must be good at tapping
the potential of the existing enterprises and at renovating and
transforming them as well as at integrating this task with the
building of new enterprises. In the next eight years, and especially in the next three years, our existing enterprises must
be the foundation for the growth of production. We must make
full use of existing equipment, make sure that complete sets
of equipment are available, introduce technical transformation
in a planned way and carry out extensive coordination among
specialized departments. This will gain us time and speed and
will save on investment. Meanwhile, the state plans to build
or complete 120 large-scale projects, including 10 iron and
steel complexes, 9 nonferrous metal complexes, 8 coal mines,
10 oil and gas fields, 30 power stations, 6 new trunk railways
and 5 key harbors. The completion of these projects added to
the existing industrial foundation will provide China with four-
teen fairly strong and fairly rationally located industrial bases.
This will be decisive in changing the backward state of our
basic industries.

In capital construction, we must keep to the principle of con-
centrating our forces and fighting a battle of annihilation to
achieve economy in our investments, high quality in our work
and short building cycles, and we must rapidly acquire the capacity to streamline production and get optimum results. With
regard to the 120 large-scale projects in the state plan for the
next eight years, the whole country, from the top levels to the
grass roots, must cooperate closely and select competent leading cadres, fine technical personnel and skilled workers for the
concerted battle to accomplish these projects successively with
greater, faster, better and more economical results.

It is essential to adhere to the policy of the simultaneous development of large, medium-scale and small enterprises. ...

In building our industry we should apply the principle of combining industry and agriculture and town and country. Where

conditions permit, the workers and staff and their families
should get organized for agricultural and sideline production,
as in the Taching Oil Field. We should as far as possible
avoid crowding the big cities with new construction units and
should build more small and medium-sized towns and cities.

3. Do a Good Job in Commerce and Develop Foreign Trade

Socialist commerce is a bridge that links industry with agriculture, urban areas with rural areas and production with consumption. It is essential to make a success of commerce, for
it promotes the rapid growth of the economy, consolidates the
worker-peasant alliance and serves to meet the people's daily
needs. Those who work in shops and supply and marketing departments are part of the working class. They are inseparably
linked with the general process of production, and since what
they do is lofty revolutionary labor, they should command the
respect of all. The commercial departments should firmly implement the policy of "develop the economy and ensure supplies," give strong support to industrial and agricultural production and wholeheartedly serve the people in meeting their
daily needs. We should organize the exchange of industrial
goods with agricultural products well, stimulate the interchange
of urban and rural products, provide the markets with adequate
supplies, appropriately expand commercial networks or centers,
increase the variety of goods on the market, and improve the
quality of service to customers. We should tighten price and
market controls and deal resolute blows to speculation and
profiteering.

There should be a big increase in foreign trade. In our expert trade, attention should be given both to bulk exports and
exports in small quantities....

4. Encourage Socialist Labor Emulation and Be Active in Technical Innovation and Technical Revolution

The masses have a vast reservoir of enthusiasm for socialism.

Socialist labor emulation is a good and important method of
bringing the initiative and creativeness of the people into full
play and of achieving greater, faster, better and more economical results in developing the economy. Each and every
locality, trade, enterprise, establishment and rural commune
and production brigade should fully mobilize the masses and
bring about an upsurge in emulating, learning from, catching
up with and overtaking the advanced units, and helping the less
advanced units.

The main aim of the labor emulation is to increase production and practice economy, that is, to strive to step up production, improve quality, raise labor productivity, economize on
materials, cut down costs and increase profits. At present,
some enterprises seek to increase production to the neglect of
the quality of products and the quantity of materials consumed,
causing much waste. This does not square with the requirement of achieving greater, faster, better and more economical
results. Failure to achieve high quality, economize on materials and provide the state with constantly increasing profits
will make it impossible for the economy to achieve sustained
and high-speed development. All enterprises are required to
reach their previous peak production levels in terms of economic and technical norms before the year is out, and those
that have already done so should strive to catch up with or surpass domestic and world advanced standards. In the course
of labor emulation, attention should be paid to combining work
with adequate rest so as to keep up the enthusiasm of the
masses. Moreover, all departments and enterprises should
break down the boundaries between trades and create more for
the state by actively undertaking the multiple utilization of resources and so turning "waste" into wealth. We must resolutely combat the spendthrift style, which pays no attention to
quality and economic accounting, and the prodigal bourgeois
style of indulgence in extravagance and waste. We must foster
the fine tradition of waging hard struggles and building the
country with diligence and thrift.

For our economy to develop at high speed, we must break

free from conventions and use advanced techniques as much as possible. The broad masses have inexhaustible creative power and are fully capable of making a great leap forward in science and technology by relying on their own strength....

5. Strengthen Unified Planning and Give Full Play to the Initiative of Both the Central and Local Authorities

Planned economy is a basic feature of the socialist economy. We must resolutely put an end to the anarchy resulting from the interference and sabotage of the "gang of four" and bring all economic undertakings into the orbit of planned, proportionate development. In formulating plans, we must follow the mass line, and both the central departments and the localities should do more investigation and study, endeavor to strike an overall balance, make the plans bold as well as sound and allocate manpower, material and money where they are most needed so that the various branches of the economy develop in coordination. A strict system of personal responsibility must be set up at all levels, from the departments under the State Council to the provinces, municipalities and autonomous regions right down to the grass-roots units, so that each leading cadre has his clear-cut responsibilities and nothing is neglected. Fulfillment of the state plan will thus be effectively ensured. We must check up regularly on how the localities, departments and grass-roots units are carrying out their plans. We shall commend those who fulfill their plans satisfactorily and shall hold the leading cadres responsible where the plan is not fulfilled because of their poor work and bureaucracy. In the case of serious failures, necessary disciplinary action will be taken.

. . .

Given the strengthening of unified central leadership, it is necessary to develop the initiative of both the central and the local authorities. While the former must have absolute control on major issues, power should devolve on the latter with respect to minor ones. Power is to be centralized where necessary, while active support is to be given to the local authorities in undertaking what should be put in their charge. . . .

6. Uphold the Principle of "From Each According to His Ability, to Each According to His Work" and Steadily Improve the Livelihood of the People

Throughout the historical period of socialism, we must uphold the principles of "he who does not work, neither shall he eat" and "from each according to his ability, to each according to his work." In applying them we must firmly put proletarian politics in command, strengthen ideological and political work and teach and encourage everybody to cultivate the Communist attitude toward labor and to serve the people wholeheartedly. With regard to distribution, while we should avoid a wide wage spread, we must also oppose equalitarianism and apply the principle of more pay for more work and less pay for less work. The enthusiasm of the masses cannot be aroused if no distinction is made between those who do more work and those who do less, between those who do a good job and those who do a poor one, and between those who work and those who don't. All people's communes and production brigades must seriously apply the system of fixed production quotas and calculation of work-points on the basis of work done and must enforce the principle of equal pay for equal work irrespective of sex. The staff and workers of state enterprises should be paid primarily on a time-rate basis with piecework playing a secondary role, and with additional bonuses. There should be pecuniary allowances for jobs requiring higher labor intensity or performed under worse working conditions. In socialist labor emulation, moral encouragement and material rewards must go hand in hand, with emphasis on the former. As regards the reform of the wage system, the relevant departments under the State Council should, together with the local authorities, make conscientious investigations and study, sum up experience, canvass the opinions of the masses and then submit a draft plan based on overall consideration to the central authorities for approval before it is gradually implemented.

. . .

We are not yet acquainted with many of the problems that crop up in economic construction. In particular, in many respects modern production remains an unknown kingdom of necessity to us. In accordance with Chairman Mao's instructions, the leading cadres at all levels must use their brains and assiduously study Marxism-Leninism, economics, production management and science and technology so as to "become expert in political and economic work on the basis of a higher level of Marxism-Leninism." We must study hard and work well, sum up experience, attain a better grasp of the laws governing socialist economic construction, master the art of guiding and organizing modern production, raise the level of economic management and do our economic work in an ever more meticulous, thoroughgoing, practical and scientific way, thus propelling the national economy forward at high speed.

THE RELATIONSHIP BETWEEN CHINA AND OTHER COUNTRIES*

2

Mao Tse-tung

We have put forward the slogan of learning from other countries. I think we have been right. At present, the leaders of some countries are chary, and even afraid, of advancing this slogan. It takes some courage to do that; in other words, theatrical airs have to be discarded.

It must be admitted that every nation has its strong points. If not, how can it survive? How can it progress? On the other hand, every nation has its weak points. Some believe that socialism is just perfect, without a single flaw. How can that be true? It must be recognized that there are always two aspects, the strong points and the weak points. The secretaries of our Party branches, the company commanders and platoon leaders of our army have all learned to jot down both aspects in their pocket notebooks, the weak points as well as the strong ones, when summing up their work experience. They all know there are two aspects to everything. Why do we mention only one? There will always be two aspects, even ten thousand years from now. Each age, whether the future or the present, has its own two aspects, and each individual has his own two aspects. In short, there are two aspects, not just one. To say there is only one is to be aware of one aspect and to be ignorant of the other.

*From Mao Tse-tung, "On the Ten Major Relationships." Peking Review, No. 1 (January 1, 1977), 23-25.

Our policy is to learn from the strong points of all nations and all countries, learn all that is genuinely good in the political, economic, scientific and technological fields and in literature and art. But we must learn with an analytical and critical eye, not blindly, and we must not copy everything indiscriminately and transplant mechanically. Naturally, we must not pick up their shortcomings and weak points.

We should adopt the same attitude in learning from the experience of the Soviet Union and other socialist countries. Some of our people were not clear about this before and even picked up their weaknesses. While they were swelling with pride over what they had picked up, it was already being discarded in those countries. As a result, they had to do a somersault like the monkey Sun Wu-kung. For instance, there were people who accused us of making a mistake of principle in setting up a Ministry of Culture and a Bureau of Cinematography rather than a Ministry of Cinematography and a Bureau of Culture, as was the case in the Soviet Union. They did not anticipate that shortly afterward the Soviet Union would make a change and set up a Ministry of Culture as we had done. Some people never take the trouble to analyze, they simply follow the "wind." Today, when the north wind is blowing, they join the "north wind" school; tomorrow, when there is a west wind, they switch to the "west wind" school. Afterward when the north wind blows again, they switch back to the "north wind" school. They hold no independent opinion of their own and often go from one extreme to the other.

In the Soviet Union, those who once extolled Stalin to the skies have now in one swoop consigned him to purgatory. Here in China some people are following their example. It is the opinion of the Central Committee that Stalin's mistakes amount to only 30 percent of the whole and his achievements to 70 percent and that, all things considered, Stalin was nonetheless a great Marxist. We wrote "On the Historical Experience of the Dictatorship of the Proletariat" on the basis of this evaluation. This assessment of 30 percent for mistakes and 70 percent for achievements is just about right. Stalin did a number of wrong things in connection with China. The "Left" adventurism pursued by Wang Ming in the latter part of the Second Revolutionary Civil War period and his Right opportunism in the early days of the War of Resistance against Japan can both be traced to Stalin. At the time of the War of Liberation, Stalin first would not let us press on with the revolution, maintaining that if civil war flared up, the Chinese nation ran the risk of destroying itself. Then when fighting did erupt, he took us half seriously, half skeptically. When we won the war, Stalin suspected that ours was a victory of the Tito type, and in 1949 and 1950 the pressure on us was very great indeed. Even so, we maintain the estimate of 30 percent for his mistakes and 70 percent for his achievements. This is only fair.

In the social sciences and in Marxism-Leninism, we must continue to study Stalin diligently wherever he is right. What we must study is all that is universally true, and we must make sure that this study is linked with Chinese reality. It would lead to a mess if every single sentence, even of Marx's, were followed. Our theory is an integration of the universal truth of Marxism-Leninism with the concrete practice of the Chinese revolution. At one time, some people in the Party went in for dogmatism, and this came under our criticism. Nevertheless, dogmatism is still in evidence today. It still exists in academic circles and in economic circles too.

In the natural sciences, we are rather backward and here we should make a special effort to learn from foreign countries. And yet we must learn critically, not blindly. In technology I think at first we have to follow others in most cases, and it is better for us to do so, since at present we are lacking in technology and know little about it. However, in those cases where we already have clear knowledge, we must not follow others in every detail.

We must firmly reject and criticize all the decadent bourgeois systems, ideologies and ways of life of foreign countries. But this should in no way prevent us from learning the advanced sciences and technologies of capitalist countries and whatever is scientific in the management of their enterprises.

In the industrially developed countries they run their enterprises with fewer people and greater efficiency, and they know how to do business. All this should be learned well in accordance with our own principles so that our work can be improved. Nowadays, those who make English their study no longer work hard at it, and research papers are no longer translated into English, French, German or Japanese for exchange with other countries. This too is a kind of blind prejudice. Neither the indiscriminate rejection of everything foreign, whether scientific, technological or cultural, nor the indiscriminate imitation of everything foreign as mentioned above, has anything in common with the Marxist attitude, and they in no way benefit our cause.

In my opinion, China has two weaknesses, which are at the same time two strong points.

First, in the past China was a colonial and semicolonial country, not an imperialist power, and was always bullied by others. Its industry and agriculture are not developed and its scientific and technological level is low, and except for its vast territory, rich resources, large population, long history, The Dream of the Red Chamber in literature, and so on, China is inferior to other countries in many respects and so has no reason to feel conceited. However, there are people who, having been slaves too long, feel inferior in everything and do not stand up straight in the presence of foreigners. They are just like Chia Kuei in the opera The Famen Temple who, when asked to take a seat, refuses to do so, giving the excuse that he is used to standing in attendance. Here we need to bestir ourselves, enhance our national confidence and encourage the spirit typified by "Scorn U.S. imperialism," which was fostered during the movement to resist U.S. aggression and aid Korea.

Second, our revolution came late. Although the 1911 Revolution which overthrew the Ch'ing emperor preceded the Russian revolution, there was no Communist Party at that time, and the revolution failed. The victory of the people's revolution came in 1949, more than thirty years after the October Revolution.

On this account too, we are not in a position to feel conceited. The Soviet Union differs from our country in that, first, tsarist Russia was an imperialist power and, second, it had the October Revolution. As a result, many people in the Soviet Union are conceited and very arrogant.

Our two weaknesses are also strong points. As I have said elsewhere, we are first "poor" and second "blank." By "poor" I mean we do not have much industry and our agriculture is underdeveloped. By "blank" I mean we are like a blank sheet of paper and our cultural and scientific level is not high. From the standpoint of potentiality, this is not bad. The poor want revolution, whereas it is difficult for the rich to want revolution. Countries with a high scientific and technological level are overblown with arrogance. We are like a blank sheet of paper, which is good for writing on.

Being "poor" and "blank" is therefore all to our good. Even when one day our country becomes strong and prosperous, we must still adhere to the revolutionary stand, remain modest and prudent, learn from other countries and not allow ourselves to become swollen with conceit. We must not only learn from other countries during the period of our First Five-Year Plan, but must go on doing so after the completion of scores of five-year plans. We must be ready to learn even ten thousand years from now. Is there anything bad about that?

. . .

SELF-RELIANCE AND MAKING FOREIGN THINGS SERVE CHINA*

3

Notes on Studying Chairman Mao's
"On the Ten Major Relationships"

Lo Yuan-cheng

In his work "On the Ten Major Relationships," Chairman Mao pointed out: "Our policy is to learn from the strong points of all nations and all countries, learn all that is genuinely good in the political, economic, scientific and technological fields and in literature and art. But we must learn with an analytical and critical eye, not blindly, and we must not copy everything indiscriminately and transplant mechanically. Naturally, we must not pick up their shortcomings and weak points." Chairman Mao also taught us: "Rely mainly on our own efforts while making external assistance subsidiary." On the question of the relationship between China and other countries, Chairman Mao has scientifically summed up the experience of China's revolution and construction and formulated for us a policy conforming to revolutionary dialectics. While emphasizing development of China's national economy on the basis of self-reliance, this policy also affirms the importance of learning from foreign countries and "making foreign things serve China" in our socialist construction.

Owing to long years of oppression by the three big mountains — imperialism, feudalism and bureaucrat-capitalism — in old China, the productive forces developed at a very slow pace, and science and technology lagged far behind some countries. To rapidly transform the backward features of China

*From Peking Review, No. 28 (July 8, 1977), 9-11.

after the founding of the People's Republic of China, on the basis of persevering in maintaining independence and keeping the initiative in our own hands and relying on our own efforts, we have learned from foreign countries in a planned way and with our own emphasis and selection and introduced some new techniques into China so that the good experience of foreign countries can serve China's socialist construction. This gives full expression to the unity of opposites in the relationship between "making foreign things serve China" and relying on our own efforts.

Following Chairman Mao's instructions, China has imported in the last twenty years or so equipment and technology urgently needed in the development of China's national economy and sciences. Premier Chou also issued many important instructions on introducing advanced foreign techniques. He advocated that foreign experience should be applied analytically and critically, not mechanically. Premier Chou held that we should not place blind faith in or rely completely on foreign techniques, but should combine studying them with devising something original from them and that China should take her own road of industrial and technical development. These instructions are beneficial to speeding up the development of China's national economy, hastening the modernization of agriculture, industry, national defense and science and technology as well as catching up with and surpassing advanced world levels.

The history of science and technology shows that the creations and inventions of the world's laboring people in these fields cannot remain a monopoly of one nation for long but inevitably will sooner or later spread to all nations.

In his Dialectics of Nature, Engels listed several major inventions — the magnetic needle, printing, type, flax paper, ... gunpowder, spectacles and mechanical clocks. Of these contributions made by people of different countries, the magnetic needle, printing, gunpowder, paper and mechanical clocks were invented in China, while type was invented both in China and Korea. On the other hand, China has absorbed many foreign things in the political, economic, cultural, scientific and technical fields. For example, tomatoes, potatoes, peanuts and maize came from Latin America, cotton from Pakistan. Copernicus's theory on the solar system and Darwin's theory of evolution were sources of enlightenment for many advanced Chinese in modern history. Every nation in the world has its own merits and characteristics; otherwise it could not exist and develop. Every nation and country as it develops is bound to absorb and make use of, to a greater or lesser degree, scientific and technological achievements of other nations and countries. Learning from foreign countries and learning from others' strong points to make up our deficiencies through trade and other exchanges on the basis of equality and mutual benefit help our economy, culture, national defense and science and technology draw on good experience, make their own creations and stride forward. Presumptuous conceit and blind rejection of all things foreign are anti-Marxist and unscientific.

Ours is a country of the dictatorship of the proletariat. The superiority of the socialist system provides very favorable conditions for rapidly developing science and technology. We dare to put forward the slogan of learning from foreign countries precisely because we have full confidence in our own country, in our socialist system and in our people of all nationalities. We are ready to learn from the strong points of all countries and all nations. We want to learn all that is genuinely good and useful, and we shall always do so. This is the scientific Marxist approach.

However, the "gang of four" acted totally against Chairman Mao's teachings and his revolutionary line in foreign affairs, ignored China's economic and trade relations with over 150 countries and regions and did its utmost to sabotage our economic and technical exchanges with countries all over the world. It maliciously slandered learning from foreign countries as "servility to things foreign," the introducing of techniques from abroad as "trailing behind at a snail's pace," and it metaphysically counterposed self-reliance to learning from foreign countries and "making foreign things serve China." If we refuse to learn from foreign experience and have to do everything from scratch, it will inevitably lead to a slowdown in the development of some industrial techniques. That would really mean "trailing behind at a snail's pace!" The "gang of four" opposed the introduction of advanced techniques from abroad and even vilified the import of certain major projects approved by Chairman Mao, alleging that this tied the fate of China's industry "to others' apron strings." Chiang Ch'ing frenziedly clamored for the dismantling of a set of imported chemical fertilizer equipment installed at Taching Oil Field, viciously attacking it as "sabotaging self-reliance" and being a "disgrace to the Chinese." The gang's real intention was to create confusion on this important front of foreign trade and undermine the socialist economy so as to seize power during the ensuing disorder.

The counterrevolutionary double-dealing tricks of the "gang of four" were similar to those of the bandit gang of Trotskyites. Lenin pointed out after the October Revolution the importance of obtaining as quickly as possible from the capitalist countries the means of production, such as locomotives, machinery, and electrical equipment. He also stressed the necessity to adopt everything that is truly valuable in European and American science. However, Trotsky frenziedly attacked these directives of Lenin's and vilified them on the grounds that the economy of the Soviet state would "always be under the control of world economy." In a direct rebuff, Stalin sharply denounced Trotsky's counterrevolutionary absurdities: "To depict a socialist economy as something absolutely self-contained and absolutely independent of the surrounding national economies is to talk nonsense" (The Seventh Enlarged Plenum of the ECCI). Stalin's criticism of Trotsky is entirely applicable to the "gang of four."

We must resolutely adhere to Chairman Mao's line and learn from foreign countries on the basis of self-reliance. This means absorbing the good experience and techniques from abroad for our own use so as to enhance our self-reliance capabilities and build China into a powerful, modern socialist country before the end of this century.

SPEED UP THE MODERNIZATION
OF NATIONAL DEFENSE*   **4**

Editorial by Jen-min jih-pao, Hung-ch'i, and
Chieh-fang chun-pao Celebrating the Fiftieth
Anniversary of Founding of the PLA

At a time of great joy, when the Third Plenary Session of
the Tenth Central Committee of the Communist Party of China
has ended in success and when the Eleventh National Congress
of the Party will be convened soon, the whole Party, the whole
army and the people of all nationalities throughout the country
are celebrating the fiftieth anniversary of the founding of the
Chinese People's Liberation Army with great enthusiasm and
jubilation.

On this brilliant festival day, we deeply honor the memory
of our great leader and teacher Chairman Mao Tse-tung,
founder of the People's Liberation Army. We honor the memory of our esteemed and beloved Premier Chou En-lai, Chairman Chu Teh of the Standing Committee of the National People's Congress, Vice Chairman K'ang Sheng of the CCP Central Committee, and Vice Chairman Tung Pi-wu of the NPC
Standing Committee, who dedicated all their energies throughout their lives to the revolutionary cause of the Chinese people.
We honor the memory of Comrades Ho Lung, Ch'en I, Lo Jung-
huan and Yeh T'ing, and Comrades Fang Chih-min and Liu
Chih-tan and other proletarian revolutionaries of the older
generation who made outstanding contributions to the founding
and development of our army. We shall always remember the
martyrs who fell heroically during the people's war of libera-

*From Peking Review, No. 32 (August 5, 1977), 15-17.

tion and the people's revolution. We salute the commanders and fighters of the People's Liberation Army, the militia of the whole country, and the workers, peasants and intellectuals who have contributed to building our national defense.

The fifty years of the People's Liberation Army were years of struggle under the great banner of Chairman Mao. The growth of our army, an army that has developed from nothing and has grown from small to big and from weak to strong, is the result of the victory of Chairman Mao's revolutionary line over opportunist lines. In the initial stage of Party building, Ch'en Tu-hsiu denied the need for armed struggle. As a result, the vigorous first great revolution met with debacle when Chiang Kai-shek started the counterrevolution. In 1927, with the triumph of Chairman Mao's revolutionary line over Ch'en Tu-hsiu's Right opportunist line, the Nanchang Uprising, the Autumn Harvest Uprising, the Canton (Kwangchow) Uprising and armed uprisings in other areas took place, and there was the march to the Chingkang Mountains. Chairman Mao founded the first contingent of the Workers' and Peasants' Red Army and set up the first rural revolutionary base area, and blazed the new path of encircling the cities from the countryside and seizing political power by armed force. Later, however, Wang Ming's "Left" opportunist line occupied the dominant position, and this brought extremely heavy losses to our Party and army. The Tsunyi Meeting of 1935 put an end to the domination of Wang Ming's "Left" opportunist line and established Chairman Mao's leadership throughout the Party and army, thereby enabling our Party and army to steer clear of danger to safety. From then on, our army developed and grew in strength, and finally defeated the Japanese imperialists and Chiang Kai-shek and seized political power throughout the country. Since the founding of New China, the People's Liberation Army, the staunch pillar of the dictatorship of the proletariat, has defended the motherland and the socialist revolution and socialist construction. During the Great Cultural Revolution, Lin Piao worked hand in glove with the "gang of four" to practice revisionism and splittism, engage in intrigues and conspiracies,

oppose the Party and disrupt the army in an attempt to destroy
our great wall. In 1971, Chairman Mao led us in smashing the
Lin Piao anti-Party conspiratorial clique, winning great victory in the Party's tenth two-line struggle. Chairman Hua, carrying out Chairman Mao's behests, led us in 1976 in shattering
the Wang-Chang-Chiang-Yao anti-Party conspiratorial "gang
of four," winning the great victory in the eleventh two-line
struggle. This victory saved the revolution and the Party and
smashed the gang's plot to usurp the leadership of our army
and destroy our great wall. History proves that the banner of
Chairman Mao is the banner of unity and victory. It is the
sacred duty of the whole Party, the whole army and the people
throughout the country to hold high and defend the great banner
of Chairman Mao at all times.

To hold aloft the great banner of Chairman Mao, we must
build up our army and strengthen our national defense in accordance with Chairman Mao's military thinking and line.
Chairman Mao was the greatest Marxist of our time; he inherited, defended and developed Marxism-Leninism in all
fields, including military affairs. He greatly enriched the
treasure house of Marxist-Leninist military theory with his
concepts of the people's army and people's war, his strategy
and tactics for people's war, his thesis that the Party com-
mands the gun, his principles for political work in the army
and his statements that efforts should be made to build powerful ground, air and naval forces and that we should make some
atom and hydrogen bombs. All these are our precious assets
as well as weapons of struggle for the oppressed people and
nations of the world, particularly for those of the Third World.
Over the decades, Chairman Mao led our army in waging protracted, arduous and tortuous struggles, summed up its rich
experience and wrote many important military works to form
a comprehensive system of military thinking. We must have
an accurate and all-round understanding of his military thinking and use it to guide our army building and defense construction.

At present the two hegemonic powers, the Soviet Union and

the United States, are fiercely contending with each other, the factors for war are increasing and the Soviet revisionists, in particular, have not given up their wild ambition to subjugate our country. We must therefore strengthen army building and speed up the modernization of our national defense. Chairman Mao pointed out: "We are stronger than before and will be stronger still in the future. We will have not only more planes and artillery but atom bombs too. If we are not to be bullied in the present-day world, we cannot do without the bomb." The four modernizations (of agriculture, industry, national defense and science and technology) put forward by Premier Chou in accordance with Chairman Mao's instructions include the modernization of national defense. Wang, Chang, Chiang and Yao opposed the Party and tried to disrupt the army, and seriously undermined army building and defense construction. When we wanted to prepare against war, they said this was "not taking class struggle as the key link"; when we wanted to push ahead with defense industry, they said this was following "the theory that weapons decide everything"; when we wanted to strengthen military training, they said this was a "purely military viewpoint"; when we wanted to consolidate the army, they said that was "restoration"; when we wanted to carry forward the army's fine traditions, they said that was "restoration of the old," and so on and so forth. What they wanted was to destroy the People's Liberation Army which is the pillar of the dictatorship of the proletariat, so that our country would once again be reduced to a semicolonial and semifeudal country to be partitioned by others at will. The smashing of the "gang of four" has swept away the biggest obstacle to army building. We can now march forward under the guidance of Chairman Mao's military thinking and along his line on army building, do a good job of building our army and strengthening national defense.

Holding high the great banner of Chairman Mao, Chairman Hua has set forth a series of measures for grasping the key link in running the army well and called on us to strive to "accelerate the revolutionization and modernization of the People's

Liberation Army." The commanders and fighters of the army
should respond to the call of Chairman Hua and the Party Central Committee and carry through to the end the great political
revolution of exposing and criticizing the "gang of four." They
should seriously carry out education in the "ten should-or-
shouldn'ts,"* distinguish correct from erroneous lines, do
away with the revisionist trash of the "gang of four" and Lin
Piao politically, ideologically and organizationally, and eliminate its pernicious influence. They should carry forward the
fine traditions of our army, strengthen ideological and political
work, undertake hard training, put forward strict demands and
help train more fighters like Lei Feng** and more companies
like the "Hard-Boned 6th Company." *** The army should rely
on the people, and the people should support the army. There
should be closer unity between the army and civilian organizations and between the army and the people. "The whole nation
should learn from the People's Liberation Army; the Liberation Army should learn from the people of the whole country."
"If the army and the people are united as one, who in the world
can match them ?"

To build up a modern national defense, we should correctly
handle the relations between defense construction and economic
construction. A strong national defense must have a strong
economy as its base. "Only with the faster growth of economic construction can there be greater progress in defense
construction." If agriculture, industry and science and technology do not make progress, how can national defense be
modernized? The People's Liberation Army should help and
take an active part in building the socialist economy. To show

---

*This refers to ten questions including: Should or shouldn't
we uphold the principle that the Party has absolute leadership
over the army, should or shouldn't we strengthen revolutionary
discipline and should or shouldn't we inherit and carry forward
the fine traditions of our Party and army.

**See issue No. 15, 1977, Peking Review.

***See issue No. 25, 1977, Peking Review.

concern for economic construction means to show concern for
defense construction. The workers, peasants and intellectuals
throughout the country should work hard to accomplish the four
modernizations before the end of the century. Producing more
grain, iron and steel, petroleum and other industrial and agricultural products and developing science and technology means
contributing to building our national defense.

We modernize our national defense solely for defense. Chairman Mao taught us: "Dig tunnels deep, store grain everywhere,
and never seek hegemony." We do not seek hegemony now, and
even when we have become strong economically and have modernized our national defense in the future, we will never seek
hegemony or become a superpower. Our principle is: "We will
not attack unless we are attacked; if we are attacked, we will
certainly counterattack." The Soviet revisionists recently
made a big hue and cry, slandering us as "bellicose." Messrs.
Soviet revisionists, you frenziedly engage in arms expansion,
make a show of force, reach out your hands everywhere, carry
out aggression against others, and station a large number of
troops and set up many military bases on the soil of other
countries. Isn't that bellicose? We tell the people the facts
about your contention for hegemony and have made some
preparations against a war of aggression. Should we be called
"bellicose"? Your gangster logic can hoodwink and intimidate
nobody!

In celebrating Army Day, our hearts are turned to our compatriots in Taiwan, flesh of our flesh, who are living in misery.
Taiwan must be liberated; our motherland must be reunified.
This represents the general trend of development and the common aspiration of the people. No one can obstruct it. When
and how to liberate Taiwan are entirely the internal affairs of
China and brook no foreign interference whatsoever.

The present situation in our country is fine, and it is getting
better and better. We have full confidence in building up a
powerful national defense since we have Chairman Mao's revolutionary line as our guide, since we are led by our wise leader
Chairman Hua with Vice Chairman Yeh, Vice Chairman Teng

and other central leading comrades working in concert with him, since we have 800 million industrious, brave and intelligent people, since we have the heroic and combat-worthy People's Liberation Army trained in its fine traditions and since we are supported by our achievements in economic construction in the past two decades and more. Let us rally more closely around the Party Central Committee headed by Chairman Hua, hold aloft the great banner of Chairman Mao and strive to speed up the modernization of our national defense.

Selected bibliography

Barnett, A. Doak. Communist China and Asia: Challenge to American Policy.
    New York: Harper and Brothers, 1960.
    _____, ed. Communist Strategies in Asia: A Comparative Analysis of
    Governments and Parties. New York: Praeger Publishers, 1963.
    _____. China Policy: Old Problems and New Challenge. Washington,
    D.C.: Brookings Institution, 1977.
    _____. China and the Major Powers in East Asia. Washington, D.C.:
    Brookings Institution, 1977.
Chen, King C. Vietnam and China. 1938-1954. Princeton, N.J.: Princeton
    University Press, 1969.
Chiu, Hungdah, ed. China and the Question of Taiwan: Documents and Analy-
    sis. New York: Praeger Publishers, 1973.
Cohen, Jerome Alan, and Hungdah Chiu. People's China and International
    Law, 2 vols. Princeton, N.J.: Princeton University Press, 1974.
Copper, John F. China's Foreign Aid: An Instrument of Peking's Foreign
    Policy. Lexington, Mass.: D. C. Heath, 1976.
FitzGerald, Stephen. China and the Overseas Chinese: A Study of Peking's
    Changing Policy. Cambridge: Cambridge University Press, 1972.
Gittings, John. Survey of the Sino-Soviet Dispute. London: Oxford Univer-
    sity Press, 1968.
Griffith, William E. Albania and the Sino-Soviet Rift. Cambridge, Mass.:
    MIT Press, 1963.
    _____. The Sino-Soviet Rift. Cambridge, Mass.: MIT Press, 1964.
    _____. Sino-Soviet Relations, 1964-1965. Cambridge, Mass.: MIT
    Press, 1967.
Gurtov, Melvin. China and Southeast Asia — the Politics of Survival.
    Lexington, Mass.: D. C. Heath, 1971.
Halpern, A. M., od. Policies Toward China: Views from Six Continents.
    New York: McGraw-Hill Book Co., 1965.
Hinton, Harold C. Communist China in World Politics. Boston: Houghton
    Mifflin, 1966.

_____. China's Turbulent Quest: An Analysis of China's Foreign Relations Since 1945. New York: Macmillan, 1970.

_____. Peking-Washington: Chinese Foreign Policy and the United States. Beverly Hills, Calif.: Sage Publications, 1976.

Hsiao, Gene T., ed. Sino-American Détente and Its Policy Implications. New York: Praeger Publishers, 1974.

Hsiung, James C. Law and Policy in China's Foreign Relations. New York: Columbia University Press, 1972.

Hsüeh, Chün-tu, ed. Dimensions of China's Foreign Relations. New York: Praeger Publishers, 1977.

Jo, Yung-Hwan, ed. Taiwan's Future? Tempe, Arizona: Center for Asian Studies, Arizona State University, 1974.

Johnson, Cecil. Communist China and Latin America, 1959-1967. New York: Columbia University Press, 1970.

Kau, Michael Y. M., et al. "Public Opinion and Our China Policy," Asian Affairs, January-February 1978. pp. 133-147.

Klein, Donald W. & Clark, Anne B. Biographic Dictionary of Chinese Communism. Two vols. Cambridge, Mass.: Harvard University Press, 1971.

Lall, Arthur. How Communist China Negotiates. New York: Columbia University Press, 1968.

Larkin, Bruce D. China and Africa, 1949-1970. Berkeley, Calif.: University of California Press, 1971.

Lovelace, Daniel D. China and "People's War" in Thailand, 1964-1969. Berkeley, Calif.: University of California, Center for Chinese Studies. Research Monograph, No. 8, 1971.

Maxwell, Neville. India's China War. New York: Pantheon Books, 1970.

Mozingo, David P. Chinese Policy Toward Indonesia, 1949-1967. Ithaca, N.Y.: Cornell University Press, 1976.

Passin, Herbert. China's Cultural Diplomacy. New York: Praeger Publishers, 1962.

Robinson, Thomas W. "The Sino-Soviet Border Dispute," The American Political Science Review, December 1972, pp. 1175-1202.

Scalapino, Robert A. "China and the Balance of Power," Foreign Affairs, January 1974, pp. 349-385.

Simmonds, J. D. China's World: The Foreign Policy of a Developing State. New York: Columbia University Press, 1970.

Simmons, Robert. The Strained Alliance: Peking, P'yongyang, Moscow, and the Politics of the Korean War. New York: The Free Press, 1975.

Taylor, Jay. China and Southeast Asia: Peking's Relations with Revolutionary Movements. New York: Praeger Publishers, 1976.

Tsou, Tang, ed. China in Crisis. Vol. 2: China's Policies in Asia and America's Alternatives. Chicago: University of Chicago Press, 1968.

Tsou, Tang, and Morton H. Halperin. "Mao Tse-tung's Revolutionary Strategy and Peking's International Behavior," The American Political Science Review, March 1965, pp. 80-99.

Van Ness, Peter. Revolution and Chinese Foreign Policy: Peking's Support for Wars of National Liberation. Berkeley: University of California Press, 1970.

Whiting, Allen S.. China Crosses the Yalu: The Decision to Enter the Korean War. New York: Macmillan, 1960.

_____. The Chinese Calculus of Deterrence: India and Indochina. Ann Arbor, Mich.: University of Michigan Press, 1975.

Williams, Jack F., ed. The Taiwan Issue. East Lansing, Mich.: Asian Studies Center, Michigan State University, 1976.

Wu, Yuan-li. The Strategic Land Ridge: Peking's Relations with Thailand, Malaysia, Singapore, and Indonesia. Stanford, Calif.: Hoover Institution Press, 1975.

Yu, George T. China's African Policy: A Study of Tanzania. New York: Praeger Publishers, 1975.

Zagoria, Donald S. The Sino-Soviet Conflict, 1956-1961. Princeton, N.J.: Princeton University Press, 1962.

_____. Vietnam Triangle. New York: Pegasus, 1967.

About the editor

Educated in China and the United States, King C. Chen received an M.A. from the University of Virginia and a Ph.D. in political science from The Pennsylvania State University. He has taught at State University of New York and Brown University and is currently Professor of Political Science at Rutgers University.

Professor Chen was a Senior Fellow of the Research Institute on Communist Affairs (now the Research Institute on International Change) at Columbia University (1973), where one of his projects evolved into the present volume. His publications include Vietnam and China (1969), The Foreign Policy of China (1972), and others.